THE HUNTER'S GAME COOKBOOK

THE HUNTER'S GAME COOKBOOK

BY

Jacqueline E. Knight

WINCHESTER PRESS

WINCHESTER is a Trademark of Olin Corporation used by
Winchester Press, Inc. under authority and control of
the Trademark Proprietor.

Published by Winchester Press
205 East 42nd Street
New York, N.Y. 10017

Printed in the United States of America

Library of Congress Cataloging in Publication Data

Knight, Jacqueline E
  The hunter's game cookbook.

  Includes index.
  1. Cookery (Game) I. Title.
TX751.K55   641.6′9′1   77-20923
ISBN 0-87691-252-8

Dedication

To game-management people everywhere
who make hunting still possible.

CONTENTS

CONTENTS

CONTENTS

CONTENTS

INTRODUCTION

Throughout man's long history on this earth he has been, for the most part, a carnivore, a meat eater. Some of his earliest records, painted on cave walls, depict hunting activities. Early man was not a herdsman; thousands of years passed before he learned that animals could be domesticated, making the hunting of wild animals unnecessary for sustenance.

Modern man, however, continues to hunt. In some cases he does it to supplement a sparsely filled larder, but in most cases man hunts for a much more complicated reason. Buried in his subconscious is the desire to pit himself against the wild, whether it be a bird or a beast. It is a matter of great gratification to him to stalk a quarry in its own habitat, an often alien world without sidewalks and signposts. The feeling of oneness that a hunter experiences when by himself with nature is perhaps inexplicable to nonhunters, yet may well be the most important part of the total hunting experience. Certainly most of the more than 15,000,000 licensed hunters in the United States recognize this and acknowledge it.

Today's hunter contributes to the economy of his state in many ways. His license fees support and improve the game he hunts; the money he spends on food and lodging, clothing, and equipment is important to many a small town. And he makes a significant contribution to the family larder.

People often lose sight of one important point when comparing game meat and domestic meat. Game meat is the ancestor of our domestic meat. All meat animals were at one time wild. Man has domesticated, interbred, and crossbred them over many years to produce what we accept quite naturally as market meat. In just the last century, market meat included the flesh of wild animals and birds, and market hunting was quite legal in many areas. Nowadays only a few high-priced, specially licensed markets may even carry "wild" meat, which comes from herds and flocks of normally wild species which are being raised for profit. They could contradictorily be called domestic wild game and are the sources of the "pheasant under glass" and "venison steak" found on expensive menus in a scattering of larger cities.

Too many people make the mistake of comparing domestic and game meat. They are *not* the same, any more than beef and lamb are the same. Each species is different, having a different texture and flavor, and these differences should be recognized and appreciated for what they are. This does not mean that game meat cannot be prepared in many of the same ways as domestic meats. As a matter of fact most of it can be. Many of our domestic meat recipes are actually hand-me-downs from the days when game meat was "normal" fare and domestic meat the rarity. The most important difference between the meats, generally, is that game, because of its greater activity and frequently lesser food supplies, yields meat that is leaner than domestic meat. This is true in all species, from wild Canada goose compared to the domestic variety to venison compared to beef.

Many people profess to dislike game meat because of a "gamy" flavor. By definition, this means that the game meat has been kept uncooked, and unpreserved, until almost tainted. I don't like high-flavored meat either, even though I have in this book included a few English-style methods of handling game birds. The English traditionally and by preference hang a bird without cleaning; with some species they even cook and eat birds with the viscera.

Many a hunter, unfortunately, must take much of the blame for unsatisfactory meals from game. All too often it is because the hunter does not take care of his bag promptly that those at the table dislike the results of a hunting trip. Because of this, I have begun each section of this book with Field Notes important to the hunter, the cook, and the diners; if they are not followed everyone will be disappointed. No recipe in the world can make improperly handled game a satisfactory dish.

Included in the Field Notes are clues on how to judge the game's age. Old game, quite naturally, is usually tougher than the young; if the hunter can tell the cook its age, the cook's job is much easier and the results are much better. The hunter would also be well advised to tell the cook the basic details of how the game was taken; any game that has been panicked will have a system charged with adrenaline. Game that is taken without prior fright is much better eating.

For those new to game cookery, or those who are encountering some species for the first time, I would recommend that your first dish be the most simple so that you really get to know the natural texture and flavor of the particular species. In future preparation of the same game meat, you will know how to adjust seasonings and flavorings to please those you are serving. After all, no recipe, except for a bakery product, needs to be followed in minute detail. Cooking offers great latitude to your imagination and inventiveness. First, however, you must know what you are dealing with.

Recipes in the sections that follow are grouped according to the size of the piece of meat involved. The larger pieces, roasts, for instance, or whole birds, are dealt with first, then cuts and half birds, then cubed meat and birds cut into serving portions. Particularly with a bird, at least one part of it is frequently too badly shot up to put on the table. That part is best discarded or saved to make stock. In the case of a few stray pellets, they are easy enough to pop out with a sharp-pointed kitchen knife.

Cast iron is one of the best cooking materials for any meat recipe. It distributes heat evenly and makes slow simmering possible—particularly important with tougher meats. Perhaps the most versatile cast-iron implement is the Dutch oven with a rack and tight-fitting lid. Use it without the rack for quick browning. To deglaze the bottom, pour in some liquid, bring to a simmer while stirring to loosen particles stuck to the bottom. Then put the rack under the ingredients to keep them from sticking. Deglazing makes the finished dish richer in flavor and gives it better color.

A pressure cooker is a valuable tool to the cook with limited time. Many of these recipes can be converted to use in the pressure cooker: reduce the liquid called for to about half a cup more than you want in the finished dish and cook under 15 pounds pressure for about one-third the time called for in the standard cooking method. Again, it is a good idea to deglaze the bottom of the pressure cooker before sealing the top.

Where it is practical, I have indicated the point at which a recipe may be held or a dish may be frozen. As with much cooking, it is not only possible but practical to prepare several meals at one time, freezing the extra servings for future use. Some of the recipes, as a matter of fact, are freezer recipes: the time-consuming tasks are done on a slack day and all that's required before eating is the defrosting and finishing. Remember *not* to freeze cooked potatoes (they turn mushy) or dishes with mayonnaise (which separates).

Game meat, whether a supplement to increasingly expensive domestic meat or an added benefit to time spent out-of-doors, is excellent eating when properly cared for all along the way. I hope this guide will show hunters and cooks alike that path.

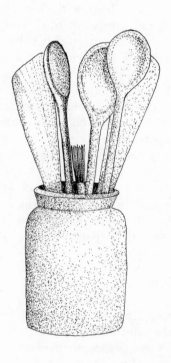

TABLE OF WEIGHTS AND MEASURES

U. S. Customary	Metric
1 teaspoon	4.95 milliliters
1 tablespoon (3 teaspoons)	14.8 milliliters
2 tablespoons (1 liquid ounce)	29.6 milliliters
1 jigger (1½ liquid ounces)	44.4 milliliters
¼ cup (4 tablespoons)	59.2 milliliters
½ cup (8 tablespoons)	118.4 milliliters
1 cup (16 tablespoons)	236.8 milliliters
1 pint (2 cups)	473.6 milliliters
1 quart (2 pints)	947.2 milliliters
1 gallon (4 quarts)	3.788 liters
1 ounce, dry (2 tablespoons)	28.35 grams
¼ pound (4 ounces)	113.37 grams
½ pound (8 ounces)	226.74 grams
1 pound (16 ounces)	453.59 grams
2.21 pounds (35.3 ounces)	1 kilogram

OVEN TEMPERATURE CONVERSION

Fahrenheit	Celsius
200	93
225	107
250	121
275	135
300	149
325	163
350	177
375	191
400	204
425	218
450	232
475	246
500	260

Water boils at 212 degrees Fahrenheit at sea level. Water boils at 100 degrees Celsius at sea level.

CHAPTER 1

IMPORTANT GENERALITIES

The importance of tending to game as soon as it is killed cannot be overemphasized. Whatever the game, it must be cleaned and cared for immediately. It should be cooled as quickly as possible; bird and small-game hunters would be wise to carry a thermal box with a bag of ice cubes in it in their vehicle, putting their game into it as soon as they can. Big-game hunters should prop open chest cavities so that as much air will circulate as possible and should carry the game on a rack on the top of their vehicle well away from engine and passenger compartment heat.

Game meats all freeze just as well as domestic varieties, and a freezer stocked from a successful hunting season can provide many excellent meals. The freezer life of game meats is similar to that of domestic meats; refer to your owner's handbook for the recommended storage time for meats and birds, keeping in mind that quality deteriorates if they are kept too long. In some states there is a legal time limit on the freezer storage of game. This is usually spelled out in the state's hunting regulations; some states, for instance, limit the storage time of game meats to six months. I do not know of any inspection of home freezers that enforces this measure, but presumably commercial freezer lockers are subject to official inspection.

Whatever your freezer facilities, be sure to identify your game meat packages. The best method, along with labeling as to type and cut, is to note the game license number under which it was taken. Many commercial meat cutters who process game for hunters keep records of license numbers and assign seasonal numbers to the packages they make up. In this case it is not necessary to add the license number as well. That is cross-referenced in the cutter's records.

If you pack your own game for the freezer, pack fully trimmed meats in meal- or portion-sized packages. Before wrapping, carefully wipe off all bone and bone-marrow dust from the meat. Any saw used to cut bones is bound to spread some dust across the cut and many people feel that this dust, particularly from the marrow, is what imparts a so-called "gamy" taste. Steaks can be packed together with two sheets of wax paper or plastic film between so that they separate easily. Always double-wrap the meat, using the drugstore fold for both wrappings. To make a drugstore fold, lay the food on a sheet of foil large enough to bring up on the long side and fold together at least twice. Continue folding down until tight against the food. Crease each end into points and fold inward at least twice. Again continue folding until close against the food to exclude as much air as possible. Seal tightly, label and date, and freeze as quickly as possible.

To save space in your freezer, and to preserve as much moisture in the meat as possible, it is wise not to cut the meat any smaller than necessary. This means that even if you intend to have hamburger from that deer, freeze the meat in chunks and grind it just before using. One of the most practical kitchen appliances is an electric grinder. While meat can be ground for hamburger or sausage with the old-fashioned hand-cranked kind, it is much easier and quicker to use electric power.

Game meat is not only considerably leaner than domestic meat,

2

but in the case of deer, elk, and antelope, the fat is not the most palatable; it is closer to tallow than to good, edible beef suet. A pleasantly flavored fat must inevitably be added to this meat for hamburger and sausage as well as for larger cuts such as roasts. There are several domestic fats that are good and a number of ways to use them.

Beef suet is, I feel, the most compatible with big game. It can be sliced thin and laid in a blanket over a roast. Sometimes the sheet must be pinned on with skewers to keep it in place, or tied on under the cords used for rolling a boned roast. This technique, which is called "barding," is also used for game birds, with bacon or salt pork frequently used in place of the suet. If the game is not to be kept in a freezer more than a few weeks, it can be barded before freezing, but it is best to bard it just before cooking with fresh fat.

"Larding" is another technique of adding necessary extra fat. In this case lard, beef suet, bacon, or salt pork is chilled and cut into thin strips to be put into a larding needle. This long, tapered tube is pushed into the meat; when withdrawn it leaves a line of fat. This line can be put straight through a roast or "stitched" to the outside in ½- to 1-inch sections, in which case it is called "piqueing."

One technique I often use is to melt or render the fat I intend to use, mix in any desired herbs and spices, let the fat solidify again, and then cut it. This method puts flavoring through as well as outside a large piece of meat. This sometimes means freezing the fat, since melting softens the texture and it doesn't hold too well in a needle. Much the same effect, however, can be obtained by rolling the strips of fat, at room temperature, in seasonings, and chilling before threading.

Naturally, for burgers, loaves, or sausage, the additional fat is ground in with the game meat. Beef suet is undoubtedly best for burgers while pork fat is the usual addition to sausage. People who are on medically dictated diets should follow the recommendations of their physicians as to the choice of alternate ingredients.

Canning is a method of preservation that has somewhat gone out of favor, and logically, I think. The canning process is also a cooking process, limiting the end uses of the meat. Keep in mind that any meat must be canned under pressure for safety, using either the cold- or hot-pack method. Use the guide that came with your pressure cooker for directions in preparing and processing the meat, or refer to the United States Department of Agriculture's

3

"Home Canning of Meat" pamphlet, available from your county extension office.

Smoking is primarily done with larger game birds such as turkey and pheasant. If the smoking is done as a cooking process the end results are exotic fare indeed. Cold-smoked birds are also unusual when finished by roasting. As with any smoking process, always use hardwood with a smoke that will complement the meat's basic flavor. Many people prefer to use smoke-flavoring ingredients when cooking their game bag in any number of ways; this method is much more flexible and less time-consuming than actually using a smoker unit.

A temporary smokehouse is frequently set up at primitive hunting camps. The smoking process is, after all, a good preservative. If the weather is on the warm side during an extended hunt, it may well be wisest to use this form of protection. More than one elk or deer has been saved by smoking.

CHAPTER 2

BIG GAME

FIELD NOTES

The big-game hunter frequently admits to looking primarily for a trophy head. This holds true with all the species in this category (with the exception of buffalo) since there are several organizations that keep size records for them. Trophy heads, however dramatic over a fireplace, unfortunately mean that the game taken is far from being young; it is an older adult animal that has been around for at least several years.

Also, unless the animal was completely unaware of danger until the single killing shot dropped him, chances are that the resulting meat will not be of the highest quality. When an animal is aware of danger, the heart rate increases tremendously to supply the muscles with fuel to get away from that danger. The body is charged with a massive dose of adrenaline to increase the physical load capacity, and the nervous system is under extreme tension. Blood vessels in the internal organs constrict, redistributing the blood to the muscles and flesh, including the steaks, tenderloin, etc. This fuel in turn is converted into energy and waste products of lactic acid and pyruvic acid accumulate in the meat.

An improperly placed shot will not only wound and panic an animal, but it can also ruin a great deal of meat for the table. A paunch shot particularly is to be avoided. Rupturing the intestines releases bodily wastes that are almost impossible to remove from the meat.

Older animals, understandably, are apt to be tough. They can be excellent eating, but their age should be taken into consideration when choosing a cooking method. Long, slow, moist cooking is best for older game of all species, birds as well.

Venison is the prime target of big-game hunters all over this continent and includes deer (whitetail, mule, blacktail), elk, moose, and caribou—all species that shed antlers annually. Horned animals such as pronghorn antelope and mountain goat and sheep are in much smaller supply. All animals in this category, however, are handled in the field in basically the same way.

Even though you may want the head of any big-game animal for a trophy, the first thing that should be done is to eviscerate the animal. It is sheer thoughtless waste to think only of that trophy. Eviscerating is easily done on the smaller animals such as pronghorn, while doing an elk or moose may well call for the use of an ax as well as a very sharp knife.

If there is any slope to the land at all, position the animal so that the head is higher than the tail. Some hunters (and how-to-do-it articles in reputable publications) make no mention of the musk glands on some of these animals. These should, of course, be cut out carefully, unless the lower part of the leg (from the hock down) is removed completely.

To continue with the eviscerating, cut the belly open from the breastbone to the pelvis. Avoid cutting the abdominal wall by holding the knife, cutting edge up, in the palm of the hand with the forefinger under the point, or "bed" the back of the knife between the first two fingers. This keeps the point from digging downward and places the hand between the skin and the belly wall. Cut around the anus; pull back the skin and cut through the belly membrane carefully for access to the intestines. Cut the anus free and tie it off with a cord. If the animal is a buck, cut the genitals away. Tie off the bladder. Reach into the body and slice through the diaphragm in the chest. Cut the windpipe and gullet at the throat and, holding them in the hand, pull backward. At this point the animal can be turned, tipping out all the intestines. With a knife or ax split the pelvis. The breastbone should also be split at this time unless you want a full shoulder mount of your trophy.

The cavity and flesh should be well washed, as should the variety meats: heart, liver, and kidneys. These should be put into plastic bags for transporting. Prop the entire cavity open as wide as possible and hang the carcass to cool. Cut away all you can of the blood-clotted flesh.

If you want the head for mounting, do not try to skin it. Taxidermists prefer to do it and do it well. For a full shoulder mount a cut should be made through the hide behind the forelegs around the barrel and also around the top of the forelegs. At the point where the barrel cut meets at the top of the shoulder, a cut should begin straight up the top side of the neck toward the base of the skull. This should end in a "Y" to the base of each antler. To keep it simple, the hunter should skin the cape up to the termination point of the cut at the base of the antlers, leaving the ears, skull, etc., intact. Naturally the throat is also skinned, although there's little left within it at this point.

The neck should be severed at the last joint, just at the base of the skull, with a heavy knife or saw; don't swing an ax at that point. If it is going to be several days before you can get the head to a taxidermist, salt it generously. If it's going right to a taxidermist, simply roll it up, fleshy side under. Do not seal it in a plastic bag or other airtight container; this will cause rot.

If preferred, the head can be cut off as close to the shoulders as possible, without skinning, and then kept cold—or even frozen—until it can be professionally attended to.

Many people recommend skinning big game in the field. Personally, I don't go along with this practice, even though I recognize that removing the hide cools the flesh more quickly and that the hide is more easily skinned while the kill is fresh. If the game is going immediately to "civilization"—a cool room for hanging—I prefer to transport it in its hide. I feel that this helps protect the meat from foreign substances.

If the carcass is to be hung out of doors, it is particularly important to protect it from a variety of problems. Flies, if it's warm enough for them to be out, will "blow" and spoil the meat. To help prevent this, sprinkle all exposed flesh very generously with black pepper. This can easily be washed off when the animal is

7

butchered. If the hide has been removed it is also wise to wrap the carcass in cheesecloth. This is very porous and allows good air circulation.

Meat hanging outdoors is of course inviting to predators. While little can be done beyond mounting a guard against the larger ones, something can be done about birds. A few years ago a friend of mine dropped a big elk just before dark. He managed to quarter it and cache it in a couple of trees before going to get pack animals to bring it out the next day. I went to give him a hand packing and was almost as upset as he was to discover that birds had practically finished off the tenderloin. One Canada jay was impudent enough to come for the last few scraps as we stood there. Later, too late to do any good with this particular animal, we discovered that if he had laid some fresh fir-tree tips in the cavity the birds would have left it alone.

Too many people do not realize that big-game meat should be hung. Right here at home I have neighbors who, every successful deer season, will have a steak from the animal the night of the day they shot it. While this is all well and good when you are in a camp and the game you shoot is your active larder, it does not provide the best eating. In my mind, only the variety meats should be eaten right away; the bulk of the carcass should be hung (skinned) in a controlled environment such as a butcher's cold room, just above freezing temperature.

The best of beef is hung, and big-game meat should undergo just such tender loving care to provide the best eating. Hanging time, even under controlled conditions, is a variable thing. Some insist three days is enough; others insist on a matter of weeks. Personally, my system is to figure, even for a smaller animal such as a pronghorn, at least four days, assuming it came right from the field to the plant. Depending on the age of the animal, I mentally set a minimum hanging time, then make it a practice to check it every few days. I know when I first started doing this with the locker out in Wyoming the boys thought me rather a nuisance. They were sure they would know when the meat was ready to cut. At any rate, I kept it up until I thought it was ready.

My test is to draw a sharp-pointed knife very gently down the meatiest part of a ham. As soon as that point is followed by a single almost clear bead of moisture, I consider the meat ready to cut. This is my test and I am sure there are others equally reliable.

Cutting up game for storage is really not as complicated or difficult as many think. True, it's much easier to tell the man at the locker plant how thick you want your steaks and then pick them up all wrapped and flash frozen, but many people do their own cutting.

Within the obvious limitations, for all practical purposes all four-legged game can be cut the same way. Large animals—moose, caribou, elk in the venison group—are almost always quartered in the field. They are just so plain big that they present transportation problems if they are not reduced in bulk, if not in number of pieces.

Nothing exotic is required in the line of tools. While commercial butchers cut while the carcass is hanging by both hind legs, it is perfectly practical to do it on a protected countertop. A meat saw is necessary as well as a sharp, narrow-bladed knife.

Boning the meat before packaging makes a great deal of sense since it reduces the amount of space needed in the freezer and prevents a gamy taste some feel is caused by bone marrow. To cut and bone a venison follow these steps.

The first cut is to remove a front shoulder. Lift the leg up from the chest and cut the meat attaching it to the side of the ribs. Work the knife back and forth to cut the connective tissue between the leg and rib cage. The last cut will separate the top of the shoulder blade from the withers.

Discard, if it has not already been removed, the lower, bony part of the leg. Cut the shoulder or blade roast from the leg by severing the leg at the joint; move the shoulder blade up and down to locate it and cut through it. Trim to eliminate all fat and make a neat piece of meat; the bone is not removed from this cut. Save good trimmings for stew and hamburger. Frying steaks can be cut from the shoulder roast as well; the muscles on each side of the bony ridge on the shoulder blade can be removed and sliced 1/4 to 3/8 inch thick.

To separate the arm roast from the shank, prepare to saw the leg bone by cutting the meat down to the bone. Make this cut just above the "point" on the leg. Saw through the bone. Clean off bone dust, trim the arm roast, and it's ready for packing or cooking.

Trim the meat from the heavy tendons and tissue of the shank. This meat is good for grinding.

Turn the animal so that you are working along the spine to remove the backstrap or loin from one side of the backbone. First cut the flank loose just in front of the hind leg and extend the cut all the way to the backbone. Use the vertical spines of the backbone as a guide and cut forward along these until you reach the base of the neck. Then make a side-of-the-rib cut parallel to the second cut directly over the point where the ribs curve down to join the backbone. The loin lies in the groove between the junction of the ribs and the vertical spines of the backbone. Remove it by cutting it loose from the ribs. Lift the loin and start cutting and peeling it from the groove, continuing forward until the loin ends or the base of the neck is reached.

Lay the loin on a table and trim it by pulling off the fat, odd-grained meat, and tough tissue, starting from one end. Cut enough of the connecting strands to allow a good hand hold. The loin will still be encased in a thin connective tissue. Remove the loosely attached meat near the neck end of the loin. This loose meat is good for grinding or stew but lacks the tenderness of good steaks. It is best, if possible, to package the loin whole, or in family-sized packages. Cut the steaks (a generous inch thick) just before cooking.

Remove the flank by cutting it free from the backbone and adjoining ribs. (The other side nearest the hind leg was cut free when making the first cut in removing the loin.)

Remove the neck by sawing the backbone off just in front of the point of the shoulder. Neck meat makes excellent minced meat, stew, or grinding meat, or it can be roasted.

Remove the side of the rib from the backbone. Use the saw and cut the ribs loose at the point where they curve en route to connecting with the backbone. Cut all the way to the base of the neck.

The side of rib can now be cut up or put aside while you turn and cut the other side of the carcass. Use the saw to cut off the lower, flatter rib plate. These plates can be barbecued whole or separated into 2- or 3-rib sections. Long ribs can also be cut into shorter sections if desired. The layer of meat on the ribs is usually left on, but it can be removed and used for jerky, grinding, stew, or tiny steaks. Enough meat will be left between the ribs for barbecuing even if this meat is removed.

Remove the tenderloin by lifting and cutting it free from the backbone. The two tenderloins are located on each side of the backbone and just forward of the pelvic area; they are small in diameter relative to their length. This is the most tender meat and it makes excellent steaks. To make the steaks larger in diameter, butterfly them. Cut the first steak almost but not all the way through, leaving tissue connecting the two pieces. Make the next cut all the way through the tenderloin. The two steaks are laid open connected on one side.

Saw the backbone off just in front of the hind legs. It can be cut into sections and used for stock or soup. The meat scraps can be used for stock or soup, or picked off and used for minced meat, headcheese, or grinding.

Separate the two hind legs by sawing through the middle of the backbone. Use the spinal cord in the backbone as a guide in making the saw cut.

To remove the rump roast (at the top of the leg), locate the ball and socket joint that connects the pelvic bones with the large leg bone. Feel the joint as you raise and lower the rump roast. Cut down to the ball and socket joint and work the knife through it. Make the cut as vertical as possible, but leave enough meat on the rump for a meal. (It can be sawn, but a knife is neater for this job.) Remove the fat and sharp projections of pelvic bone before cooking or packing. If you prefer, the meat can be removed and cut into steaks, cubed, or ground.

Cut the sirloin tip from the remainder of the hind leg. Set the leg in a vertical position and remove the kneecap by cutting it loose from the underside. If it's difficult to get the knife under the kneecap, cut directly to the large leg bone. Lay the leg flat on the table and use the leg bone as a guide for the knife while cutting off the large chunk of meat. Notice the large white bone in the meat; start at the kneecap and, keeping the knife in a vertical plane against it, cut the meat away from the bone with short strokes. When the sirloin has been removed, remove the connective tissue and extra meat from it. The remaining chunk of sirloin tip will be enclosed in a thin connective tissue and will resemble a football in shape. The sirloin tip is excellent as a roast or it can be cut into steaks—if they are to be fried, thin ones, not over 3/4 inch thick. The meat is also good in chunks or ground.

To remove the round just below the rump roast position on the hind leg, start by cutting the connective tissue that separates the shank from the round and the bone. Cut the tendon and shave and cut the meat loose from the leg bone. This takes a bit of maneuvering around the joints, but keep at it. Next separate the boned round into its individual muscles, each of which is enclosed in an envelope of connective tissue. Cut the connective tissue to separate the muscles, avoiding cutting the meat as much as possible. Chunks of trimmed round can be made into steaks or roasts. Steaks are best cut thin. Trimmings are good for grinding.

Most extension services of states with good deer hunting publish bulletins with their particular local ways of cutting and trimming.

11

The directions above come from Oregon State University's Co-operative Extension Service. A query to your favorite hunting state's university or agricultural extension service may well bring a more recent publication.

The cutting and trimming of any animal inevitably leads to a considerable reduction in weight from live weight to finished and packed. With the average big-game animal, this can range from a 35% loss to as much as 50%; if the animal is badly shot up, it can run even higher. If you take your animal to a processor, the loss in net weight is rarely due to his keeping a few prime steaks for his own use!

Age estimations of antlered game are all too often predicated on the number of points on a buck. With animals that shed antlers (as opposed to horns, which are not shed), this is one of the least accurate measures. Game departments of states that check on the ages of game taken rely on the number of teeth and their condition. They check the back or "cheek" teeth in the lower jaw. A six-month-old fawn deer has only four full-sized teeth on either side. A yearling (about 18 months old in its first legal hunting season) has five fully developed teeth to a side with a sixth and last tooth visible but not yet fully out of the jawbone. From 2½ years on, all six teeth are fully visible and the amount of wear they show is the only measure of age.

VENISON

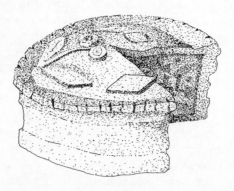

This category of antlered game covers animals in a wide range of sizes, yet all of them can be cooked in the same way. So far as that goes, domestic beef can be used in these recipes as well—if you can afford it!

Sizes of the animals must, of course, be an average. Younger examples will be smaller, and frequently the females run considerably smaller than the males of comparable age. Keeping this in mind, live weight of a whitetail deer will range as low as 40 pounds for a subspecies of the Coues whitetail to 300 pounds for a Northeastern one. A blacktail deer will run between 150 to 200 pounds, while the mule deer, which some consider the same species as the blacktail, will go from 250 to 300 pounds. The various major subspecies of caribou (often called reindeer) range from 200 to 300 for a Barren Ground one to 300 to 400 for a Woodland to 450 to 600 for a Mountain caribou. The elk, also known as the wapiti, ranges from 700 to 1,000 pounds live weight. The moose, averaging from 900 to 1,400 pounds, is the largest antlered game on this continent.

As noted, there is considerable difference between live weight and packed-for-the-freezer weight, but there's a lot of good eating to be had from all except the very smallest animal. If the animal has been carefully killed, cared for, hung, and cut, there is no reason for marinating. The only need for marinating is to tenderize meat or to soak in special flavorings. If you have any question as to whether a particular antlered animal will need marinating, cook and eat *first* a steak from a tender cut. This will give you a good indication of the condition of the rest of the meat.

Additional recipes for marinades and sauces to serve with the meat can be found in Chapter 5.

VENISON ROASTS AND RIBS

ROAST LOIN OF VENISON

3 to 5 lbs. tender loin of venison
¼ cup flour seasoned with ½ tsp. salt and ¼ tsp. pepper
2 or more slices salt-pork fat
1 bay leaf

Dust meat with seasoned flour; put on a rack in open roaster. Cover with salt pork; put bay leaf on top. Use a meat thermometer and roast at 350° to 185° on meat thermometer, 35 to 40 minutes per pound. Serve with Colbert Butter.
SERVES 6 to 8.

13

All large roasts such as rib roasts and racks can be cooked the same simple way. A 3- to 4-lb. rib roast of prime buck or doe should roast at 350° for approximately 25 minutes per pound for rare.

SMOTHERED VENISON ALBERTA

3 lbs. tender cut venison
½ cup seasoned flour
2 tbsps. sweet butter
1 tbsp. vegetable oil

2 tbsps. grated horseradish
1½ tsps. celery seeds
1 tsp. onion salt
2 cups solid-pack peeled tomatoes

Roll roast in seasoned flour and brown in butter and oil in a Dutch oven. Mix horseradish, celery seeds, and onion salt into tomatoes; pour on meat. Cover and simmer undisturbed over very low heat for 3 hours, until very tender.
SERVES 6 to 8.

SAUERBRATEN

4 lbs. round, rump, or chuck of
  venison
1½ cups red-wine vinegar
½ cup dry red wine
2 onions, sliced
2 carrots, sliced
3 whole cloves
3 allspice berries

1 bay leaf
1 tbsp. peppercorns
1 tbsp. salt
8 tbsps. butter
1 tbsp. cooking oil
9 tbsps. flour
1 tbsp. sugar
⅔ cup crushed gingersnaps

Make a marinade with vinegar, red wine, onions, carrots, cloves, allspice, bay leaf, peppercorns, and salt. Marinate meat in it, covered and in refrigerator, for 3 days, turning occasionally. Remove meat and pat dry; reserve marinade. Brown meat in 4 tablespoons of the butter with the cooking oil in a Dutch oven, sprinkling meat with 5 tablespoons flour as it is turned. Heat marinade and pour over meat; cover, reduce to a gentle simmer, and cook until tender, about 3 hours. Strain off cooking liquid and skim off fat. Keep meat warm while finishing sauce. Melt remaining 4 tablespoons butter, blend in 4 tablespoons flour and the sugar, and cook gently until lightly browned. Slowly stir in cooking liquid and cook, stirring, until smooth and thickened. Add the gingersnaps and pour over meat. Cook gently for 30 minutes.
SERVES 4 to 6.

IDAHO SPICED ROUND

5 to 6 lbs. elk round roast
1 cup onion vinegar
1 tbsp. chile powder
1 tbsp. salt
1 bay leaf
1 tsp. ground cloves

1 tsp. ground allspice
½ cup flour seasoned with ½ tsp.
    salt and ¼ tsp. pepper
3 tbsps. bacon fat
3 tbsps. soy sauce

Cook vinegar with chile powder, salt, bay leaf, cloves, and allspice, then cool. Pour over meat and add cold water to cover. Refrigerate and let marinate overnight. Wipe meat dry; strain marinade and reserve 2 cups of it. Roll meat in the seasoned flour, brown in half the bacon fat. Put meat on a roaster rack and rub with remaining bacon fat mixed with soy sauce. Pour 1 cup of reserved marinade into pan. Reduce remaining 1 cup marinade over high heat to ½ cup. Roast meat at 350° for 20 to 25 minutes per pound, basting with reduced marinade every 30 minutes.
    SERVES 10 to 12.

DRY-ROASTED RIBS

3-inch section of ribs from young
    tender elk
4 tbsps. butter, softened
1 tsp. garlic salt

1 tbsp. sugar
½ tsp. pepper
6 (or more) bacon strips

Rub top and ends of ribs with butter. Sprinkle with a mixture of garlic salt, sugar, and pepper; do not rub in. Lay on bacon strips to cover thoroughly; let the bacon hang over the ends. Cook at 300° for 20 minutes per pound, basting every 30 minutes.
    SERVES 1 or 2.

ELK IN A BLANKET

5 lbs. rump roast
¼ lb. sweet butter
pinch of cayenne
1 tsp. minced parsley
2 tsps. lemon juice
3 cubes (½-inch size) beef suet
1 cup flour
3 to 4 tbsps. cold water
1 cup undiluted cream of
    mushroom soup, hot

½ cup tart grape jelly,
    melted
¼ cup gooseberry jelly,
    melted
1 cube of vegetable extract,
    dissolved in water
½ cup heavy cream, whipped
    (optional)

15

Cream the butter, add cayenne and parsley, and work in lemon juice. Wipe roast with a damp cloth. Make deep slits in the roast and insert cubes of suet. Make a pastry of flour and water; roll out to a sheet large enough to encase roast. Smear butter mix on roast, wrap in pastry, and seal seams. Bake on a roaster rack at 300° for 2½ hours. Remove lower part of pastry blanket to allow juices to escape into pan. Add soup and jellies, all heated, to pan with dissolved cube of vegetable extract. Increase heat to 450° and cook for 30 minutes, basting every 7 to 10 minutes. Add the whipped cream just before serving, if desired.

SERVES 10 to 12.

MULE DEER RIB ROAST

3 to 4 lbs. rib roast
¼ tsp. sage seasoning
1 garlic clove, mashed
¼ tsp. dried marjoram
3 tbsps. olive oil
1 baking potato per person

1 tsp. salt (if not using salt pork)
beef fat or salt-pork blanket to
    cover
1 small onion per person
paprika

Stir sage seasoning, garlic, and marjoram into oil. Let stand at room temperature for 30 minutes. Scrub potatoes and put into a 350° oven. Rub ribs well with oil mixture until all is used. Sprinkle with salt if using beef fat. Cover with fat blanket and tie on. Roast in oven with potatoes, allowing 1½ hours for the potatoes and 25 minutes per pound for the ribs. Mince onion and use to top potatoes; dust ribs with paprika 30 minutes before they are done.

SERVES 4 to 6.

DESERET POT ROAST

4 lbs. mule deer rump or round
    roast
¼ cup flour seasoned with 1 tsp.
    salt and ¼ tsp. pepper
½ lb. salt pork, diced
2 cups cold water

1 bay leaf
1 tbsp. wine vinegar
4 potatoes, quartered
4 carrots, quartered
8 small white onions
1 yellow turnip, quartered

Rub seasoned flour into the meat. Render ½ cup fat from salt-pork bits; remove bits. Brown meat in rendered fat, turning often.

16

Add water, bay leaf, and vinegar. Cover and cook slowly until tender, about 3 hours. Add potatoes, carrots, onions, and turnip for last 30 minutes.

SERVES 8 to 10.

WYOMING MOOSE ROAST

roast of desired size	2 cups tomato juice
seasoned flour	2 cups dry red wine
fat for browning	1 can (8 oz.) mushrooms, drained
2 bell peppers	1 tbsp. pickling spices
2 onions	3 garlic cloves
5 celery ribs	salt and pepper
½ lb. salt pork	

Dust roast with seasoned flour, brown in hot fat. Grind together the bell peppers, onions, celery, and salt pork, keeping all the juices. Cook the ground mixture and juices together, covered, for 1 hour. Add tomato juice, wine, and drained mushrooms. Make a spice bag with pickling spices and garlic cloves. Put the meat in a large Dutch oven or casserole with a cover, add the spice bag, and pour the liquid mixture over and around the meat. Season to taste. Cook the roast, covered, in 250° oven until done to your taste; a large roast may take as much as 7 hours at this temperature. Baste occasionally. Thicken sauce for gravy if desired.

POLISH LOIN OF VENISON AU NATUREL

4 to 5 lbs. loin of venison	ground pepper, juniper berries,
olive oil	thyme
juice of 1 lemon	2 cups red wine
2 or 3 onions, sliced	salt
1 celery root, sliced	4 to 6 oz. larding salt pork
1 parsley root, sliced	4 tbsps. butter, melted

Rub meat with oil, sprinkle with lemon juice. Cover with onion slices, celery root, and parsley root, dust with pepper, juniper, and thyme. Wrap in cheesecloth. Pour on the wine and refrigerate for 2 days. Turn occasionally. Unwrap and discard vegetables but do not rinse meat. Rub with salt, lard with salt pork, and roast at 300° for 2 hours, basting with butter. Serve with drippings or sauce.

SERVES 10 to 12.

17

VENISON ROAST FILET

4 to 5 lbs. venison tenderloin (do not use frozen meat)
6 to 8 tbsps. butter, softened
salt and pepper

Smear tenderloin generously with butter; sprinkle with salt and pepper. Put into a shallow pan and roast at 450° to 500° for about 25 minutes. Remove and keep warm for 5 minutes before slicing at least ½ inch thick.
    SERVES 12 to 14.

VENISON FILET WELLINGTON

4 to 5 lbs. venison tenderloin (do not use frozen meat)
6 to 8 tbsps. butter, softened
salt and pepper
1½ to 2 cups pâté, preferably pâté de foie gras
1 recipe pastry for a 2-crust pie, or equivalent of puff paste

Prepare and cook tenderloin as in Venison Roast Filet. Remove meat from the oven and cool completely. Spread the filet with a good layer of pâté and wrap completely in a layer of pastry about ⅛ inch thick. Trim the edges of the pastry and seal together. Put the covered filet on a baking sheet and bake at 450° to 500° for about 15 minutes, or until the pastry is lightly browned. Slice at least ½ inch thick.
    SERVES 12 to 14.

ROAST LEG OF VENISON

6 to 7 lbs. leg of venison
salt and freshly ground black
    pepper
2 onions, sliced thin
2 carrots, sliced thin
3 celery ribs, chopped
2 shallots, chopped
3 parsley sprigs, chopped
2 garlic cloves, crushed

1 large bay leaf, crumbled
1 tsp. dried rosemary
½ tsp. dried thyme
6 peppercorns, crushed
6 juniper berries, crushed
3 cups dry red or white wine
1 cup wine vinegar
½ cup olive oil

Dust meat well with salt and pepper. Mix vegetables, herbs, and spices, and put half in the bottom of a deep narrow bowl. Put in the venison and spread the remaining mixture over the meat. Mix wine, vinegar, and oil, and pour over all. Marinate refrigerated for 2 days, turning several times each day. Drain meat and reserve ½ cup marinade for sauce if desired. Pat meat dry with paper towels. Roast at 375°, allowing about 12 minutes per pound for rare venison. Serve with Pepper or Poivrade Sauce.

SERVES 10.

VENISON SHOULDER ROAST

1 shoulder, boned, rolled, and tied
1 lemon, cut into halves
½ tsp. salt
2 garlic cloves, slivered
¼ cup flour seasoned with ½ tsp. onion salt and ¼ tsp. pepper

beef-fat blanket to cover
2 onions, cut into halves
4 celery ribs, chopped
4 small bay leaves

Rub meat with cut lemon, dust with salt. Insert garlic slivers with a sharp knife. Dust with seasoned flour and tie on fat blanket. Put in a roaster, without a rack. Put onions, celery, and bay leaves around, not on, meat and roast, uncovered, at 350° for 3½ to 4½ hours; do not use any liquid. Allow 22 to 27 minutes per pound. Remove fat blanket for the last 30 minutes of cooking.

SPANISH STUFFED EYE OF THE ROUND (BOLICHE)

4 lbs. eye of the round
1 chorizo sausage, chopped
¼ lb. cooked ham, chopped
1 garlic clove, minced
¼ cup chopped Spanish onion
1 small green pepper, seeded and chopped

salt and pepper
paprika
3 tbsps. bacon drippings
¾ cup hot water
1 bay leaf
4 whole cloves

Run a long sharp knife through the center of the round, but not through the opposite end, to form long pocket. Make a stuffing of sausage, ham, garlic, onion, and green pepper. Stuff into pocket firmly but lightly. Skewer and lace open end. Sprinkle well on all sides with salt, pepper, and paprika. Brown well in drippings in a Dutch oven, turning often. Add hot water and deglaze pot. Add bay leaf and cloves. Cover pot and bake at 350° for about 2½ hours, basting occasionally, until meat is fork tender.

SERVES 8 to 10.

BRAISED VENISON

2½ to 3 lbs. venison rump roast, larded with pork fat
2 cups red Burgundy wine
¼ cup olive oil
1½ cups sliced celery
1½ cups sliced carrots
1½ cups sliced onions
¼ cup whiskey
¼ cup condensed chicken broth
1 tbsp. crushed juniper berries
1 small bay leaf

Marinate roast in wine and olive oil for 24 hours. Turn 2 or 3 times while marinating. Remove and pat dry. Brown in a Dutch oven with no additional fat. Remove. Sauté sliced celery, carrots, and onions in remaining rendered pork fat in a Dutch oven for 10 minutes. Add venison, whiskey, chicken broth, juniper berries, bay leaf, and marinade. Cover and cook in a 300° oven for 30 minutes. Turn meat and cook at 250° for 1½ hours more. Remove meat and reduce sauce by half. Strain sauce and pour over meat.
SERVES 8.

SCOTTISH MARINATED ROAST VENISON

5 to 6 lbs. leg or saddle of venison
salt and pepper
1½ cups claret
1 cup vinegar
juice of 3 lemons
½ cup melted butter
1 cup rich venison stock
walnut catsup or lemon juice

Rub roast with salt and pepper. Marinate in claret, vinegar, and lemon juice for 4 to 6 hours, turning frequently. Roast venison in 450° oven for 30 minutes, basting often with marinade blended with melted butter. Reduce heat to 300° and roast until cooked to taste. A leg or saddle of this size should take about 45 minutes to 1 hour for rare. Remove meat to a platter. Stir venison stock into pan juices and boil until slightly reduced. Skim off fat and season with walnut catsup or lemon juice to taste. Serve sauce on the side.
SERVES 6 to 8.

ROAST SADDLE OF VENISON

5 to 6 lbs. saddle of venison
¼ lb. fresh pork fat cut into
  ⅓-inch-wide strips
4 cups buttermilk
1 onion, sliced
4 tbsps. butter
2 tbsps. oil
1 tsp. salt

1 tsp. crushed juniper berries
½ tsp. pepper
1 cup venison or beef stock
1 cup sour cream
2 tbsps. flour
1 to 2 tbsps. chokecherry or
  red-currant jelly
lemon juice

Lard venison with pork fat. Soak venison in buttermilk for at least 24 hours. Drain and dry thoroughly. In a roasting pan just large enough to hold meat, brown onion in butter and oil; remove onion and reserve. Brown meat on all sides. Remove meat and rub all sides with mixture of salt, juniper berries, and pepper. Return reserved onion to pan and put meat on top. Roast at 450° for 45 minutes to 1 hour, or until top is browned and crisp. Transfer to a hot platter. Strain pan juices, pressing onion through sieve; skim off as much fat as possible. Add stock to juices and use to deglaze pan. Add sour cream blended with flour. Cook, stirring, until hot and well blended. Add jelly, and lemon juice to taste.

    SERVES 6 to 8.

SADDLE OF VENISON

5 to 6 lbs. saddle of prime deer
2 tbsps. lard, softened
1 tbsp. brown sugar

½ cup flour seasoned with
  1½ tsps. onion powder and
  ½ tsp. pepper

Rub all sides of meat with lard and dust with seasoned flour. Roast at 450° for 30 minutes. Reduce heat to 325° and roast for 1½ hours. Dust lightly with brown sugar and roast for 30 minutes more.

    SERVES 6 to 8.

SIERRA SADDLE OF VENISON

5 to 6 lbs. venison saddle
vinegar
3 tbsps. sweet butter
2 tbsps. lard
1 tbsp. garlic juice

½ tsp. ground cloves
¼ tsp. pepper
dash of cayenne
1 tsp. honey
2 tsps. Spanish paprika

21

Wipe meat with a vinegar-dampened cloth. Melt together the butter and lard; add garlic juice, cloves, pepper, and cayenne, and spread on meat. Top meat with a double thickness of cheesecloth long enough to tuck under meat, to act as a wick for the fat. Roast at 300° for 25 minutes per pound. At 20 minutes before meat is done, remove the cheesecloth; spread meat with honey and dust with paprika. Roast at 450° for the remaining 20 minutes, basting every 5 minutes with the juices.

SERVES 6 to 8.

POLISH BRAISED SHOULDER OR BREAST OF VENISON

4 lbs. boned, rolled, and tied meat, marinated (perhaps Basic Red Wine)
salt
10 peppercorns, ground
20 juniper berries, ground
1 tsp. dried thyme
1 onion, sliced

6 bacon strips, diced
1 cup dry red wine
20 prunes, pitted
1 sour apple, cored, pared, and diced
10 walnuts
2 tbsps. pumpernickel bread crumbs

Drain meat and reserve marinade. Sprinkle meat with salt, and rub with mixed ground peppercorns, juniper berries, and thyme. Sauté onion in bacon. Lightly brown meat. Add ¼ cup marinade, the wine, prunes, apple, walnuts, and crumbs. Simmer, covered, until meat is tender and sauce is thickened, 1½ to 2 hours.

SERVES 8 to 10.

CANADIAN ROAST LEG OF VENISON

6 to 7 lbs. leg roast, marinated (perhaps from Idaho Spiced Round)
4 onions, sliced
4 carrots, diced
6 celery ribs, sliced
6 small bay leaves
1 cup water

½ lb. salt pork, sliced
salt and pepper
¼ lb. butter
1 cup flour
3 cups sour cream
1½ cups currant jelly
1½ cups dry red wine

Put onions, carrots, celery, and bay leaves in a baking dish; add water. Top with marinated meat, skin side up. Brown at 500° for 20 to 30 minutes. Turn meat over, cover with salt pork, and season. Insert meat thermometer. Reduce heat to 375° and roast for 30 minutes per pound until internal temperature reaches 180°. Remove meat, strain juices, and skim off fat. Melt butter, blend in flour, and add pan juices. Gradually add sour cream, jelly, and wine. Simmer until thickened.

SERVES 12 to 14.

CHEYENNE VENISON POT ROAST

4 to 5 lbs. rump or round of venison
½ cup salt-pork drippings
½ cup flour seasoned with ½ tsp. salt and ¼ tsp. pepper
1 tsp. paprika
1 tbsp. garlic vinegar

2½ cups venison or beef stock
1 bay leaf
2 yellow turnips, diced
4 potatoes
4 onions
6 carrots
1 tsp. celery salt

Heat drippings in a Dutch oven. Roll meat in seasoned flour. Rub in flour so meat absorbs as much as possible. Dust with paprika. Brown meat on all sides in drippings. Add vinegar, 2 cups stock, bay leaf, and turnips. Cover and cook at 300° for 2 hours. Add potatoes, onions, carrots, and celery salt, cover again, and cook for 45 minutes. Make 1 cup of thickening with 1 tablespoon of remaining seasoned flour, the remaining ½ cup cold stock, and the pot liquid. Blend all together and cook for 15 minutes.

SERVES 8 to 10.

PENNSYLVANIA VENISON POT ROAST

3 to 4 lbs. rump or shoulder of venison
2 tbsps. flour
2 tbsps. brown sugar
½ tsp. paprika
¼ tsp. pepper
4 tbsps. sweet butter

½ cup venison or beef stock, hot
1 rib celery, chopped
1 onion, chopped
1 onion per person, quartered (optional)
1 potato per person, quartered (optional)

Blend flour, brown sugar, paprika, and pepper; sprinkle over the meat. Brown meat in butter in a Dutch oven. Add stock, celery, and onion. Cover, roast at 375° for 3 to 3½ hours. Quartered onions and potatoes can be added for last half hour, if desired.

SERVES 6 to 8.

RACK OF VENISON

4 to 5 lbs. rack of venison,
    marinated (perhaps Wine
    Vinegar)
bacon

1 cup dry red wine
½ cup beef stock
1 tbsp. beurre manié

Lard with bacon. Roast, using marinade for basting, at 350° for about 20 minutes per pound for rare. After 45 minutes add heated wine and continue basting. Skim off excess fat from pan juices, add beef stock, and thicken with beurre manié.
SERVES 8 to 10.

OLYMPIA ROAST VENISON

2½ lbs. boneless venison
1 onion, sliced
1 cup oil
½ cup lemon juice

1 tsp. salt
6 tbsps. sherry
bacon
1 tbsp. horseradish

Make a marinade with onion, oil, lemon juice, salt, and 3 tablespoons sherry. Marinate meat in it, in the refrigerator, for 24 hours. Drain meat. Roast, covered with 3 slices of bacon, at 350° for 20 to 30 minutes per pound until tender, basting with the marinade. Remove to platter; stir horseradish and remaining 3 tablespoons sherry into pan liquid and heat through.
SERVES 8 to 10.

CANADIAN POT ROAST

4 lbs. top round roast, marinated
    (use same marinade as for
    Olympia Roast Venison)
¼ cup flour seasoned with 2 tsps.
    salt and ⅛ tsp. pepper
⅛ tsp. ground cloves
¼ cup chopped suet
4 cups dry red wine

4 cups venison or beef stock
6 carrots, sliced
4 onions, sliced
6 celery ribs, sliced
1 cup seedless raisins
flour
butter

Wipe meat with a damp cloth; dredge with seasoned flour mixed with cloves. Try out suet in a Dutch oven until golden. Brown meat. Add wine and stock, and cook over low heat, covered, for 3 to 5 hours until tender. Add carrots, onions, celery, and raisins for the last 30 minutes. Remove meat; strain liquid, skim off fat, and measure liquid. For each cup, use 2 tablespoons each of flour and fat; blend flour and butter and cook until light brown. Stir in liquid slowly and cook, stirring, until thickened. Simmer for 5 minutes.

SERVES 8 to 10.

HUNGARIAN VENISON POT ROAST

4 to 5 lbs. rump or shoulder of
   venison
6 or more strips of salt pork or
   bacon
2 garlic cloves, slivered
salt and pepper
flour
3 tbsps. olive oil

1 onion, chopped
1 carrot, chopped
1 celery rib, chopped
1 parsley sprig
1 tsp. dried oregano
1 cup beef bouillon
1 cup sour cream
1 tbsp. Hungarian paprika

Lard the roast with at least 6 strips of salt pork or bacon. Make small slits in the outside of the roast and insert the garlic slivers. Sprinkle liberally with salt and pepper and roll in flour. Brown the roast in the hot oil in a Dutch oven, turning meat until uniformly browned on all sides. Add vegetables, herbs, and bouillon. Cover and simmer for another 30 minutes, or until tender. Remove meat to a hot platter and keep warm. Reduce the pan liquid to about ¾ cup; vegetables can be strained out if desired. Add sour cream and paprika to liquid and blend well; bring just to the boiling point. Serve with sliced meat.

SERVES 8 to 10.

NEW ENGLAND SIMMERED VENISON

6 lbs. young venison roast, larded
   with ¼ lb. salt pork
¼ lb. butter
salt and pepper
4 cups milk

2 cups water
beurre manié
½ cup sour cream
½ cup red wine

Brown meat well in butter. Dust with salt and pepper. Add milk and water. Cover and simmer for 3 hours. Thicken gravy with beurre manié; boil for 10 minutes. Add sour cream and wine.

SERVES 10 to 12.

EARLY AMERICAN VENISON

5 to 6 lbs. shoulder of venison,
    boned, rolled, and tied
¼ lb. mutton or lamb fat,
    pounded flat
1 cup port wine
½ tsp. salt

½ tsp. pepper
¼ tsp. ground allspice
1 tbsp. butter
1 tbsp. flour
water

Soak fat in wine for 1 hour; wrap fat around meat and tie. Put meat in a Dutch oven; sprinkle with salt, pepper, and allspice. Pour on the wine from the fat. Start to cook over low heat. As soon as the wine begins to simmer, stir in butter kneaded with flour. Cook, covered, for 3 to 4 hours, or until tender. Check and add water as needed. Remove meat; skim fat from juices before serving as gravy.

SERVES 10 to 12.

ROAST VENISON WITH GARLIC GRAVY

4 lbs. venison roast, boned,
    rolled, and tied
salt and pepper
4 tbsps. butter
2 tbsps. brown sugar

1 tbsp. vinegar
1 garlic clove, mashed
½ cup water
⅛ tsp. dried thyme
½ bay leaf, crumbled

Sprinkle meat with salt and pepper and put in a roaster. Roast at 450° for 30 minutes, turning several times to brown evenly. Melt butter; add brown sugar, vinegar, garlic, and water. Heat to boiling; add thyme and bay leaf, and pour over meat. Reduce heat to 350° and continue to roast, basting occasionally, until done. Strain gravy. Can be thickened with 1 tablespoon flour if desired.

SERVES 8 to 10.

DANISH ROAST VENISON LEG

6 to 7 lbs. leg of venison
6 oz. salt pork
1 tsp. salt
¼ tsp. pepper

½ tsp. ground ginger
1 tbsp. cooking oil
½ lb. butter
2 cups venison or beef stock, hot

Wipe meat with a damp cloth; dry. Lard with salt-pork strips dipped into 1 teaspoon salt, ¼ teaspoon pepper, and the ginger. Rub meat with oil, put on a roaster rack. Melt butter and pour over meat. Bake at 350° until tender, for 2½ to 3 hours, basting with a mixture of stock and butter. Serve with gravy made from pan juices.

Serves 12 to 14.

VENISON SLICES

Chops are never thought of when talking about beef, but any big-game cutter knows that game chops come from the same place on the animal that pork, veal, or lamb chops come from. Rather than trimming the loin off the bone, saw the section into chops of the desired thickness, or leave the loin whole for a roast. From one loin you can get three different chops: shoulder-end, center (the choice ones), and leg-end chops. Steaks, of course, may come from several different cuts.

BASIC BROILED VENISON

1-inch-thick young, tender chops or steaks
cooking oil
pepper
garlic salt (optional)

Brush chops with oil, and dust with pepper, and garlic salt, if desired. Put on a greased broiler rack in preheated broiler. For rare, cook almost within reach of heat source for 5 to 7 minutes per side; for well done, put 3 to 4 inches below heat source for 12 to 15 minutes per side.

BASIC PAN-BROILED VENISON

1-inch-thick young, tender chops or steaks
salt
garlic salt (optional)

Sprinkle the bottom of a heavy iron skillet well with table salt and preheat. (Meat can be dusted with garlic salt if desired.) Cook meat to desired degree of doneness over high heat, turning once.

LATIN AMERICAN FILETE A LA PLANCHA

tender, thick steaks
coarse salt
water

Coat a *heavy-gauge aluminum* griddle thickly with *coarse* salt. Sprinkle well (off the fingers) with water. Put pan over high heat.

When water is evaporated and salt forms a sheet and "pops," add steak. Turn only once to put second side onto salt. Cook to desired degree of doneness. Salt does not sink into meat, and griddle rinses clean.

TROPHY VENISON STEAKS OR CHOPS

venison steaks or chops
garlic salt
freshly ground pepper

cooking oil
red wine

Marinate meat (with Sangria). Pound a bit of garlic salt and freshly ground pepper into meat; rub with oil. Sear in a hot iron pan until brown; add ½ cup red wine. Cover and bake at 300° for at least 1 hour, adding wine as needed to keep meat moist.

CARIBOU CUTLETS IN CREAM SAUCE

3 lbs. tender steaks, 1½ inches
  thick, cut into serving pieces
½ cup flour seasoned with ½ tsp.
  salt and ¼ tsp. pepper
2 tbsps. sweet butter

1 tbsp. vegetable oil
1 cup sour cream
1 tsp. onion salt
½ tbsp. soy sauce
dash of cayenne

Dredge meat with seasoned flour and brown in combined butter and oil over low heat to form a crust. When brown, add sour cream, onion salt, soy sauce, and cayenne. Simmer slowly, covered, for about 1½ hours until done.

SERVES 6 to 8.

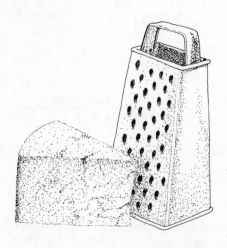

MT. HOOD ELK SCALLOPINI

1½ lbs. elk steak, cut into serving pieces ⅜-inch thick
seasoned flour
1 egg, beaten
⅓ cup light cream
1 cup fine cracker crumbs

1 cup grated Parmesan cheese
⅓ cup minced parsley
¼ cup cooking oil
1 garlic clove, minced
½ cup sherry
½ cup venison stock or water

Pound pieces well. Dredge meat with flour, dip into blended egg and cream, then into crumbs mixed with cheese and parsley, coating well. Heat oil and garlic, add meat, and brown. Pour in sherry and stock and cover. Bake at 375° for 45 minutes to 1 hour.
SERVES 3 or 4.

GOLD RUSH CASSEROLE

1½ lbs. elk bottom round
1 baking potato, peeled and diced
2 cups boiling consommé
1 tbsp. pickling spices
½ cup flour seasoned with ½ tsp. salt and ¼ tsp. pepper

¼ cup salt-pork fat
1 tbsp. melted bacon fat
2 tsps. vinegar
½ tsp. brown sugar
½ cup catsup
dash of pepper sauce

Boil potato in consommé to a paste; strain, reserving both consommé and potato paste. Bring consommé to a gentle simmer in a Dutch oven with the pickling spices in a cheesecloth bag. Cut meat into serving pieces, dredge with seasoned flour, and brown in salt-pork fat over high heat. Add to Dutch oven and simmer, covered, for 1 hour. Baste well with mixture of 2 tablespoons pot liquid, the bacon fat, vinegar, and brown sugar, and cook, covered, for 1 hour more. Remove spice bag, and add potato paste, catsup, and pepper sauce. Cook slowly for 30 minutes to thicken.
SERVES 2.

COLORADO CHICKEN-FRIED ELK STEAK

½-inch-thick top round steaks, wiped with a damp cloth
½ cup fine bread crumbs mixed with ½ tsp. salt, ¼ tsp. pepper, and 1 crushed bay leaf

1 egg, beaten with 1 tbsp. water
3 tbsps. butter
3 tbsps. lard or cooking oil

Dip steaks into seasoned crumbs, then into egg, then into crumbs again. Drain, let dry for 30 minutes. Melt butter and lard together and fry the steaks over medium heat for 10 minutes per side, turning them only once.

ELK SCHNITZEL HOLSTEIN

1 egg per person
anchovy filets

paprika
capers

Prepare chicken-fried elk steaks as in recipe for Colorado Chicken-Fried Elk Steak. Top each steak with a fried or poached egg and 1 or 2 anchovy filets. Dust with paprika and garnish with capers.

MONTANA SMOTHERED STEAKS

4 elk rib steaks
1 tbsp. olive oil
1 tsp. celery salt
½ cup flour seasoned with ½ tsp.
   salt and ¼ tsp. pepper
2 tbsps. sweet butter
½ cup chopped onion

1 tbsp. salt butter
½ cup mushroom pieces
1 tsp. onion juice
½ cup sour cream
¼ tsp. Kitchen Bouquet, or
   1 tbsp. currant jelly

Wipe steaks with a damp cloth. Brush both sides with oil and pile steaks one on top of the other for 1 hour before cooking. Brush with oil every 20 minutes. Add celery salt to seasoned flour and dredge steaks with mixture. Let steaks stand spread out for about 15 minutes before melting sweet butter and sautéing onion. Remove onion and fry steaks for 5 minutes on each side; remove steaks to broiler rack, spread onion on top. Cook 6 inches below heat source at 350° for 30 minutes. When almost done, pour juices into a skillet, add salt butter, and sauté mushrooms over low heat. Add onion juice and 1 teaspoon seasoned flour per steak; mix well with mushrooms until flour is absorbed. Add sour cream and blend. Simmer, uncovered, for 10 minutes. Add Kitchen Bouquet or currant jelly. Serve 1 steak per person, with sauce spooned over.

SERVES 4.

NEW BRUNSWICK STEAK

1 top round moose steak, ¾ inch
   thick
¼ cup flour seasoned with ½ tsp.
   salt and ¼ tsp. pepper
2 tbsps. sweet butter

½ cup chopped onion
2 tbsps. flour
½ cup sour cream
1 cup canned mushrooms with
   liquid

Dredge steak with seasoned flour; brown quickly in sweet butter. Remove steak and sauté onion in same pan until soft. Return steak, cover skillet, and simmer for 45 minutes. Blend 2 tbsps. flour into sour cream, add mushrooms with can liquid, and pour over steaks. Cover skillet and simmer for 30 minutes.

SERVES 4 to 6.

VENISON À LA FLAMANDE

4 lbs. venison, sliced 1 inch thick
4 tbsp. butter
3 cups chopped onions
2 tbsps. flour
2 cups beer
1 tbsp. cider vinegar

1 tbsp. sugar
2 tsps. salt
1 bay leaf
½ tsp. dried marjoram
2 tbsps. minced parsley

Brown meat in butter in a Dutch oven. Remove meat and sauté onions in same pan until brown. Stir in flour, beer, vinegar, sugar, salt, bay leaf, and marjoram; bring to a boil. Return meat to pot, cover, and cook over low heat for 2½ hours, or until very tender. Sprinkle with parsley.

SERVES 8 to 10.

VENISON TERIYAKI

2 lbs. lean steak from a young animal, cut 1¼ inches thick, then
    sliced thin with the grain and cut into 5-inch-long strips
½ cup soy sauce
1 garlic clove, mashed
1 tbsp. green ginger root, minced

Marinate strips for several hours in mixture of soy sauce, garlic, and ginger root. Weave strips onto bamboo skewers and broil on a hibachi only long enough to heat through. Serve rare.

SERVES 4 to 6.

POLISH STEAKS IN WINE

6 individual loin steaks, 1 inch
    thick
3 tbsps. butter
1 onion, sliced

ground pepper
ground juniper berries
ground thyme
½ cup dry white wine

31

Brown steaks quickly in hot butter. Put in casserole in layers with onion slices, seasoning each meat layer with pepper, juniper, and thyme. Add browning butter mixed with wine. Simmer, covered, for 30 minutes.

SERVES 6.

WYOMING SWISS STEAK

2 lbs. round steak, cut ½ inch
    thick
3 tbsps. flour seasoned with 2 tsps.
    salt and dash of pepper
3 tbsps. hydrogenated vegetable
    shortening

1 onion, sliced
1 can (3 oz.) mushrooms
¾ cup water
½ cup sour cream

Cut meat into serving pieces. Dredge with seasoned flour and brown in hot shortening. Lay onion slices on meat; add mushrooms and ½ cup water. Cover and simmer until tender, about 1 hour. Remove meat. Stir in sour cream and ¼ cup water; deglaze pan and heat, but do not boil.

SERVES 6.

VENISON STEAK ST. HUBERT

4 venison round steaks, up to 9 oz.
    each, cut ¾ inch thick
2 cups dry white wine
¾ cup 5% acidity vinegar
½ cup olive oil
¼ cup water
2 carrots, sliced
2 onions, sliced

2 shallots, chopped
1 garlic clove, chopped
2 bay leaves
⅛ tsp. pepper
⅛ tsp. dried thyme
small pinch of ground cloves
butter

Make a marinade of the wine, vinegar, oil, water, carrots, onions, shallots, garlic, bay leaves, pepper, thyme, and cloves. Marinate steaks in the refrigerator for 1 day. Remove and dry. Sauté steaks in thin layer of hot butter until brown on both sides. Serve rare with Pepper Sauce.

SERVES 4.

WYOMING ZESTY CASSEROLE

2 lbs. meat, cut into strips $\frac{1}{2}$ x 1 x
   3 inches
seasoned meat tenderizer
$\frac{1}{2}$ tsp. garlic powder
1 cup seasoned flour
$\frac{1}{4}$ lb. butter
1 green pepper, chopped

1 large onion, chopped
1 can (3 oz.) mushrooms
1 can ($10\frac{3}{4}$ oz.) condensed cream
   of celery soup, undiluted
3 tbsps. white wine
4 tbsps. orange juice

Season meat well with tenderizer and garlic powder; roll in seasoned flour and brown in butter. Put meat into a baking dish. Combine green pepper, onion, mushrooms, soup, wine, and juice, and pour over meat. Cover dish and bake at 350° for $1\frac{1}{2}$ hours.
   SERVES 4 to 6.

VENISON SCALLOPINI

2 lbs. thin slices of round steak,
   pounded paper thin
2 eggs, beaten
$\frac{1}{2}$ tsp. seasoned salt
$\frac{1}{4}$ tsp. pepper
1 garlic clove, mashed

2 tbsps. cold water
$\frac{1}{2}$ cup flour
2 tsps. paprika
$\frac{1}{4}$ lb. sweet butter
2 slices of pimiento, minced
$\frac{1}{2}$ cup grated Parmesan cheese

Blend eggs, seasoned salt, pepper, garlic, and water. Mix flour and 1 teaspoon paprika. Dredge meat with flour, then dip into egg mixture. Sauté in hot butter, turning frequently. When meat is browned, sprinkle with pimiento and put skillet into 350° oven for 15 minutes. Dust with some of the Parmesan and return to the oven for 5 minutes. Serve with hot pasta, with rest of cheese and butter from skillet and sprinkle with remaining paprika.
   SERVES 6 to 8.

STUFFED VENISON SLICES

2 lbs. venison, sliced thin
$2\frac{1}{2}$ cups fresh bread crumbs
6 tbsps. melted butter
1 medium onion, minced
6 tbsps. minced parsley
2 tbsps. minced boiled ham

4 egg yolks
2 tbsps. grated Parmesan cheese
pinch of dried thyme
$\frac{1}{2}$ tsp. salt
$\frac{1}{4}$ tsp. pepper
3 tbsps. melted sweet butter

Brown 2 cups of the crumbs in 6 tablespoons melted butter. Remove. Sauté onion, parsley, and ham in the same butter. Mix with crumbs, egg yolks, cheese, thyme, salt, and pepper. Put 1 tablespoon stuffing on each slice of meat, roll up, and skewer. Dip into melted sweet butter, then into remaining ½ cup of crumbs. Bake in greased dish at 350° until done, about 1 hour.

SERVES 4 to 6.

BARBECUE VENISON BUNS

venison steak, cut into very thin slices
1 cup catsup
1 tsp. dry mustard
¼ cup red-wine vinegar
1 tbsp. Worcestershire sauce
1 garlic clove, mashed
Tabasco to taste

In a chafing dish make a sauce of the catsup, dry mustard, vinegar, Worcestershire sauce, garlic, and Tabasco. Simmer steak slowly in the sauce. Serve with warmed, split, small buns.

HARBOUR ISLAND STEAKS

2½ lbs. thin venison steaks
½ cup flour seasoned with 1 tsp. salt, 3 tsps. paprika, and ¼ tsp. pepper
6 tbsps. butter
1 garlic clove, sliced
2 tsps. curry powder
1 tsp. Worcestershire sauce
1 tsp. dry mustard
½ can (4 oz.) tomato purée
1 can (10¾ oz.) consommé, undiluted
1 leaf of oregano, or 1 small bay leaf, crumbled
1 cup sherry

Roll steaks in seasoned flour and brown in least possible amount of butter. Remove to a Dutch oven or roaster. Make gravy of remaining flour with garlic, curry powder, Worcestershire sauce, mustard, purée, consommé, and oregano or bay leaf. Simmer in skillet with remaining butter for 15 minutes, and pour over steaks. Bake, covered, at 300° for 3 to 3½ hours. Add sherry and bake, covered, for 1 hour more.

SERVES 5 or 6.

VENISON STEAKS WITH ANCHOVY CREAM

6 steaks, about ½ lb. each
2 cups dry white wine
½ cup vinegar
¼ cup water
1 carrot, chopped
1 onion, chopped
2 bay leaves
½ tsp. pepper
¼ lb. butter
1 cup heavy cream
¼ lb. cream cheese
¼ cup chopped anchovies
3 tbsps. brandy

Make a marinade of wine, vinegar, water, carrot, onion, bay leaves, and pepper. Bring to a boil, then cool. Put steaks in marinade in glass or enamelware dish and chill for 24 hours. Remove, dry well. Sauté steaks in butter on both sides until brown but still rare. Remove to a heated platter. Stir cream, cream cheese, anchovies, and brandy into pan fat and cook over very low heat until smooth. Pour over steaks.

SERVES 6.

LOIN CHOPS BORDELAISE

2 chops
2 tbsps. butter
2 tbsps. chopped onion

1 cup dry red wine
salt and pepper

Pan broil chops lightly. Cook onion in butter for 5 minutes, or until onion is soft. Add wine and simmer for 5 minutes. Season to taste and pour over chops.

SERVES 1 or 2.

STUFFED CHOPS

4 double chops
3 cups fresh bread crumbs
1 cup peeled and diced apple
1/4 cup chopped celery
1 tbsp. grated onion
1 tsp. salt

1/2 tsp. pepper
1 cup milk
1 egg, beaten
2 tbsps. pork drippings
2 apples, unpeeled, cored, and
    halved

Make a pocket in each chop. Make a stuffing of bread crumbs, peeled and diced apple, celery, onion, salt, pepper, milk, and egg. Pack stuffing into greased pan and bake at 350° for 1 hour. Cool. Dust chops with salt and pepper and braise in 2 tablespoons pork drippings. Stuff chops and skewer. Put on rack in pan and top each with 1/2 cored, unpeeled apple, cut side down. Cover dish and bake at 350° for 1 1/2 to 2 hours.

SERVES 4.

YANKEE BREADED STEAKS OR CHOPS

4 steaks or chops, 1 1/2 inches thick
2 eggs, beaten
1 tbsp. maple syrup
1 tbsp. water
1 cup coarse dry crumbs

1 tsp. onion salt
1/2 tsp. pepper
1 tbsp. lard
2 tbsps. sweet butter

Wipe meat with a damp cloth. Beat eggs, syrup, and water together. Mix crumbs with onion salt and pepper. Dip meat into egg mixture, then into crumbs, again into eggs, then again into crumbs. Melt lard and butter in a Dutch oven and brown meat on both sides. Cover and bake at 300° for 2½ to 3 hours.
SERVES 4.

VENISON POLONAISE

6 chops	6 juniper berries
1 onion, sliced	½ tsp. dried thyme
2 carrots, sliced	½ cup vinegar
4 shallots, chopped	¼ cup olive oil
4 parsley sprigs	red wine
1 tsp. salt	4 tbsps. butter
6 peppercorns, crushed	1 cup sour cream

Combine chops with onion, carrots, shallots, parsley, salt, peppercorns, juniper, thyme, vinegar, oil, and enough red wine to cover. Let stand, refrigerated, for 24 hours. Drain chops, reserving ½ cup of the strained marinade. Wipe chops dry. Cook chops in hot butter for 4 minutes on each side, or to desired degree of doneness. Remove to heated platter. Add reserved marinade to skillet and bring to a boil. Stir in sour cream and heat. Adjust seasoning and serve sauce separately.
SERVES 6.

VENISON CUBED

Stews are familiar favorites to peoples all over the world. They are easy to make and lend themselves to almost infinite variety. They do, however, take time, and any processing that can be done ahead is of assistance to the cook. One trick is particularly applicable to venison, which is leaner than beef, and that is to coat the pieces well with liquid fat—melted butter or cooking oil—and then cook with the liquid used for the stew. Preliminary browning is eliminated, and it is unnecessary to deglaze the pan or transfer the meat to another cooking dish. Stew can be cooked either on top of the stove or in a moderate oven, covered, of course, so that it does not dry out. With any stew, make sure that the cubes are as uniformly sized as possible. If this is done, all the meat will be equally well cooked, with no over- or underdone pieces.

Where practical, use the best cuts that you can; stringy parts are tough. Wine is usually, but not always, added early in the cooking so that the full flavor is released and the alcohol is evaporated. Use herbs and spices to accent flavor, not to dominate it, and always check for seasoning before serving, particularly when the stew has been warmed up. Don't forget that stews are inevitably better the second time around. Whether cooking the first time, or warming up, be sure that the stew does no more than simmer; only occasional bubbles should rise to the surface of the liquid. Always skim off any fat from the surface before serving. Skim it several times during the cooking, or remove the hardened fat if the stew is chilled before reheating. A Dutch oven is invaluable for stews; the heavy pan prevents scorching and a close-fitting lid keeps the moisture in.

NOME CARIBOU CASSEROLE

2 lbs. caribou top round, cut into
  2-inch cubes
½ cup flour seasoned with ½ tsp.
  salt and ¼ tsp. pepper
2 tbsps. sweet butter
1 tbsp. vegetable oil
2 baking potatoes, sliced thin
2 large onions, sliced thin

1 cup canned mushrooms
½ lb. ham, cut into julienne strips
½ tsp. dried rosemary
½ tsp. ground sage
½ tsp. dried marjoram
½ cup (approx.) cream of
  mushroom soup, undiluted

Roll meat in seasoned flour and fry brown in butter and oil over low heat. Put a layer of potato, then a layer of onion and mushrooms in a buttered casserole; top with layers of ham and caribou. Continue layering, sprinkling with rest of flour and herbs. Cover and bake at 325° for 30 minutes. Add enough soup to cover. Bake for 1 hour more, until tender.

SERVES 6 to 8.

OLD-TIMER STEW

2 lbs. elk shoulder, cut into
  bite-sized cubes
1 cup flour seasoned with ½ tsp.
  salt and ½ tsp. pepper
3 cups water
2 tsps. wine vinegar
½ cup tomato juice
2 tsps. lemon juice
1 tsp. paprika

½ lb. salt pork, minced
1 onion, minced
1 small garlic clove, minced
2 tsps. brown sugar
¼ cup heavy port wine
1 cup diced potatoes
½ cup chopped onion
1 cup chopped celery
dash of dried thyme

Roll cubes of meat in seasoned flour. Boil the water, add vinegar, tomato juice, lemon juice, and paprika, and simmer slowly for 15 minutes. Render salt pork in a Dutch oven. Add minced onion and garlic and cook until onion is transparent. Add brown sugar. When absorbed, add the floured meat and brown over high heat. Add water mix to meat. Cover and simmer for 2¾ hours. Add some tomato juice, if needed, to keep moist. After 2½ hours, remove half of the liquid and stir in wine. Add potatoes, onion, celery, and thyme to the stew. Slowly brown 1 tablespoon of remaining flour in the sweet butter; add the removed half of the liquid slowly. Cook, stirring, to thicken. If too thick, thin with tomato juice. Stir thickened gravy into Dutch oven for rest of cooking time, until meat and vegetables are tender.
SERVES 4 to 6.

PRESSURE COOKER ELK STROGANOFF

2 lbs. elk, in bite-sized cubes	2 cans (3 oz. each) mushrooms
seasoned flour	with liquid
3 tbsps. butter	1 tbsp. prepared horseradish
1 onion, sliced	½ to 1 tbsp. Kitchen Bouquet
	1 cup sour cream

Roll meat cubes in seasoned flour. Melt butter and cook onion until soft. Add meat cubes. Drain mushrooms and add to meat. Add enough water to the mushroom liquid to make ½ cup. Add with horseradish, Kitchen Bouquet, and sour cream to meat and onion. Stir well, seal cooker, and cook at 15 pounds pressure for 20 minutes. Cool quickly.
SERVES 4 to 6.

MULE DEER POT PIE

2 lbs. mule deer meat, cut into 1-inch cubes	1 cup boiling water
4 tbsps. sweet butter	½ cup seedless raisins, blanched
1 large onion, sliced	1 cup cooked and diced carrots
1 garlic clove, diced	1 cup new potatoes, cooked
4 tbsps. salt butter	1 cup peas, cooked
1 tbsp. flour	½ tsp. salt
2 tbsps. milk	¼ tsp. pepper
	3 cups biscuit dough

Melt sweet butter in a Dutch oven and sauté meat, turning often, for 10 minutes. Add onion and garlic. In a separate pot melt salt butter, blend in flour and milk and slowly add boiling water. When thickened, add raisins and pour over meat. Cover and bake at 375° for 2½ hours. Remove from oven. Pour stew into a 4-quart casserole with the carrots, potatoes, and peas. Season and cover with a thin layer of rich biscuit dough. Bake at 425° until biscuit topping is golden brown, 10 to 15 minutes.

SERVES 8 to 10.

SWEET AND SOUR VENISON

4 lbs. venison, cut into bite-sized cubes
2 cups wine vinegar
2 cups water
1 tbsp. sugar
1 cup diced carrots
2 garlic cloves, split

2 tbsps. chopped parsley
2 whole cloves
4 small onions, sliced
3 tbsps. seasoned flour
3 tbsps. rendered beef fat
1 cup sherry

Boil vinegar, water, and sugar for 2 minutes. Put carrots, garlic, parsley, cloves, and two of the onions in a crock and pour on the hot marinade. When cool, add meat cubes, cover dish, and refrigerate for 24 hours. Drain meat and pat dry; reserve marinade. Roll meat in seasoned flour and brown in rendered fat in a Dutch oven. Add remaining 2 onions, the marinade vegetables, and 1 cup marinade. Bake at 350° for 1 hour, stirring often. Add more marinade as necessary to finish gravy. When meat is tender, add sherry and simmer for 10 minutes.

SERVES 8 to 10.

HUNTSMAN'S RAGOUT OF VENISON

2 lbs. venison, cubed
1 cup dried kidney beans
1 onion, studded with 2 cloves
1 bay leaf
1 garlic clove
flour seasoned with salt, pepper, and paprika

4 to 5 tbsps. chopped beef suet
1 onion, minced
red wine
1 cup (approx.) sour cream

Soak beans in water to cover overnight. Drain beans and put in a heavy kettle with studded onion, bay leaf, garlic, and salted water to cover. Bring to a boil and simmer until tender, about 2 hours. Dust meat with seasoned flour. Try out beef suet, and brown meat in the fat. Add minced onion, cover with wine, and bring just to a boil. Cover, reduce heat, and simmer for 1½ to 2 hours, or until meat is tender. Add drained beans, mix, and correct seasonings. Serve with a spoonful of sour cream on each portion.

SERVES 6 to 8.

ATLANTA VENISON SUPREME

2 lbs. top round of venison, cut into ½-inch cubes
4 tbsps. sweet butter
2 tbsps. seasoned flour
1 cup heavy cream

1 tbsp. minced parsley
1 tbsp. minced chives
½ cup dry sherry
3 tbsps. grated Swiss cheese

Melt butter in a Dutch oven. Add meat and cook, covered, at low simmer for 30 minutes. Remove lid, and increase heat to sauté meat. Remove meat. Blend seasoned flour into drippings. Add cream and cook, stirring, until thick. Add parsley and chives and return meat. Cover and bake at 350° for 1 hour. Add sherry and blend in. Sprinkle with cheese, cover dish again, and cook for 20 minutes.

SERVES 6 to 8.

FIREPOT

2 lbs. filet or top sirloin, cut into 1-inch cubes (do not use frozen meat)
2 cups strong chicken broth
2 cups dry white wine
1 onion, thinly sliced
3 celery ribs with leaves, chopped
1 garlic clove, minced
½ tsp. salt

10 peppercorns, crushed
8 juniper berries, crushed
2 parsley sprigs
1 tsp. dried tarragon or 1 tbsp. fresh
½ tsp. dried thyme or 2 sprigs fresh
1 bay leaf

Three days before serving, heat broth and wine to bubbling. Add onion, celery, garlic, salt, peppercorns, juniper berries, parsley, tarragon, thyme, and bay leaf. Bring to a boil again. Remove from heat, cool, then refrigerate, covered. Just before serving, strain liquid through the finest sieve. Bring to a boil, pour into firepot or fondue pot, and place over heat. Keep simmering slowly. Arrange meat cubes attractively on a platter. Provide fondue forks and dipping sauces: Bearnaise, Sweet-Sour, hot mustard, Tomato, Horseradish, curried mayonnaise, hollandaise, sour cream with chives, chili sauce. Each diner holds his meat cubes on a fork in

the simmering pot until it achieves the desired degree of doneness
—preferably rare.

SERVES 4 to 6.

FONDUE

2 lbs. venison tenderloin or sirloin, cut into ¾-inch cubes (do not use
   frozen meat)
peanut oil

Heat 1½ inches peanut oil in a fondue pot over high heat to 400°.
Each guest skewers meat cubes onto a fondue fork and cooks them
to his taste in the hot oil. Serve dipping sauces such as those for
Firepot on the side.

SERVES 6.

NEBRASKA CURRIED VENISON

2 lbs. venison steak, cut into 1-inch cubes	2 tbsps. sugar
	1 bay leaf
2 large onions, minced	pinch of dried basil
4 tbsps. butter	pinch of dried thyme
5 tbsps. curry powder	pinch of ground allspice
1 can (24 oz.) tomatoes, undrained	salt and pepper
2 tbsps. white vinegar	1 cup light cream

Fry onions in butter until light brown. Add meat cubes and curry
powder and fry until well browned. Add tomatoes, vinegar, sugar,
bay leaf, basil, thyme, allspice, salt, and pepper, and bring to a
boil. Reduce heat, cover, and simmer for at least 1 hour. Remove
from heat when done. Add cream and stir in lightly. Serve with
rice and curry condiments: peanuts, raisins, grated coconut, sliced
bananas, apple slices, etc.

SERVES 6 to 8.

LANCASTER CASSEROLE

2 lbs. meat, cut into 1-inch cubes	4 oz. crumbled Bleu cheese
2 tbsps. cooking oil	3 tbsps. diced green pepper
3 tbsps. butter	3 tbsps. diced pimiento
¼ cup flour	8 oz. broad noodles, cooked and
1 tsp. salt	drained
1½ cups milk	

Brown meat cubes slowly in oil. Melt butter in a saucepan and blend in flour, salt, and milk. Cook, stirring, until thickened. Add cheese and stir melted. Blend in green pepper and pimiento. Add with meat to noodles, and pour all into a greased 2-quart casserole. Bake at 350° for 30 minutes.

SERVES 6 to 8.

FRENCH GAME LOU PASTIS EN POTT (POTTED WINE STEW)

Cook in a large pot, at least 5-quart size, cast-iron or porcelain-enameled Dutch oven or a casserole with a tight lid. Try *never* to empty the pot; it is best when new ingredients, including wine, are added and the ingredients are cooked with the base from the last stew. The pot can be kept refrigerated for a few days, or it can be frozen, the base slipped out and freezer-wrapped. When ready to remake the pot, return to the original cooking dish, coated with salt pork or bacon fat to prevent sticking. This dish is made over a two-day period.

2 lbs. venison or beef chuck or bottom round, cut into 1½-inch cubes
2 lbs. stewing-quality pheasant or chicken, cut into serving pieces
½ lb. salt pork or bacon, thickly sliced
6 carrots, sliced
3 whole bay leaves
small bunch of parsley, leaves scissored coarsely
¼ cup fresh thyme leaves, snipped, or 2 tsps. dried
6 figs, fresh or dried, cut into halves
2 lbs. onions, sliced
salt and pepper
MSG (optional)
1 lb. mushrooms
3 garlic cloves, minced
¼ lb. shallots, minced
½ cup Cognac, warmed
red Bordeaux wine

Rub 1 slice of salt pork or bacon all over inner walls of the pot; line bottom with more pork slices. Spread 3 carrots in even layers on pork. Add bay leaves. In even layers, snip on the parsley and thyme. Make a layer of figs. Make an even layer with one-third of the onions. Add half of the venison chunks and sprinkle with salt and pepper (and MSG if desired). Add second third of sliced onions. Add half the pheasant pieces in an even layer. Sprinkle with salt and pepper (and MSG if desired). Remove the stems from half of the mushrooms and tuck into spaces in the pot. Sprinkle on the garlic and shallots. The pot should now be about half full. Flame the Cognac, pour over the layers, and let flames die out. Pour on the red Bordeaux barely to cover the ingredients. Put on the lid and set pot in the middle of a 325° oven. Let bubble gently; check after 1 hour to make sure that it is bubbling *gently;* increase or reduce heat by 25° to control. *Do not stir pot at any time.* Cook this way until the liquid level is reduced by half, 3 to 4 hours, depending on type of dish. When liquid level is correct, remove from oven, let cool, then refrigerate overnight.

The second day, set oven at previous day's temperature. Fill pot to within ½ inch of the top by adding, as on the day before, 3 carrots, 1 pound venison, remaining onions, pheasant, and mushrooms. Season with salt and pepper (and MSG). Add more red wine, again barely to cover. Cover pot and cook as on the day before until liquid is again reduced by half. The dish now may be served, but is much better if it is first cooled, then refrigerated for 3 days, then reheated. To serve, serve the meat pieces from the top first, carefully digging down to get the sauce from the base of the pot. From 8 to 10 people can empty this pot, but it always is best to try to limit the number of servings so that the pot is only half emptied. To continue the cooking cycle after the first meal, defrost the remainder and again make layers in roughly the same proportions. Small game can be used, sausages, other birds, other big game, with vegetables, always adding more red wine barely to cover and cooking until the liquid is reduced by half. Never add more wine when only reheating, only when adding new meat and vegetables.

BRANDIED STEW

3 lbs. meat, cut into 1½-inch cubes

salt and freshly ground pepper

3 tbsps. butter

6-inch strip of orange rind, 1 inch wide

1½ lbs. small white onions (silverskins)

⅓ cup condensed beef broth, undiluted

1 large garlic clove, crushed

½ cup brandy

6 carrots, cut into ¼ x ¼ x 2-inch sticks

2 tbsps. minced fresh parsley

1 tbsp. grated lemon rind

Season meat generously with salt and pepper. Melt butter and heat until it foams and begins to brown. Add meat, turning to coat all sides with butter. Add orange rind and arrange onions over the meat. Stir together the broth, garlic, and half the brandy, and add to meat. Cover and cook over very low heat, without stirring, for 2½ hours, or until meat is very tender. Add carrots, pushing them down into liquid; cover and simmer for 30 minutes, or until carrots are tender. Just before serving remove meat and vegetables to a serving dish or shallow soup plates. Stir parsley and remaining brandy into liquid. Check seasoning and ladle over meat and vegetables. Garnish with lemon rind.

SERVES 6 to 8.

FREEZER STEW BASE

4 to 5 lbs. venison, cut into 1-inch cubes
1½ cups chopped onions
6 tbsps. rendered beef suet
1 cup flour seasoned with 2 tbsps. salt and ½ tsp. pepper
boiling water or unseasoned beef or venison stock

Soften chopped onions in rendered suet; remove to a stew pot. Flour meat cubes and brown well on all sides in hot suet. Remove to stew pot and cover generously with water or stock. Cover pot and simmer for 1½ hours. *Or* do in pressure cooker at 15 pounds pressure for 25 to 30 minutes, with liquid barely to cover. Cool. When cooled, remove hardened fat from top. Package in freezer containers, either pints or quarts. Defrost before continuing with finishing steps.

MAKES 3 quarts.

HARVEST STEW

1 pint Freezer Stew Base
1 cup seasoned stock
2 pkgs. (10 oz. each) mixed frozen vegetables, not thawed

Add stock to base and slowly bring to a boil. Add frozen vegetables to pot after stew liquid starts to bubble. Cover and simmer for 20 minutes. If you like, add 1 or 2 cubed, parboiled potatoes for the last 10 minutes.

SERVES 4 to 6.

BAVARIAN STEW

1 qt. Freezer Stew Base	1 head of cabbage, cut into
1 tsp. caraway seeds	6 wedges
¼ cup wine or cider vinegar	6 small gingersnaps, crushed
	½ cup warm water

Bring stew to simmer; add caraway seeds, vinegar, and cabbage. Cover and simmer for 35 to 40 minutes. Remove cabbage and meat and add gingersnap crumbs, softened in warm water, to thicken stew liquid. Return meat and cabbage, and mix gently.
SERVES 6.

EAST INDIAN STEW

1 qt. Freezer Stew Base	1 cup sour cream
8 small white onions	1½ tsps. curry powder, or to taste
1 cup diced green pepper	⅛ tsp. cayenne pepper

Bring stew to simmer; add onions and green pepper. Cover and simmer for 30 minutes. Combine sour cream, curry powder, and cayenne with a few spoonfuls of hot liquid, then stir into pot.
SERVES 6.

SWEDISH STEW

1 qt. Freezer Stew Base
3 large potatoes, cut into ½-inch dice
2 cups yellow turnips, cut into ½-inch dice
¼ cup catsup
1½ cups beer

Parboil potatoes for 5 minutes. Bring stew base to simmer; add potatoes, turnips, catsup, and beer. Cover and simmer for 30 minutes, or until vegetables are tender.
SERVES 6.

SPANISH STEW

1 qt. Freezer Stew Base	½ tsp. pepper
1 cup chopped onions	1 cup chopped peeled tomatoes
1 cup diced green peppers	1½ cups canned garbanzos, with
¼ cup olive oil	liquid
2 garlic cloves, crushed	½ cup chopped pimientos
1 tsp. salt	cornstarch (optional)

Sauté onions and green peppers in oil with garlic, salt, and pepper for 5 minutes. Add to simmering stew base with tomatoes and garbanzo liquid, and simmer for 30 minutes. Add garbanzos and pimientos. Thicken with cornstarch dissolved in a bit of water if desired.

SERVES 6.

MEAT AND KIDNEY STEW

1 qt. Freezer Stew Base
1 lb. cleaned kidneys, cut into
    ½-inch slices
1 tbsp. vinegar
3 tbsps. flour seasoned with ½ tsp.
    salt and dash of pepper
3 tbsps. cooking oil

⅛ tsp. dried basil or oregano or
    rosemary
1 cup diced carrots
½ cup slivered celery
1½ cups boiling venison or beef
    stock

Sprinkle kidney slices with vinegar and let stand for 2 hours. Dredge with seasoned flour and brown in oil with herb of your choice. Add to simmering base with vegetables and stock. Cover and simmer for 15 minutes.

SERVES 6 to 8.

STEWED VENISON STROGANOFF

1 qt. Freezer Stew Base
1 can (3 oz.) mushrooms with
    liquid

1 tbsp. prepared horseradish
1 cup sour cream
1 tsp. Kitchen Bouquet

When base begins to simmer, add mushrooms, horseradish, sour cream, and Kitchen Bouquet. Cover and simmer very gently for 20 minutes, stirring from time to time.

SERVES 6 to 8.

MY EASY STEW

2 lbs. venison, cut into bite-sized
    cubes
2 onions, sliced
2 tbsps. beef suet, rendered
seasoned flour
1 cup red wine
1 cup venison or beef stock

2 tbsps. hot catsup
2 bay leaves
1 can (8 oz.) potatoes, drained and
    rinsed
2 cans (8 oz. each) vegetables of
    your choice, drained

Sauté onions in suet until soft. Flour meat and brown. Add wine, stock, catsup, and bay leaves. Cover and simmer for 1½ to 2 hours, or until tender. Add drained canned potatoes and vegetables. Cook slowly 20 minutes more.

SERVES 6 to 8.

OVEN STEW PATTERN

2 lbs. meat, cut into 1-inch cubes
seasoned flour
2 tbsps. cooking oil or melted
    butter

2 cups raw vegetables (carrots, potatoes, celery, etc.) cut into chunks
2 cups liquid (broth, tomato juice, wine, and/or water)

Dredge meat with seasoned flour and mix well with oil in a Dutch oven. Bake at 400° for 30 minutes, stirring once, to brown. Add raw vegetables and liquid and bake, covered tightly, at 350° for 1¾ hours. (If canned vegetables are used, add them for the last 30 minutes of cooking.)

SERVES 4 to 6.

MEXICAN CHILE CON CARNE

Chile is all too often made with ground meat. While it can be done that way, this is the better way.

3½ lbs. top round, cut into
    ½-inch dice
5 tbsps. lard
2 cups chopped onions
4 garlic cloves, minced
4 tbsps. chile powder
1½ tsps. dried oregano
1½ tsps. ground cumin seed
1 tsp. crushed hot red pepper

2 cups venison or beef broth
1 can (1 lb. 13 oz.) whole tomatoes
6 oz. tomato paste
1 tbsp. salt
1 tsp. sugar
1 to 2 tbsps. yellow cornmeal (optional)

Pat meat dry with paper towels. Heat 3 tablespoons of the lard in a Dutch oven. When hot, add all the meat at once. Sear it for 3 or 4 minutes, turning constantly, until all pieces are lightly browned. Transfer meat to a bowl. Add remaining lard to pot, and heat; sauté onions and garlic until onions are wilted, but do not brown. Stir in chile powder, oregano, cumin seed, and red pepper, and mix well to coat onions. Add broth, tomatoes with juice, tomato paste, salt, and sugar. Break up tomatoes with the back of a spoon. Return meat to pot, cover, and simmer for 40 to 50 minutes, until meat is very tender. Cool, cover, and refrigerate overnight. To serve, bring slowly to a boil, reduce heat, and simmer until heated well through. (If stew is too liquid, do this final cooking without a lid.) Stew can also be thickened with cornmeal, if desired. To do this, sprinkle on top of the stew, starting with about 1 tablespoon, and stir in. Also, canned or cooked red kidney beans can be added.

SERVES 6 to 8.

BURGOO

2 lbs. venison
1 large pheasant, squirrel, or duck
salt
2 potatoes, cubed
2 turnips, cubed
2 carrots, cut into thick slices
2 celery ribs, chopped
2 or 3 tomatoes, chopped
1 cup fresh lima beans
1 cup fresh corn kernels

1 cup sliced okra (fresh preferred)
½ small head of cabbage, shredded
4 small red peppers, seeded
1 small green pepper, seeded and cut into strips
½ cup chopped parsley
2 tsps. dried thyme
pepper

Cover meat and bird with salted water (1 tablespoon salt per quart). Bring to a boil, reduce heat, and cover. Simmer for 2 to 3 hours, or until tender. Cut meat from bones and cube. Return meat to broth; add vegetables and parsley. Bring to boil; add thyme and pepper to taste. Cover, reduce heat, and simmer until vegetables are very tender, 45 minutes. Correct seasonings.

SERVES 6 to 8.

SCOTTISH MINCED PIES

2 lbs. venison, cut into ¼- to ½-inch dice
1 cup minced onions
2 tbsps. beef drippings
2 tsps. salt
dash of pepper

½ tsp. mixed herbs of your choice
2 tbsps. flour
1 cup beef bouillon
pastry for 2-crust, 9-inch pie, uncooked

Cook onions in drippings until golden. Add meat, salt, pepper, and herbs. Cook, stirring, until browned. Add flour and cook, stirring, for 1 minute. Add bouillon and simmer until thick. Cool. Line a 6-cup pie pan (or 12 4-ounce custard cups for individuals) with pastry, leaving a bit of overhang. Fill to within 1 inch of the top, fit on top crust, and seal. Trim, and slash or prick top for steam vents. Bake at 400° for 10 minutes; reduce heat to 350° and continue baking until browned. If making individual pies, allow to cool slightly and slip out of cups. Serve hot or cold. This freezes well; reheat on a cookie sheet.

SERVES 8.

Minced meat (which incidentally has many more uses than just the traditional holiday pie) should be made of meat that is finely minced, *not* ground.

NEW ENGLAND MINCED MEAT

4 lbs. lean venison in one piece	4 lbs. raisins
2 lbs. beef suet in one piece	3 lbs. dried currants
4 lbs. (about) Baldwin apples, pared, cored, and minced	½ lb. citron, minced
	1 tbsp. grated mace
3 quinces, pared, cored, and minced	1 tbsp. ground cinnamon
	1 tbsp. ground cloves
3 lbs. sugar	2 nutmegs, grated
2 cups molasses	1 tsp. pepper
2 qts. fresh cider	brandy or grape juice to taste

Cover meat and suet with boiling water and cook, covered, until tender, several hours. Cool in the cooking water. Remove cake of suet, dice into ¼-inch bits and reserve. Mince meat into ½-inch dice and add to twice the volume of minced apples. Add quinces, sugar, molasses, cider, raisins, currants, citron, and minced suet. Reduce the meat cooking liquid by boiling to 1½ cups, and add to apple mixture. Heat gradually, stirring occasionally, and cook slowly for 2 hours. Add mace, cinnamon, cloves, nutmeg, pepper, and brandy or grape juice and simmer for 20 minutes. Freezes very well.

MAKES 6 to 8 quarts.

If the minced meat is to be frozen, it is best to eliminate the brandy and add it after thawing.

Variation

1 lb. lean chuck, minced into ¼- to ½-inch pieces	¼ lb. butter
2½ cups water	1 tsp. grated lemon rind
4 apples (4 cups chopped)	2 tbsps. lemon juice
15 oz. seedless raisins	2 tsps. salt
11 oz. dried currants	2 tsps. ground cinnamon
4 oz. candied citron, minced	1 tsp. grated mace
1¾ cups brown sugar	½ tsp. ground cloves
½ cup molasses	1½ cups sweet cider

Simmer meat in the water for 30 minutes; stir in remaining ingredients and simmer, stirring often, for about 1 hour, or until slightly thickened. Ladle into two 1-quart jars, cool, and cover tightly. Store in refrigerator for at least 4 weeks to ripen and mellow. Can then be frozen.

MAKES 2 quarts.

OLD NEW ENGLAND MINCED MEAT

3 qts. diced venison, cut into ¼- to ½-inch dice	1 lb. white sugar
1 qt. beef suet, minced	1 pint black molasses
6 qts. peeled, cored, and chopped apples	1 pint boiled cider
5 lbs. seedless raisins, minced	½ cup lemon juice
1 lb. citron, minced	¼ cup salt
1 pint minced candied orange peel	1 qt. dark rum
2 lbs. brown sugar	½ cup ground cloves
	¼ cup ground cinnamon

Simmer all but rum, cloves, and cinnamon 2 hours; then remove from heat and stir everything together. Keep in a crock in a cool place, stirring often, or process in Mason jars or freeze.

MAKES 6 to 8 quarts.

BAYOU MINCED MEAT

2 lbs. venison, cut into cubes	juice of 2 oranges
1 lb. beef suet, cut into cubes	juice of 1 lemon
3 lbs. apples, peeled, cored, and cut into chunks	2 tbsps. grated orange rind
1 lb. currants	2 tbsps. grated nutmeg
½ lb. citron	1 tbsp. ground cloves
2 lbs. brown sugar	1 tbsp. ground cinnamon
	1 pint whiskey or cider

Grind meat, suet, apples, currants, and citron through the coarse blade of a grinder once. Mix thoroughly with sugar, orange juice, lemon juice, orange rind, nutmeg, cloves, cinnamon, and whiskey or cider. Let stand at room temperature for 1 hour. Bring to a boil and cook for 30 minutes, stirring constantly, at medium heat. Put into canning jars and proceed with canning process.

Makes 3 to 5 quarts.

MINCED MEAT SOUP

⅓ cup minced meat
1 can (10¾ oz.) condensed
  tomato soup

1 soup-can water
1 tsp. lemon juice
½ tsp. grated lemon rind

Blend soup and water. Add minced meat, lemon juice, and rind. Heat, stirring from time to time. Garnish with a dollop of whipped cream on each serving if desired.

Serves 2 or 3.

MINCED MEAT STUFFING (excellent for duck)

2¼ cups minced meat
1 cup minced onion
¾ cup minced celery
6 oz. butter
12 cups ¼-inch bread cubes
  (about 18 slices)

1 tbsp. salt
1 tbsp. poultry seasoning
¼ to ½ tsp. pepper
¾ cup (about) water

Sauté onion and celery in butter for about 5 minutes. Stir in bread cubes, salt, poultry seasoning, and pepper. Add water and toss gently until well moistened.

Makes 12 cups.

MINCED MEAT OATMEAL COOKIES

1⅓ cups minced meat
1¼ cups sifted all-purpose flour
¾ tsp. baking soda
½ tsp. salt

½ cup hydrogenated vegetable
  shortening
1 cup brown sugar
1 egg
1½ cups rolled oats

Sift flour, baking soda, and salt together. Cream shortening and gradually add brown sugar, beating until fluffy. Beat in egg and stir in minced meat. Gradually add sifted ingredients, blending well. Stir in oats. Drop by teaspoon about 2 inches apart, onto a greased cookie sheet. Bake at 350° until lightly browned, about 15 minutes.

MAKES 48 cookies, 2-inch size.

GLAZED MINCED MEAT MOUNDS

½ cup minced meat
1 cup all-purpose flour
½ tsp. baking soda
¼ tsp. salt
½ tsp. ground cinnamon
¼ tsp. grated nutmeg

½ cup chopped pecans
5½ tbsps. butter, softened
⅓ cup dark brown sugar
1 egg
1 tbsp. sour cream

Mix flour, baking soda, salt, cinnamon, nutmeg; add pecans and set aside. Cream butter and brown sugar together until light and fluffy; add egg and beat well. Combine mixtures, minced meat, and sour cream, and mix well by hand. Drop by heaping teaspoon to form mounds on a cookie sheet, leaving 2 inches between mounds. Bake at 400° for 10 to 12 minutes; break one to be sure it is done inside. Remove, and while still hot, spread with Vanilla Glaze. Loosen from sheet with pancake turner. Cool completely and store airtight. These freeze well, also ship well. They are good keepers and stay fresh longer than hermits.

MAKES 18 mounds.

VANILLA GLAZE

1½ cups confectioners' sugar
dash of salt
1 tsp. vanilla extract

2 tbsps. butter, melted
2 tbsps. light cream or 1 tsp.
   evaporated milk

Stir all ingredients briskly to make a smooth paste; a bit more cream may be needed. Can be stored for a few hours in an airtight jar, refrigerated, if desired.

MINCED MEAT BROWNIES

½ cup minced meat
¼ lb. butter, softened
1 cup sugar
2 eggs
1½ oz. unsweetened
   chocolate, melted and cocled

1 tsp. vanilla extract
½ cup chopped nuts
¾ cup all-purpose flour
¼ tsp. salt

Cream butter and sugar together until light and fluffy. Add eggs, one at a time, beating well after each addition. Stir in minced meat, chocolate, vanilla, and nuts. Add flour and salt and mix well. Spoon into a greased 9-inch-square pan and bake at 350° for about 30 minutes. Cool in the pan on a rack, then cut into squares. Roll in confectioners' sugar, if desired.

MAKES 16 squares.

MINCED MEAT REFRIGERATOR COOKIES

¾ cup minced meat
6 oz. butter, softened
1 cup sugar
1 egg
3 cups all-purpose flour
1 tsp. ground cinnamon

½ tsp. baking soda
½ tsp. salt
1 tsp. grated orange rind
½ tsp. vanilla extract
½ cup chopped walnuts

Cream butter and sugar together until light and fluffy. Beat in egg. Sift together flour, cinnamon, baking soda, and salt; add to creamed mixture. Mix until crumbly. Add orange rind, vanilla, minced meat, and walnuts; dough will be sticky. Dampen hands in cold water; divide dough into halves and shape each into a roll about 1½ inches in diameter; shape on wax paper to keep from sticking. Wrap each roll separately in wax paper. Refrigerate until well chilled. (Can be frozen at this point.) With a sharp knife dipped into cold water, cut into slices about ¼ inch thick. Put on greased cookie sheets. Decorate tops as desired with maraschino cherries, walnut halves, etc. (or cookies can be frosted after baking). Bake at 350° for about 10 minutes, or until edges are golden. Remove at once from sheets and cool on a rack.

MAKES 5 to 6 dozen.

DANISH MINCED MEAT COFFEE CAKE

2 cups minced meat
3 to 3½ cups all-purpose flour
⅓ cup granulated sugar
¾ tsp. salt
2 pkgs. active dry yeast
¾ cup water

⅓ cup milk
6 tbsps. butter
1 egg, at room temperature
1½ tsps. grated orange rind
2 cups confectioners' sugar
3 tbsps. orange juice

Thoroughly mix 1 cup flour, the granulated sugar, salt, and undissolved yeast. Combine water, milk, and butter in a saucepan and heat over low heat until liquids are warm (120° to 130°); butter need not melt. Gradually add to dry ingredients and beat with electric mixer at medium speed, scraping bowl occasionally. Add egg and ½ cup flour, or enough to make a thick batter. Beat at high speed for 2 minutes, scraping bowl sides occasionally. Stir in additional flour to make a soft dough. Cover and let rise in a warm place free from drafts until doubled in bulk, about 40 minutes.

Combine minced meat and orange rind. Stir raised dough down and turn onto a well-floured board; divide into halves. Roll one half into a rectangle 16 x 12 inches and put on a greased jelly-roll pan. Spread minced meat mix over dough. Roll remaining dough in the same way and cover top of minced meat; seal edges. Snip surface of top dough in several places with scissors for steam vents. Cover and let rise in a warm place, free from drafts, until doubled in bulk, about 40 minutes, or until done. Lift from sheet at once and let cool on rack. Combine confectioners' sugar with orange juice, mix to spreading consistency, and spread over cooled cake. To serve, cut into 2-inch squares.

MAKES 1 coffee cake.

MINCED MEAT LOAF

1 cup minced meat	¾ cup brown sugar
3 cups sifted all-purpose flour	1½ cups chopped walnuts
3½ tsps. baking powder	2 eggs
½ tsp. salt	½ cup milk
¼ tsp. baking soda	⅓ cup vegetable oil

Sift flour, baking powder, salt, and baking soda; stir in brown sugar and walnuts. Beat eggs well and stir in milk, oil, and minced meat. Add milk mix all at once to flour mixture; stir just until evenly moist. Spoon into greased loaf pan (9 x 5 x 3 inches) and bake at 350° for 1 hour, or until center tests done. Cool in the pan on a rack for 10 minutes. Loosen around the edges with a knife and turn out onto rack to cool thoroughly. Wrap airtight and store overnight to mellow. Cut into thin slices.

MAKES 1 loaf.

MINCED MEAT AND PUMPKIN PIE

1½ cups minced meat	½ tsp. grated nutmeg
pastry for 1-crust, 9-inch pie, unbaked	½ tsp. ground allspice
1 egg white	½ cup heavy cream or evaporated milk
1 egg	1 cup canned (or mashed, cooked) pumpkin
½ cup sugar	
½ tsp. ground ginger	

Line 9-inch pie pan with pastry. Flute a high rim of the dough around pie dish; prick bottom and sides lightly with a fork and brush the inside with a little unbeaten egg white. Chill until dry. Spread minced meat over bottom of shell. Combine whole egg, sugar, ginger, nutmeg, and allspice, and beat until light. Fold in cream and then pumpkin. Stir until very smooth. Pour over minced meat and bake at 400° for 30 minutes; reduce heat to 350° and bake for 30 minutes longer, or until custard tests done. Insert a knife near the edge of the dish. If knife comes out clean, the custard will be solid all the way through when cooled. Cool on a rack. Serve warm or cold, with cream, whipped or sour, if desired.

SERVES 6 to 8.

STEAMED MINCED MEAT PUDDING

1½ cups minced meat
1¾ cups all-purpose flour
2 tsps. baking powder
1 tsp. salt
½ tsp. ground cinnamon

¼ lb. butter, softened
1 cup sugar
2 eggs
⅔ cup evaporated milk
confectioners' sugar

Mix flour, baking powder, salt, and cinnamon. Cream butter and sugar together until light and fluffy. Add the eggs, one at a time, to the creamed mixture, beating well after each addition. Add dry ingredients alternately with evaporated milk, beating smooth after each addition. Stir in minced meat and pour into a greased 1½-quart pudding mold or ovenproof casserole. Grease inside of lid, or bottom of a double sheet of foil, and cover dish. (If using foil, tie on well.) Set dish on a rack in a kettle and pour in enough boiling water to come halfway up the mold. Cover kettle and steam for 1½ hours; add about 20 minutes more if the mold has no tube. Unmold and serve warm dusted with confectioners' sugar. If made well ahead of serving, can be reheated in the top part of a double boiler for about 1 hour.

SERVES 8.

MINCED MEAT MOUSSE

½ cup minced meat
1 envelope unflavored gelatin
2 tbsps. cold water
⅓ cup boiling water
4 egg yolks

½ cup sugar
4 cups heavy cream, whipped
    until it holds a peak
2 oz. rum

Sprinkle gelatin on cold water and let stand for about 5 minutes to soften. Pour in the boiling water and stir to dissolve gelatin. Beat yolks thoroughly and gradually beat in the sugar until the mixture is thick and creamy. Stir in the dissolved gelatin. Fold in the whipped cream, minced meat, and rum. Put into a 6-cup mold and chill for about 2 hours, or until set.

SERVES 6 to 8.

SPANISH EMPANADAS DE NAVIDAD

FILLING:

1 cup minced meat	1 tbsp. brandy
1½ tsps. cornstarch	1 tbsp. Cointreau

Gradually stir minced meat into cornstarch in a small saucepan; add brandy and Cointreau and bring to boiling, over medium heat, stirring constantly. Reduce heat and simmer for 3 minutes. Remove from heat.

PASTRY:

2 cups sifted all-purpose flour	½ tsp. salt
2 tbsps. sugar	⅓ cup shortening
2 tsps. baking powder	⅓ cup (approx.) ice water

Sift flour with sugar, baking powder, and salt. Cut in shortening to cornmeal consistency. Add ice water, 1 tablespoon at a time, tossing lightly with a fork after each addition, until dough can be shaped into a ball. Divide into halves. Keeping 1 ball wrapped in wax paper, roll out the other to a sheet about ⅛ inch thick and cut with 3½-inch round cutter. Put about 1 teaspoon filling on half of the round, moisten the edge, and fold over; seal with a fork. Put on a cookie sheet. Repeat with remainder. Bake at 375° until golden brown, about 15 to 20 minutes. Serve warm or cold.

MAKES about 24.

MINCED MEAT NUT SQUARES

1½ cups minced meat	¾ cup hydrogenated vegetable
1¼ cups light brown sugar	shortening
1½ cups rolled oats	¾ cup chopped pecans or walnuts
2 cups sifted all-purpose flour	1 egg yolk
½ tsp. salt	1 tbsp. water

Combine sugar, oats, flour, and salt, and cut in shortening. Add nuts. Press half this mix into a 9-inch-square pan; spread with minced meat. Sprinkle remainder of first mix on top. Combine egg yolk and water and brush over crumbs. Bake at 400° for 20 to 25 minutes, or until lightly browned. Cool and cut into 2-inch squares for cookies, or 3-inch squares and top with whipped cream for dessert.

MAKES 16 cookies, 9 desserts.

MINCED MEAT ALMOND CRUNCH

3 cups minced meat
1 cup light brown sugar
1½ cups all-purpose flour
1 tsp. baking soda
½ tsp. salt

½ cup hydrogenated vegetable
  shortening
1¾ cups rolled oats
1 cup slivered almonds

Combine sugar, flour, baking soda, and salt. With pastry blender or knives, cut in shortening to the consistency of coarse cornmeal. Mix in oats. Sprinkle half of this onto bottom of lightly greased pan (15 x 10 inches); pat down well. Spread on minced meat and top with remainder of first mix. Top with almonds and pat into place. Bake at 325° for 45 minutes. Let cool in the pan on a rack, then cut into squares. Store, covered, for several days before serving, either plain or topped with soft ice cream or with cheese wedges.

MAKES 15 squares, 3½-inch size.

APRICOT AND MINCED MEAT FLAMBÉ

18 oz. minced meat
8 oz. canned apricot halves

¼ cup apricot brandy

Drain juice from fruit into saucepan. Stir in minced meat, and heat carefully to boiling. Dice apricot halves and add to hot sauce. Heat brandy separately; ignite and carefully pour over hot sauce. When flame dies by itself, ladle over ice cream, angel, sponge, or pound cake.

MAKES about 3½ cups.

MINCED MEAT FLAMBÉ

1½ cups minced meat

¼ cup warm kirsch

Heat minced meat in top part of a double boiler over gently boiling water for 45 minutes. Transfer to chafing dish to keep warm. Just before serving, ignite the kirsch and pour over minced meat. Serve over vanilla ice cream or baked custard.

MAKES 1½ cups.

MINCED MEAT TOPPING

1 cup minced meat   1 to 2 tsps. grated lemon rind
2 tbsps. light corn syrup

Simmer minced meat, syrup, and lemon rind together for 10 minutes. Serve hot over sponge cake, ice cream, gingerbread, cooked or canned fruits.

MAKES 1 cup.

VENISON GROUND

Ground meat is the base for many popular dishes. It also uses up irregular or small pieces of meat that otherwise would be wasted. These pieces can be trimmings from tender roasts, or bits and pieces from the neck and other tough cuts. Grinding is a good way to make tough meat more palatable. The fact remains, however, that better cuts of meat make better ground meat.

It is perfectly acceptable to use ground venison, with some added fat such as beef fat, without adding any other meats. Some people prefer to mix ground venison with domestic meats. The decision to use domestic meats with venison is entirely a matter of personal taste, as are the proportions of domestic to game meat. Personally, I prefer to use only game meat, moistening it for cooking with beef fat from roasts or steak cuts. Since I prefer ground meat to be lean, I will grind no more than 15% beef fat by weight with even the leanest game meat cuts.

Whether the meat and fat is ground only once or twice is another personal decision. Assuming that the fat and game meat is cut into relatively small pieces and well mixed before putting through the grinder, a good mix can be obtained by one grinding, which is what I prefer to use. A second grinding will make a more cohesive mix.

When it comes to meatballs and meat loaves, many people prefer to blend in other meats, just as they do with beef. If this is the way you like these ground meat dishes, make your meat mixes just as you do with beef, following the same proportions and using pork, lamb, or veal with the venison and fat. If this is your choice, it's best to buy the domestic meat in chunks. Then it can be cubed in the same size as the venison and the total mix ground once only. If you buy the domestic meats already ground, the venison and beef fat will have to be ground, then blended with the domestic meats and the mix reground. It is difficult to make a smooth blend of raw ground meats any other way.

Since the combinations of meat are a matter of choice, in all the following recipes you may use either venison and beef fat in your preferred proportions (I would recommend starting with 15% beef fat to venison by weight) or venison with beef fat and domestic meats.

Meatballs are familiar all over the world, and there's not a single version that doesn't lend itself to the use of venison. For any of these recipes, use venison ground (preferably just before use) to your family's taste with beef fat. Of course, any meatball mixture can be formed into burger patties as well.

Meat loaves can be made of practically any of the meatball mixes. Simply form them into loaves and bake at 350° to doneness (about 1 hour) with a sauce. The sauce can be undiluted canned cream soup, if you wish.

Cooked meatballs, both appetizer size and main-dish size, are good to keep on hand in the freezer. These are not highly seasoned; the flavor accent comes from the sauce in which they are heated. Oven cooking, incidentally, makes them less greasy than frying.

OVEN MEATBALLS

2 lbs. venison, ground　　　　　2 eggs
½ cup fine dry bread crumbs　　1½ tsps. salt, or part garlic salt
½ cup milk

Combine everything in a bowl and mix lightly to blend thoroughly. For appetizers, shape into balls about the size of large marbles. For main-course portions, form into balls the size of golf balls. Bake on cookie sheets in 500° oven for 4 or 5 minutes for appetizer balls, 7 to 9 minutes for main-course meatballs. Freeze on cookie sheets; bag when well frozen. Heat the meatballs, frozen or defrosted, in sauce in the top part of a double boiler until heated through. Serve appetizer meatballs in a chafing dish with sauce. Sauce suggestions: Sweet-Sour, Curry, Bleu Cheese, Italian Tomato, Stroganoff, Teriyaki.

MAKES about 100 appetizer balls, or about 24 main-course balls.

Meatballs can also be frozen in sauces, then reheated.

CHINESE SWEET AND SOUR MEATBALLS

2 lbs. venison, ground
1 tsp. salt
⅛ tsp. white pepper

½ cup peanut oil
1 large green pepper, diced

BATTER

2 eggs, beaten
¼ cup flour

⅛ tsp. white pepper
1 tsp. salt

DOUBLE RECIPE OF SWEET-SOUR SAUCE

Form very small balls of meat with ½ teaspoon salt and the pepper. Dip into batter, and sauté in the oil with ½ teaspoon salt. Make Sweet-Sour Sauce. Pour sauce over meatballs and freeze; or continue by sautéing the green pepper in oil and adding to sauce; simmer for 10 minutes. If frozen, thaw, heat, and continue with green pepper.
SERVES 8.

CURRIED MEATBALLS

2 lbs. venison, ground
2 tbsps. curry powder
1 tsp. ground coriander
1 tsp. ground ginger
¼ tsp. ground cloves
¼ tsp. ground cinnamon
⅛ tsp. pepper

½ tsp. salt
1 tbsp. butter
2 tbsps. cooking oil
½ cup minced onion
2 garlic cloves, mashed
2 cups venison or beef stock
1 tbsp. tomato paste

Form the venison, curry, coriander, ginger, cloves, cinnamon, pepper, and salt into balls, and brown in the butter and oil. After sautéing, add onion and garlic. Combine stock and tomato paste and pour over meat mixture. Freeze; or cover and simmer for 20 minutes. If frozen, thaw and simmer, covered, for 30 to 35 minutes. Serve with rice and curry condiments such as peanuts, raisins, coconut, pine nuts, etc.
SERVES 8.

ITALIAN MEATBALLS

2 lbs. venison, ground
1 cup seedless raisins
1 garlic clove, mashed
1 tsp. ground oregano
1 tsp. dried basil
1 cup minced onion

3 eggs, lightly beaten
½ cup grated Cheddar cheese
½ cup grated Romano cheese
1 tbsp. sugar
½ cup pine nuts or sunflower
  seeds

Plump raisins by soaking in hot water for 10 to 15 minutes; drain. Blend all ingredients lightly and refrigerate, covered, for 1 hour. Shape into balls and sauté in oil. Serve or freeze.

SERVES 8.

SPANISH MEATBALLS

2 lbs. venison, ground
1 cup raw short-grain rice
½ cup minced onion
1 tsp. salt
¼ tsp. pepper
4 tbsps. olive oil
Spanish Sauce

Blend venison, rice, onion, and seasoning. Form into balls. Brown in olive oil; remove. Add to Spanish Sauce. Freeze; or cover and simmer for 30 minutes; for 50 minutes if frozen and thawed.

SERVES 8.

CHEESE-FILLED MEATBALLS

2 lbs. venison, ground
1 cup grated Cheddar cheese
¾ tsp. ground ginger
½ cup minced onion
1 tsp. salt
⅛ tsp. pepper
¼ tsp. garlic powder
oil
4 cups meatless spaghetti sauce

Blend Cheddar cheese with ginger and form into small balls (or use 1 cup Roquefort or Bleu cheese with 2 to 3 tablespoons minced parsley). Blend meat, onion, salt, pepper, and garlic powder and form into balls around cheese balls. Sauté in oil. Heat spaghetti sauce and add meatballs. Freeze; or cover and simmer gently for 20 minutes; for 30 to 35 minutes if frozen and thawed.

SERVES 8.

VENISON RAGOUT

1½ lbs. venison, ground
½ cup grated onion
5 tbsps. butter
1 cup bread crumbs
1 cup light cream
1 egg, lightly beaten
1½ tsps. cornstarch
1 tsp. salt
½ tsp. grated mace
¼ tsp. grated nutmeg
2 tbsps. olive oil
3 tbsps. flour
2 cups Burgundy wine
1 cup venison or beef stock
1 tsp. tomato paste
½ cup sour cream (optional)

Sauté the onion in 1 tablespoon butter until golden. Combine onion with meat, crumbs, light cream, egg, cornstarch, salt, mace, and nutmeg. Shape into about 40 small balls. Melt remaining butter with oil, add meatballs, and sauté until brown. Remove meatballs from pan. Stir flour into pan; add Burgundy, stock, and tomato paste; bring to a boil, stirring. Return meatballs and simmer, covered, for 20 minutes. Sour cream can be gently stirred in just before serving if desired.

SERVES 6.

WYOMING MULE DEER TARTAR TOAST

1 lb. venison, freshly ground (do not use frozen meat)	4 tbsps. butter, softened
3 tbsps. light cream	1 tsp. salt
1 tbsp. onion juice	1/4 tsp. pepper
8 thick slices of bread	1 tbsp. garlic salt
	4 slices of raw bacon, diced

Blend cream and onion juice gently into meat. Toast 1 side of each slice of bread under broiler. Butter untoasted sides; sprinkle with salt, pepper, and garlic salt, and toast just long enough to melt butter. Spread meat on buttered side all the way to the edges, and top with diced bacon to cover well; use more bacon if needed. Put 3 inches below source of broiler heat and broil for 8 to 10 minutes.

SERVES 4.

DELUXE BURGERS

1/2 lb. venison, ground	1/4 tsp. dried tarragon
1 tsp. red wine	salt and pepper
1/4 tsp. dried marjoram	butter
1/4 tsp. dried thyme	

Blend wine into meat and form into an oblong loaf. Sprinkle with marjoram, thyme, tarragon, salt, and pepper, and let stand at room temperature for 30 minutes. Sear on all sides in hot butter. Serve very rare.

SERVES 1.

VENISON À LA FOCHE

1 lb. venison, ground	3 cups hot venison or beef stock
1/4 lb. lean bacon	1/4 tsp. Kitchen Bouquet
1/4 cup seasoned flour	2 slices of hot toast
1 tbsp. sweet butter	1 tsp. minced parsley
8 to 10 oysters, breaded	

Brown the bacon, remove, drain, and crumble into the venison. Reserve fat. Shape meat into 2 balls and roll in seasoned flour. Flatten to shape and size to match toast. Sauté in butter for 5 minutes per side. Remove and keep warm while frying oysters in bacon fat until golden. Blend 1 tablespoon of the seasoned flour into butter and bacon fat, add stock, and cook, stirring, until thickened. Add Kitchen Bouquet to color; add oysters and simmer for 10 minutes. Put meat on toast; top with oysters and sauce, and sprinkle with parsley.

SERVES 2.

BURGUNDY LOAF

2½ lbs. venison, ground
1 cup Burgundy wine
¼ cup minced celery
1 garlic clove
1 bay leaf
2½ cups soft bread crumbs
1 large onion, minced
1 tbsp. minced parsley

2 tbsps. dried rosemary
¼ tsp. dried thyme
¼ tsp. pepper
2 eggs, beaten
1 tsp. Worcestershire sauce
1 can (10¾ oz.) beef broth, undiluted

Combine wine, celery, garlic, and bay leaf; bring to a boil and simmer, uncovered, for about 10 minutes to reduce by half. Discard garlic and bay leaf. (This is Burgundy Sauce when strained and thickened with cornstarch, if desired.) Cool liquid completely. Mix meat, wine mix, bread crumbs, onion, parsley, rosemary, thyme, pepper, eggs, Worcestershire sauce, and half of the beef broth. Form into a loaf. Bake at 350° for 1 hour and 10 minutes. Remove meat loaf and keep warm. For sauce, mix remaining half can of beef broth with ¼ cup water and add to pan juices; stir to make pan gravy. Strain and add enough water to make 1 cup, or serve with more Burgundy Sauce.

SERVES 8 to 10.

WELLINGTON LOAF

1½ lbs. venison, ground
1 can (6 oz.) mushrooms, liquid reserved
2 eggs, lightly beaten
¼ cup chopped onion

2 tbsps. chopped green pepper
salt and pepper
1 cup biscuit mix
¼ cup mushroom liquid
⅛ tsp. poultry seasoning

Form a meat loaf 10 x 3½ inches with meat, mushrooms, eggs, onion, green pepper, seasonings to taste, and 2 tablespoons of the

mushroom liquid. Put into shallow pan. Mix biscuit mix, re-maining mushroom liquid, and poultry seasoning to form a soft dough. Roll into a sheet 12 x 8 inches and put over top and sides of loaf. Bake at 375° for 45 minutes.
SERVES 6.

Ground meats, with a variety of seasonings, fill a wide range of casings. These can be used for either appetizers or main courses.

SPICED INDIAN APPETIZERS

1½ lbs. venison, ground
butter
1 large onion, minced
3 garlic cloves, mashed
3 tbsps. curry powder
1½ tsps. salt
1½ tsps. ground ginger
1 tsp. sugar
¼ tsp. cayenne pepper

1 pkg. (10 oz.) frozen green peas, thawed
70 won ton skins or pastry sheets for ravioli
oil for deep-frying
2 cups plain yogurt
¼ cup minced chutney
1 tsp. crumbled dried mint

Brown meat in smallest amount of butter possible. Add onion, garlic, curry, salt, ginger, sugar, and cayenne, and cook, stirring, until onion is limp. Stir in peas and cook for 1 minute. Drain off and discard any fat. Cool completely. Use to fill the won ton skins or ravioli dough. Put 1 scant tablespoon on each skin, fold skin over, and seal moistened edges. Keep won tons covered with plastic film as they are filled. Refrigerate or freeze. To continue (thaw covered with film if necessary), fry in 1 to 1½ inches oil heated to 360° on frying thermometer for 1 or 2 minutes, turning, until crisp and brown. Drain well and keep warm (or can be frozen after draining). If frozen, heat on a cookie sheet in a 350° oven for 15 minutes. Serve with sauce made of the yogurt, chutney, and mint, well mixed.
MAKES 70 appetizers.

RUSSIAN APPETIZERS

1 lb. venison, ground
1 onion, minced
1 garlic clove, minced
salt and pepper
butter
2 cups all-purpose flour

1 egg, lightly beaten
1 tsp. salt
⅔ cup (approx.) water
4 tbsps. butter
¼ cup Dijon-style mustard
¼ cup white wine vinegar

Brown meat with onion, garlic, and salt and pepper to taste, in as little butter as possible. Drain off any fat or liquid. Make a dough by combining flour, egg, and salt, and gradually add the water. Knead until elastic; roll one-quarter to one-third of the dough at a time to a very thin sheet, about $\frac{1}{16}$ inch thick, and cut into 2-inch squares. Top with about $\frac{1}{2}$ teaspoon of the meat, fold over, and seal the edges. Drop about one-quarter of the dumplings at a time into a large kettle of boiling salted water; lift with a wooden spoon to keep from sticking. Boil for about 10 minutes, or just until tender. Drain well. Freeze if desired. Serve hot, dotted with remaining butter cut into very small pieces, and with a sauce made of the mustard blended with the vinegar. Thaw if frozen; heat in top part of a double boiler.

MAKES 70 appetizers.

TO PREPARE CABBAGE LEAVES FOR STUFFING

To prepare cabbage leaves, remove the core from the head of cabbage with a sharp knife. Wash the head well and put it in a pan with a tight lid with about 1 cup water. Cook, covered, until the leaves begin to soften. Remove, drain, and take the head apart, removing any hard part at the bottom of leaves.

TO STUFF CABBAGE LEAVES

On each large cabbage leaf, put about 2 tablespoons of the desired stuffing. Fold the leaf over on two opposite sides and roll up, enclosing filling completely. Either tie with white string or skewer with picks. Smaller leaves from the inside of the head can be used as a bed for further cooking of the rolls, if desired.

RUSSIAN STUFFED CABBAGE

1 lb. venison, ground	1 tbsp. flour
2 onions, chopped	1 cup sour cream
3 tbsps. butter	2 tbsps. tomato purée
salt and pepper	2 tsps. sugar
$\frac{1}{2}$ cup cooked rice	2 tbsps. vinegar, or juice of $\frac{1}{2}$
1 cup venison or beef stock	lemon
8 cabbage leaves, prepared for stuffing	

Fry onions lightly in 1 tablespoon of the butter. Add meat, season with salt and pepper, and fry for a few minutes until pink color is gone. Remove from heat and add rice and a little of the stock to bind it together. Use to fill cabbage leaves, and roll them as described above. Fry rolls in 1 tablespoon butter until lightly browned on all sides. Arrange rolls close together in a casserole or baking dish. Melt remaining butter, blend in flour, and dilute with rest of stock. Sprinkle with salt, add sour cream, tomato purée, and sugar, and bring to a boil. Mix well and remove from heat. Add vinegar or lemon juice and pour over rolls. Bake at 300° for 1 hour.

SERVES 4.

VENISON STRUDEL

2 lbs. venison, ground	3 eggs
1 small onion, minced	1½ cups shredded Swiss cheese
4 tbsps. melted butter	¼ cup minced parsley
¼ lb. mushrooms, chopped	¼ cup fine dry bread crumbs
¼ tsp. pepper	12 sheets (12 x 18 inches) of
salt	strudel or phyllo dough
½ tsp. dried oregano	melted butter
2 garlic cloves, minced	sour cream for garnish

Sauté onion in 2 tablespoons of the butter until transparent. Add mushrooms and venison and sauté, stirring until meat loses its pink color and becomes crumbly. Remove to a bowl, and season with salt, pepper, oregano, and garlic. Let cool slightly. Break in eggs and mix lightly. Mix in cheese, parsley, and crumbs; chill. Use 6 sheets of dough; keep remainder covered with plastic film or damp towel. Arrange them, overlapping, brushing with melted butter, to form a rectangle 15 x 24 inches. Spread with chilled filling to within 1½ inches of long sides, within 3 inches of short sides. Fold the 1½-inch edges over filling, then fold one of the 3-inch edges over the filling and roll from that end as for a jelly roll. Lay out remaining sheets of dough in the same fashion and fold in long sides 1½ inches. Set first roll across narrow end and roll up. Brush with remaining butter and put on a large baking sheet. Bake at 375° for 30 to 35 minutes, or until golden brown. (Can be made ahead and chilled. In that case, reheat at 375° for 15 to 20 minutes.) Slice and serve with dollop of sour cream on cut side.

SERVES 6.

Ground meat is versatile in one-dish meals.

GROUND VENISON CHILE

2 lbs. venison, ground	1 tsp. oregano
2 cloves garlic, minced	1 tsp. salt
1 tbsp. bacon fat	8 oz. tomato paste
1½ to 2 tbsps. chile powder	1 qt. water
1 tsp. cumin powder	

Sauté garlic in bacon fat, add meat and brown. Add chile, cumin, oregano, and salt, and cook, stirring, for 5 minutes. Add tomato paste and water. Bring to a boil, cover, and simmer for 1½ hours. If desired, thicken with 2 tablespoons flour or cornstarch dissolved in ¼ cup water. Freeze or add canned red kidney beans (up to equal volume) and serve.

SERVES 4 to 8.

APPLE CHILE

1 lb. venison, ground	cooking oil
2 onions, sliced	1 can (1 lb.) kidney beans
1 apple, peeled, cored, and chopped	2 tsps. chile powder

Sauté onions and apple soft in enough oil to cover bottom of skillet. Remove. Brown the meat in the same pan. Return the onion and apple. Add undrained beans and chile powder. Mix well, cover, and bake at 350° for 45 minutes.

SERVES 4 to 6.

BARBECUE

1 lb. venison, ground	1 cup catsup
1 onion, chopped	1 tsp. salt
¼ cup chopped green pepper	½ tsp. pepper
1 tbsp. butter	

Cook onion and green pepper in the butter until soft but not browned, about 5 minutes. Add meat and brown. Add catsup, salt, and pepper. Cover and simmer for 15 to 20 minutes at 350°; an electric skillet is best for this. Spoon off excess fat. Freeze or serve on split hamburger buns.

SERVES 4.

EAST INDIAN KIMA

1½ lbs. venison, ground
1 cup chopped onions
½ cup diced green pepper
4 tbsps. cooking oil
1 tsp. salt
2 tbsps. curry powder
1 cup seedless raisins

1 cup venison or beef stock
2 tbsps. cornstarch
¼ cup water
½ cup chopped pimientos
1 cup slivered nuts (pine nuts,
  almonds, or peanuts)
1 pkg. (10 oz.) frozen peas

Plump raisins by soaking in hot water for 10 to 15 minutes; drain. Sauté onions and green pepper in the oil for 3 minutes. Work the salt and curry powder into the meat, then brown meat in same oil. Add raisins and stock, cover, and simmer for 10 minutes. Soften cornstarch in ¼ cup water and add with pimientos to meat mix. Cook, stirring, until thickened. Add nuts. Freeze. To serve, reheat combined with frozen peas, cooked.
SERVES 8.

GREEK MOUSSAKA

2 lbs. venison, ground
4 to 5 lbs. eggplant, unpeeled and
  cut into ½-inch-thick slices
seasoned flour
olive oil
1 cup minced onions
1 large garlic clove, minced
1 cup tomato sauce
1 tsp. salt

½ tsp. pepper
6 tbsps. butter
6 tbsps. flour
3 cups milk, warmed
3 eggs, well beaten
salt and paprika
2 cups grated Feta, Muenster, or
  Swiss cheese
1½ cups fine bread crumbs

Dredge eggplant slices with seasoned flour and sauté them in olive oil; use as little oil as possible. Drain. Use one-third of the slices to line two 2½-qt. lasagna pans. Sauté onions and garlic in a little oil for about 3 minutes; add meat and brown. Stir in tomato sauce, salt, and pepper, and simmer for 10 minutes. Melt butter and stir in flour. Add warm milk and cook, stirring, until sauce is thick and bubbling. Beat slowly into eggs; season with salt and paprika to taste. Build layers in pans with meat, custard sauce, cheese, crumbs, and eggplant slices, ending with crumbs. Freeze or bake at 350° for 30 minutes; finish by browning under the broiler. Bake still frozen and still covered at 350° for 1 hour, then uncovered for 30 minutes; finish as above.
SERVES 10 to 12.

MEXICAN PICADILLO (HASH)

1½ lbs. venison, ground
1 onion, chopped
lard
1 cup tomato purée
3 oz. slivered blanched almonds
3 oz. raisins
2 candied citrons, diced
2 small bananas, sliced

3 oz. ripe olives, chopped
6 pickled chile peppers, minced
1 tbsp. minced parsley
salt and pepper
1 tbsp. sugar
1-inch stick, or 1 pinch,
  cinnamon
2 whole cloves

Fry onion and meat in small amount of lard. When the meat starts to brown, add tomato purée. Cook until slightly thickened. Add almonds, raisins, citrons, bananas, olives, chiles, and parsley. Season with salt, pepper, sugar, cinnamon, and cloves. Simmer slowly until sauce is thickened and meat is well done. Remove cinnamon stick before serving.
  SERVES 8.

GROUND MEAT QUICHE

½ lb. venison, ground
fat
½ cup mayonnaise or salad
  dressing
½ cup milk
2 eggs, beaten
1 tbsp. cornstarch

1½ cups grated Swiss cheese
⅓ cup sliced scallions
½ tsp. salt
dash of pepper
pastry for 1-crust, 9-inch pie,
  unbaked

Brown meat in as little fat as possible. Drain well. Blend mayonnaise, milk, eggs, and cornstarch until smooth. Stir in meat, cheese, scallions, salt, and pepper. Put into unbaked pastry in 9-inch pan. Bake at 350° for 35 to 40 minutes, or until the custard tests done (a knife inserted in center comes out clean).
  SERVES 6 to 8.

FAVORITE CASSEROLE

2 lbs. venison, ground
olive oil
8 oz. spaghetti, cooked and
  drained
1 can (1 lb.) corn, drained

1 can (1 lb.) tomatoes, chopped
  but not drained
1 small can (3½ oz.) pitted ripe
  olives, drained and chopped
fine crumbs, buttered
grated Parmesan cheese (optional)

Brown meat in as little olive oil as possible. Mix with spaghetti, corn, tomatoes, and olives in a greased casserole and bake at 350° for 1 hour. Top with buttered crumbs and grated cheese and brown under the broiler.

Serves 4 to 6.

PASTA SAUCE

½ lb. venison, ground twice
¼ lb. mushrooms
1 garlic clove, mashed
pinch of cayenne

2 tbsps. olive oil
1 can (1 lb.) tomatoes
1 tbsp. tomato purée
salt and pepper

Simmer mushrooms, garlic, cayenne, and meat in oil for 5 minutes. Strain tomatoes, reserving liquid, and add. Simmer gently for 45 minutes. Blend tomato purée with a little of the reserved tomato liquid, and add with salt and pepper to taste. Cover and cook slowly 30 minutes, stirring from time to time.

Serves 4.

SANDWICH FILLING OR PARTY SPREAD

venison, ground once without suet
  (use largest blade), or finely
  minced venison steak and roast
  trimmings
onions, minced

green peppers, minced
butter
red wine or tomato juice
mayonnaise

Mix minced onions and peppers in proportions to suit your taste, and measure enough to equal amount of ground venison. Sauté vegetables in minimum of butter until soft but not browned; remove from skillet. Brown meat well, slowly. Remove meat and deglaze pan; use tomato juice if mixture is to be used in sandwiches, red wine if for a party spread. Blend meat, onions, peppers, and pan deglazing, and cool. When cooled, add mayonnaise to desired consistency.

SAUSAGES AND LUNCHEON MEATS

Sausages and luncheon meats can be made at home. Making them at home, you can season exactly to your family's tastes. Casings (hog, beef, or sheep) can be bought at meat suppliers (or perhaps through your meat man) in several sizes. Some meat grinders have sausage-stuffing attachments that make the job easier, or you can use a metal cookie press to stuff the casings, or a large cloth pastry-decorating bag with a plain, large tip.

Sausage casings come fresh, packed in a salt brine, or dry-salted. Salted casings last indefinitely under refrigeration; fresh ones, unless frozen, will spoil in about the same length of time as fresh meat. Whichever casings you use, they must be soaked in warm water for 20 to 30 minutes to make them pliable, then cut into 2- to 3-foot sections. Fit one end of the section over the nozzle of the water faucet and run lukewarm water through the casing for about 15 seconds. Drain the casing, strip out excess water, and press out any air bubbles. To fill casings, either follow the directions with your grinder attachment, or put the sausage meat into a cookie press or pastry bag; lightly greasing the tip helps. Fit the end of the casing over the tip and press the meat mixture into it, leaving about 5 inches empty on each end of the casing to allow for knotting and tying. If the meat mixture is too dry or stiff, it will probably split the casing; add enough water or liquid to the mixture to give a consistency somewhat thinner than that for meatballs or meat loaf.

To separate into links, knot one end of the casing and tie with clean white string into the length of link specified or desired. You'll need two ties between each pair of links, somewhat separated, so that links can be cut apart without spilling out their contents.

The new clear roasting film with foil ends, now available in most markets, can also be used for forming link sausages. To do this, spoon the sausage mixture into a 14-inch-long band on an 8-inch-long piece of roasting film 18 inches wide, distributing it evenly for 1-inch diameter sausages 6 inches long. Roll up the meat tightly in the film, smoothing it with your hands to make an even, compact roll. Countertwist the foil ends of the film, turning ends in opposite directions, until a firm roll is formed; tie the end with string to close securely. Tie in equidistant places to form links. These can be refrigerated for 1 or 2 days, or frozen for up to 2 weeks.

These film casings make a good proving ground for your sausage flavorings. It is always best to test any sausage mix before storing it away for future use. A small amount can be film-cased and cooked, or some of the loose sausage can be browned in butter in a skillet. Testing at this point will let you adjust seasonings as required.

Film-cased sausages can be baked as they are. Put them in a

single layer, slightly apart, on a rack in a rimmed baking sheet. With a sharp knife or fork, prick the film at 1-inch intervals on the top. Bake at 325° until well browned, about 1 hour and 10 minutes for 6-inch sausages, 55 minutes for 2½-inch sausages. For refrigerated or thawed frozen sausages, allow 1 hour and 20 minutes, or 65 minutes, respectively. Before serving, snip the film and strip it from the links.

To freeze sausages in casings, wrap well in plastic film or foil; also overwrap film-cased sausages. Thaw completely before cooking.

Casing sausages can be fresh or smoked. If you want fresh sausages, they should be scalded before freezing or cooking. To scald them, put a single layer of sausages in a frying pan. Bring water to a boil in a kettle and pour over sausages; simmer at lowest possible heat for 20 to 25 minutes. Drain. If you intend to freeze them, cool and then wrap. These sausages are browned in butter or broiled for serving. Brush with melted butter and broil about 6 inches from the source of heat until evenly browned, turning often.

Smoking of casing sausage can be done in a covered barbecue or a smokehouse. If they are barbecue-smoked they will have a light smoke flavor and will be brown. If they are smoked in a smokehouse (18 to 20 hours at a temperature no higher than 120°), they will be stronger flavored and reddish rather than brown. After smoking they will be fully cooked and ready to eat. To smoke in a covered barbecue, build a very hot coal fire of briquettes; cover the fire with a thick layer of hickory chips. Arrange the sausages in a single layer on a rack over a foil pan (to catch drippings) and put at least 6 inches from the fire. Cover the barbecue to maintain a low fire and smoke the sausages for 2 to 3 hours.

Loose sausage meat can be formed into patties or into loaves. Luncheon meats can be packed into casings or into plastic boxes.

Some cooks recommend that sausage is best frozen with the seasoning omitted until just before cooking, but obviously the seasonings cannot be well mixed in if this procedure is followed. While adding the seasonings in the original mixing may result in some change of flavor through storage, I prefer to do it that way. Frozen, with seasonings, they will keep for up to 6 months.

Saltpeter, which is called for in many sausage recipes, is a preservative obtainable at the drugstore. *Quatre-épices*, the French seasoning, is very much the result of each Frenchman being his own chef; rarely are two such blends the same. This results in truly individualistic seasoning. You can make your own "family blend"; each of the four ingredients is commonly available. English Bangers, generally made with pork, are especially good, but there's no reason why the mixtures of seasoning should not be· used with venison in combination with pork. There are many combinations which follow in which the Banger seasoning can be substituted.

FRENCH QUATRE-ÉPICES (basic spice blend)

Blend 7 parts ground pepper to 1 part each of grated nutmeg, ground cloves, and ground cinnamon. From this starting point, corrections may be made by adding a bit more of one or another of the spices. Store in a tight-lidded jar.

ENGLISH BANGER (SAUSAGE) SEASONING

4½ tbsps. salt
4 tbsps. white pepper
½ tsp. grated mace
⅝ tsp. ground coriander

⅝ tsp. grated nutmeg
⅜ tsp. MSG
¼ tsp. ground ginger
⅛ tsp. cayenne

MAKES about ½ cup.

DIXIE VENISON SAUSAGE

2½ lbs. fat-free venison shank, ground fine
2½ lbs. pork, only 40% fat, ground fine
1½ oz. salt
¼ oz. pepper

1 small pinch of ground sage
1 small pinch of cayenne
1 tbsp. pork fat
½ tsp. onion juice
1 bay leaf, crushed
¼ tsp. garlic juice

Blend salt, pepper, sage, and cayenne, and stir thoroughly through the meat. (If meat is cubed, put with seasonings through the fine blade of a grinder three times.) Will keep refrigerated for 4 weeks.

To cook, render pork fat, season with onion juice, bay leaf, and garlic juice. Bring to high heat, add cakes made of sausage, and simmer for 10 minutes per side.

MAKES 5 pounds.

Variation

Use a small pinch of grated mace instead of sage and cayenne.

BLACK HILLS VENISON SAUSAGE

2½ lbs. fat-free venison shoulder,
  ground
1 lb. salt pork, ground
2½ tsps. ground sage

2½ tsps. (or less) salt
2 tsps. white pepper
2 tbsps. onion juice
1 tbsp. lemon juice

Blend meats by kneading with the hands, and run through fine
blade of a grinder again. Mix sage, salt, pepper, onion and lemon
juices, and add in batches to meats, again by kneading thoroughly.
Run twice more through the grinder. Pack into a bread tin and
chill well. Slice and fry.
MAKES 3½ pounds.

CREOLE VENISON SAUSAGE

1 lb. fat-free venison, ground
½ lb. fat-free veal, ground
½ lb. fat-free pork, ground
½ lb. very fat pork, ground
⅓ cup flour
1½ tbsps. seasoned salt
½ tsp. ground allspice
½ tsp. grated nutmeg

½ tsp. black pepper
⅛ tsp. dried thyme
¼ tsp. dried marjoram
1 large bay leaf, crushed
pinch of cayenne
1 large onion, minced
2 garlic cloves, mashed
2 tbsps. white lard

Mix meats with flour, salt, allspice, nutmeg, pepper, thyme,
marjoram, bay leaf, and cayenne. Knead well by hand and put
through the fine blade of a grinder. Add onion and garlic, and
put through fine grinder at least once more. Form into patties.
Fry in lard over medium heat for 30 to 40 minutes, or until well
done. (Increase the spices for truly Creole hotness.)
MAKES 3½ pounds.

PENNSYLVANIA SAUSAGE

4 lbs. venison
4 lbs. pork
4 oz. commercial pork-sausage
  seasoning

½ oz. commercial quick-action
  pickle

Grind venison 3 times through a fine blade, the pork once through
a coarse blade. Mix all ingredients and grind once more through
the sausage plate. Put into casings or form into patties.
MAKES 8 pounds.

SMOKED SWISS SAUSAGE

1½ lbs. venison, ground with 15% ½ tsp. ground allspice
 beef suet   1 cup heavy cream
¾ lb. pork, ground   1½ cups (approx.) water
2¼ tsps. plus 2 tbsps. salt 2 tbsps. brown sugar
2¼ tsps. caraway seeds

Combine meats and grind through a fine blade 3 times. Mix in the 2¼ teaspoons salt, the caraway, allspice, and cream. Add enough water to make a mixture soft enough to press into casings. Tie into 12-inch lengths. Arrange in a bowl or pan and sprinkle evenly with mixed 2 tablespoons salt and the brown sugar. Cover and refrigerate overnight. Next day, smoke for 2 hours at no more than 120°. Serve hot, or slice cold for sandwiches.

 MAKES 2 pounds.

SCANDINAVIAN SAUSAGE

2 lbs. fat-free venison, ground ½ tsp. pepper
1½ lbs. pork, ground   ½ tsp. ground ginger
1 lb. beef suet, minced   1 tsp. ground allspice
2 potatoes, cooked, peeled, and ¾ cup milk
 mashed   2 cups (approx.) water
6 tsps. plus 2 tbsps. salt 2 tbsps. brown sugar
1½ tsps. sugar

Combine meats and put through a fine blade 3 times. Mix in suet, potatoes, 6 teaspoons salt, sugar, pepper, ginger, allspice, and milk. Add enough water to give a consistency suitable for pressing into casings. Tie into 12-inch lengths. Arrange in a bowl and sprinkle with remaining salt and the brown sugar. Refrigerate overnight. Next day smoke as for Smoked Swiss Sausage. Or scald by putting into skillet, pouring on boiling water, simmering at lowest heat for 20 to 25 minutes. Drain. Serve browned or smoked, hot or cold.

 MAKES 4 pounds.

FRENCH SAUSAGE

1 lb. fat-free venison, ground 3 tsps. plus 2 tbsps. salt
1 lb. lean pork, ground   1 tsp. pepper
1 lb. beef suet, minced   ½ cup Cognac or brandy
1 large garlic clove, mashed 1 cup (approx.) water
1 onion, minced   2 tbsps. sugar
½ cup minced parsley

Combine venison and pork and put through a fine blade 3 times. Mix in suet, garlic, onion, parsley, 3 teaspoons salt, and the pepper. Add Cognac or brandy and enough water to make mixture soft enough to press into casings. Tie into 4-inch links. Arrange in a bowl and sprinkle with remaining salt and the sugar. Refrigerate overnight. Next day, scald (these are not to be smoked). Brown to serve.

Makes 2 pounds.

SWEDISH SAUSAGE

2½ lbs. venison, ground with 15% beef suet
2½ lbs. pork shoulder, ground
6 raw potatoes, ground
1 cup venison or beef broth
2 onions, ground
1 tsp. pepper
1 tsp. salt
1 tsp. ground allspice
1 tsp. grated nutmeg

Mix all with the hands. Stuff into about 5 yards of casings. Tie as desired. Let stand overnight in the refrigerator. Cover with cold water, bring to a boil, and simmer gently for 1 hour. Or put into a large roaster with cold water to cover and roast at 350° for 1 hour. Good hot or cold.

Makes 7 pounds.

COLORADO SAUSAGE

3 lbs. fat-free venison
4 tbsps. Morton's Sausage Seasoning
1 lb. beef suet
¼ cup cold water (optional)

Grind venison through coarse plate of grinder and spread on a clean surface. Sprinkle evenly with seasoning. Grind suet through medium plate, then through the finest; it should be in considerably smaller pieces than the venison. Spread suet evenly on venison. Mix all together well and grind again through medium plate. (Water can be added here, if desired. It should be if the sausage is to be stuffed into casings, but it's not necessary for loose sausage unless you like it moist.) Refrigerate for 1 to 2 days, form, wrap, and freeze.

Makes 4 pounds.

MILD SAUSAGE

5 lbs. fat-free venison
1 lb. beef suet
2 tbsps. salt
1 tbsp. freshly ground black
    pepper

1 tbsp. MSG
½ tsp. cayenne
½ tsp. saltpeter
¼ cup honey
½ cup (approx.) water

Prepare meats as in the recipe for Colorado Sausage. Mix salt, pepper, MSG, cayenne, and saltpeter, and sprinkle evenly on meat. Put seasoned meat in a bowl and add honey with enough water to make mixture somewhat sticky. Let stand at room temperature while softening casings, 20 to 30 minutes. Stuff into casings.

MAKES 6 pounds.

HOT SAUSAGE

5 lbs. fat-free venison
1 lb. beef suet
3 tbsps. salt
2 tbsps. freshly ground black
    pepper

1 tbsp. ground sage
1 tbsp. MSG
1 tsp. cayenne
1 tsp. hot paprika
red wine

Prepare meats as in the recipe for Colorado Sausage. Mix with salt, pepper, sage, MSG, cayenne, and paprika. If too mild, add a bit more paprika, a little at a time. Test by cooking a sample. If too hot, add more meat. Add just enough wine to make stuffing of casings possible.

MAKES 6 pounds.

BASIC CRÉPINETTES (also called *fagots* or *gayettes*)

Soak a piece of hog caul fat (fat surrounding the stomach and intestines) in lukewarm water to cover mixed with 1 tablespoon vinegar. Soak until the caul is pliable. Cut with scissors into 4- to 5-inch squares. Wrap each square around a heaping tablespoon of sausage meat, overlapping each edge. These can be fried as they are, dipped into beaten egg and coated with fine crumbs and fried, or broiled after brushing with melted butter. Cook long enough to cook sausage through and brown the envelope.

LEBANON (PA.) BOLOGNA

17 lbs. venison with 15% beef suet
⅔ cup melted lard
2 tsps. grated mace
½ cup salt
⅔ cup brown sugar

1 oz. pepper
2 tsps. saltpeter, dissolved in a
little warm water
2 tsps. grated nutmeg
1 tsp. ground cloves

Grind meat once through fine blade. Add all remaining ingredients and regrind. Stuff into 15- to 19-inch casings, ranging from 2½ to 4 inches in diameter. Allow to hang for several days, then smoke for 7 to 9 days in cool smoke (70° to 80° F.). After smoking, hang in cool storage area or refrigerate.
MAKES 18 pounds.

PENNSYLVANIA DUTCH SCRAPPLE

Scrapple is generally made with pork meats, and the recipe can be found on page 120. It is worth noting, however, that many Pennsylvania families use venison for up to 20% of the total amount of meat when they make scrapple after the hunting season.

VENISON BOLOGNA

10 lbs. venison with 15% beef suet,
ground
6 oz. brown sugar
6 oz. salt
2½ tsps. saltpeter, dissolved in a
little warm water

¾ tsp. black pepper
½ tsp. grated mace
¼ tsp. cayenne
1⅓ cups molasses, warmed so it
flows

Mix all ingredients and stuff into casings. Tie into links as desired. Let hang in a dry place for 2 days before smoking. Smoke three times at 7-day intervals at 120°.
MAKES 7 to 8 pounds.

PRESSED VENISON

2 lbs. venison flank steak with
15% beef suet
¼ cup vinegar
2 tsps. salt

½ tsp. peppercorns
1 small bay leaf
6 cups water

Simmer the ingredients, covered, in the water for 3 hours, or until very tender. Drain and reserve liquid. Put meat through fine blade of grinder and pack into a loaf pan, 9 x 5 x 3 inches. Strain liquid and boil to reduce to ½ cup; pour over meat. Cover with wax paper and top with a heavy weight to press down. (Uncooked rice or beans are good if the layer is deep enough.) Chill overnight. Remove from pan and slice thin. Serve as "cold cuts" or wrap and freeze.

MAKES 1½ pounds.

POLISH GAME PÂTÉ

1½ lbs. venison shoulder	4 cups vinegar
1 whole rabbit	2 tbsps. olive oil
2 carrots	½ lb. salt pork
2 onions	¼ lb. pickled tongue
1 parsley root	½ cup red wine
1 celery root	4 eggs, lightly beaten
10 peppercorns	salt and pepper
10 juniper berries	bacon slices to line mold
4 cups water	

Boil carrots, onions, parsley root, celery root, peppercorns, and juniper berries in water and vinegar; there should be enough to half cover meats. Pour most over meat, add oil, and let stand for 2 or 3 days, covered, turning occasionally. Pour the rest of the marinade over ¼ pound of the salt pork. Add remaining salt pork to the meats and simmer all, covered, in marinade until very tender, about 1½ hours. Let cool in the liquid. Bone meats and grind with marinated, uncooked salt pork; press through a sieve. Dice the cooked salt pork and tongue, and add to sieved mixture. Add wine and eggs. Mix well and correct seasonings. Line a 2-quart mold with bacon, and pour in pâté mixture. Cover and steam for 2 hours. Cool completely before unmolding. Chill and slice thin.

MAKES 8 cups.

VENISON VARIETY MEATS

Venison variety meats are the same as those from domestic animals: heart, kidneys, and liver. With the possible exception of liver, these meats are all too often ignored, even in domestic meats. Perhaps that is why they are generally lower in price than the skeletal parts. They are delicious, however, and it's a shame to ignore them, even from game.

As with domestic meat, all tubes, coarse membranes, and fat

79

must be removed. Also, as with beef, the liver is most flavorful if it is not cooked to the shoe-leather state. Give it a try when still moist with a touch of pink inside.

These are the only parts of big game that can and should be eaten without any prior hanging or freezing. Quality in these parts does deteriorate through storage, and they are best eaten quite soon. As a matter of fact, the first dish is perfect for the first successful day of hunting.

HUNTER'S REWARD

1 venison heart, cleaned and cut into finger-sized pieces
1 venison liver, cleaned and cut into finger-sized pieces
1 onion, sliced into rings

2 to 4 tbsps. butter
seasoned flour
1 cup (approx.) dry red wine
1 small can (4 oz.) mushrooms with liquid

Soften onion in butter in a skillet or Dutch oven. Shake meat with seasoned flour; shake off excess. Quickly sear meat in butter. Reduce heat; add wine and mushrooms. Cover pan and simmer gently for 15 to 20 minutes.

SERVES 2 to 4.

CALIFORNIA PICKLED HEART

1 or 2 venison hearts
1½ cups water
1 cup vinegar
2 garlic cloves

1 tsp. salt
1 tsp. whole allspice
¼ tsp. pepper
4 bay leaves

Clean hearts and soak in cold salted water (1 tablespoon to 2 quarts) for 2 hours. Wash well and drain. Put hearts in an enamelware pot with remaining ingredients, cover, and cook slowly for 1½ to 2 hours. Serve warm, or cool in liquid to serve as an appetizer.

SERVES 3 to 6 as main course.

SCOTTISH DEER HAGGIS

1 venison heart
½ lb. venison liver
¾ cup steel-cut Scottish oatmeal, toasted golden at 350°, or 1 cup quick-cooking rolled oats

3 onions, minced
1 tbsp. salt
1 tsp. pepper
¼ lb. beef suet, minced

80

Wash heart and liver. Put in salted water to cover and simmer until tender. Remove from liquid. Mince heart and grate liver. Combine meats; there should be ¾ cup. Mix in oats, onions, salt, pepper, and suet and blend well. Put into a greased baking dish and cover tightly with foil. Set baking dish in a kettle with boiling water to come up half to two-thirds of the way. Cover kettle and steam for 4 hours if using Scottish oats, for 2 hours if using rolled oats.

SERVES 6 to 8.

SKEWERED VENISON HEART

1 venison heart, trimmed and cut
in ¾- to 1-inch cubes to equal
1 lb. meat
½ cup red wine vinegar
¼ cup salad oil
1 clove garlic, pressed
½ tsp. marjoram
½ tsp. chile powder

12 slices bacon, partially cooked
but still limp, drained
1 lb. cherry tomatoes
2 green peppers, cut into 1-inch
squares
1 can (1 lb.) small white onions,
rinsed and drained

Combine the vinegar, oil, garlic, marjoram, and chile, and pour over meat. Cover and chill at least overnight, stirring several times. Drain meat. Thread 6 skewers by starting with one end of a slice of bacon, adding meat cubes, tomatoes, green pepper squares, and onions, lacing the bacon along in curves. Put skewers onto a broiler rack pan and broil 4 inches from the heat 5 to 7 minutes per side or until the meat is no longer pink when slashed.

SERVES 6.

MINUTE HEART STEAK

6 slices, ½ inch thick, of venison
heart, tenderized by pounding
2 tbsps. (approx.) prepared
mustard
salt
flour

¼ cup salad oil
2 tbsps. butter
2 tbsps. lemon juice
6 green onions, sliced, with some
tops
sour cream (optional)

Spread one side of each steak with a thin layer of mustard; salt both sides lightly. Dredge with flour; shake off excess. Heat oil over medium heat and sauté steaks without crowding for 3 to 5 minutes per side, until well browned; add more oil if needed. Remove meat and drain off oil from pan. Swirl butter and lemon juice in sauté pan; deglaze pan. Heat until slightly thickened. Pour over meat, sprinkle on onions. Serve with sour cream if desired.

SERVES 4 to 6.

SAUTÉED KIDNEY (also base for Kidney Pie)

1 or 2 kidneys	4 tbsps. bacon drippings
2 tbsps. plus 1 tsp. salt	6 oz. tomato paste
1 tbsp. vinegar	½ tsp. celery salt
1 cup boiling water	¼ tsp. pepper
1 large onion, sliced	2 tbsps. sweet butter
1 medium-sized can (6 oz.)	2 tbsps. sherry
mushrooms, drained	1 slice lemon

Six hours before cooking, immerse kidneys in 2 cups cold water with 1 tablespoon salt; let stand for 30 minutes. Remove, clean thoroughly, and put into fresh cold water with 1 tablespoon salt and the vinegar, and let stand refrigerated for 5 hours. Simmer in 1 cup water with 1 teaspoon salt for about 30 minutes. Sauté onion and mushrooms in bacon drippings; add tomato paste, celery salt, and pepper, and keep warm. Melt butter in a skillet; chop kidneys and add to butter with sherry and lemon. Cook for a few minutes. Add onion mix to skillet and let cook gently for 10 minutes, stirring often.

SERVES 2 to 4.

DEVILED KIDNEYS

1 lb. kidneys	1 tbsp. lemon juice
4 tbsps. butter	2 tsps. salt
1½ tsps. dry mustard	flour
¼ tsp. paprika	1 cup (approx.) water

Soak 1 pound kidneys as in recipe for Sautéed Kidney. Clean and cut into slices. Melt 2 tablespoons butter; mix with mustard, paprika, lemon juice, salt. Roll kidney slices in this mix, then dust with flour and brown in remaining 2 tablespoons butter. Add ¾ to 1 cup hot water, deglaze pan, cover, and simmer until tender, 25 to 30 minutes.

SERVES 2 or 3.

VENISON MIXED GRILL

Prepare venison sausage and slices of venison liver, heart, and kidney (prepared as in recipe for Sautéed Kidney). Broil until done, brushing occasionally with melted butter to prevent drying.

FLORENTINE CROSTINI (liver spread)

1 lb. venison liver (or pheasant livers, etc.), cut into chunks
1 large onion, minced
1 celery rib, minced
1 large carrot, minced
½ cup olive oil

4 tbsps. butter
1 tbsp. minced anchovy filets
2 tbsps. minced capers
pepper
broth or consommé, if served cold

Combine onion, celery, carrot, and oil in a wide skillet. Cook, stirring, over medium heat for about 15 minutes, or until vegetables are quite soft but not browned. Add meat and cook, stirring, for about 5 minutes, until liver is firm but still somewhat pink inside. Blend in butter until melted, then add anchovy. Whirl in a blender to a coarse purée, or mash in a mortar with a pestle. Blend in capers and season with pepper to taste. To serve freshly made, keep warm (on a hot tray or in a chafing dish); spread on toast or crackers. Reheat over hot water. To serve cold, cool and thin to spreading consistency with broth or consommé, adding only a bit at a time.

SERVES 8 to 10.

RED LIVER SPREAD

3 lbs. liver, cut into ¼-inch slices
1 large onion, sliced
½ tsp. salt
¼ tsp. pepper
5 tbsps. onion juice

6 tbsps. hot catsup
3 tbsps. celery salt
½ tsp. garlic salt
dash of cayenne

Simmer liver and onion in water to cover until tender; drain. Put liver and onion through meat grinder twice (easier done if allowed to cool first). Mix with remaining ingredients and put through grinder at least twice more. Keep chilled in airtight jar.

MAKES 3 cups.

PICKLED VENISON LIVER

1 lb. each of venison livers and onions	1 cup white vinegar
1 cup water	1 tbsp. mixed pickling spices

Cut venison liver into finger-sized strips. Cut onion into thin slices. Simmer liver and onion rings very gently in small amount of water until just barely cooked through. Remove and drain; put into sterilized jars or freezer containers. Cover with hot pickle liquid made by boiling water, vinegar, and mixed pickling spices. Cool and let stand, refrigerated, for at least 3 days before serving or freezing.

BAKED LIVER PÂTÉ

1 venison liver	1/4 tsp. pepper
2 tbsps. melted butter	pinch of grated nutmeg
1/2 cup diced salt pork	grated rind of 1/2 lemon
1 small onion, minced	1/2 cup diced lean bacon
2 slices bread, soaked in milk	2 eggs, well beaten
1/4 tsp. salt	bacon slices to line mold

Cover and steam over low heat half of a venison liver in butter with salt pork and onion. When tender, mince the second half of the liver, raw, and combine with bread, salt, pepper, nutmeg, lemon rind, and bacon. Mix both liver mixes well with well-beaten eggs. Line a bread loaf tin with slices of blanched lean bacon, add mix, and cover with foil. Bake at 350° for 1½ hours. Serve hot on toast.

SERVES 8 as appetizer.

GERMAN LIVER DUMPLINGS

3/4 lb. venison liver	1 small onion
1½ qts. venison or beef broth	2 eggs, beaten
5 slices of untrimmed white bread	1 tsp. salt
1 cup lukewarm milk	grated rind of 1 lemon
2 oz. beef kidney suet	1/8 tsp. dried marjoram

Crumble bread and pour milk over it. Let stand until bread is well soaked and milk is cool. Squeeze as much moisture out of bread as possible. Work liver, suet, onion, and moist crumbs through a food grinder. Stir in eggs, salt, lemon rind, and marjoram. Add additional dry crumbs, 1 tablespoon at a time, if necessary, to make a mixture that will hold shape. With wet hands form into dumplings and drop into gently boiling broth. Cover pan and simmer for 15 to 20 minutes. Serve with broth.

SERVES 6.

LIVER BISQUE

½ lb. liver, blanched (dip twice
briefly into boiling water) and
ground
4 cups venison or beef stock
1 cup chopped mushrooms
3 tbsps. butter

1 tsp. salt
⅛ tsp. paprika
2 tsps. minced parsley
1 tbsp. flour
1 cup light cream

Sauté ground liver and mushrooms in 2 tablespoons of butter for 5 minutes. Combine with stock, salt, paprika, and parsley, and simmer, covered, for 20 minutes. Melt 1 tablespoon butter, blend in flour and add a bit of soup; stir until smooth. Pour back into the soup, and bring to a boil, stirring. Reduce heat, add cream, and cook, stirring, for 5 minutes longer.

SERVES 6.

ADIRONDACK LIVER

1 lb. liver, cut into ¼-inch slices
4 cups boiling water
flour
3 tbsps. bacon drippings
1 tsp. salt

2 cups stock
3 cups onions, sliced in rings
¼ lb. sweet butter
1 cup tomato juice
1 tbsp. chopped chives

Blanch liver in boiling water, drain, and pat dry. Dredge liver with flour and sauté in hot bacon drippings until brown. Add salt and stock, cover, and simmer for 1 hour. Remove liver and keep warm. Reduce pan liquid to ¼ cup. Sauté onion rings in butter until golden. Add liver; blend the reduced liquid into tomato juice and pour over liver and onions. Cover and simmer for 30 minutes. Dust with chopped chives just before serving.

SERVES 2 to 4.

LIVER LOAF

1 lb. venison liver, cut into
chunks, or ½ lb. liver and ½ lb.
venison kidney
½ green pepper, cut into chunks
½ onion, cut into chunks
4 slices bacon, cooked crisp

2 eggs, well beaten
½ cup milk
1 cup soft bread crumbs
1 tsp. salt
½ tsp. ground sage
½ tsp. celery salt

Put liver, green peppers, onion, and bacon through the coarse blade of a chopper. Mix eggs, milk, and crumbs; add meat mixture, salt, sage, and celery salt. Mix well and pack firmly into a lightly greased loaf pan (9 x 5 x 3 inches). Bake at 350° for about 1¼ hours. Turn out and serve hot, if desired; or cool, chill, and serve with catsup. Good for sandwiches.

SERVES 4 to 6.

CANADIAN VENISON LIVER AND BACON OMELET

3 slices, ½ inch thick, of venison liver

3 slices, ¼ inch thick, of Canadian bacon

¼ cup seasoned flour

1 tbsp. lard

4 tbsps. sweet butter

4 large eggs, beaten

1 cup milk

½ tsp. salt

1 tsp. minced parsley

1 tbsp. grated maple sugar or grated Cheddar or Bleu cheese

Dredge liver with seasoned flour and brown slowly in lard with Canadian bacon slices. Melt butter in another skillet and bring to a bubble but do not let it smoke. Add meat from the other skillet and turn several times to coat with butter. Make a batter of eggs, milk, salt, and parsley, and pour over meat. Cook until golden, for 5 to 7 minutes per side, turning once. Serve with maple sugar or cheese.

SERVES 2 or 3.

PENNSYLVANIA LIVER SAUSAGE

2 to 2½ lbs. venison liver

2½ lbs. venison with 15% beef suet

6½ lbs. pork trimmings (hearts, tongues, and kidneys can also be used)

1 loaf stale bread, or 1 lb. whole-wheat flour

salt and pepper

onions (optional)

Cook meats thoroughly in water to cover; save 4 cups broth. Grind meats with bread through a fine blade. Add reserved broth. Season with salt and pepper to taste (chopped onions to taste, optional). Mace, celery seed, cardamom, and coriander are often used to add flavor. After seasoning, cool the mixture for 10 minutes, and pour into pans or crocks to set. If to be kept in casings, the second cooking is done after stuffing: simmer the sausages for 20 minutes, then dip into cold water to bleach. Hang them in a cool place to dry, or place them in crocks without bleaching and cover with hot lard to preserve. Often referred to as "pudding" meat.

MAKES 10 to 12 pounds.

LIVERWURST

1 lb. young venison liver	1 large onion, quartered
1½ lbs. pork shoulder, boned, with some fat	2 celery ribs
	6 parsley sprigs
5 cups water	1 bay leaf
¼ cup red wine	1 tsp. MSG
2 garlic cloves	1 small onion
2½ tsps. salt	1½ tsps. onion powder
¾ tsp. pepper	1½ tsps. seasoned salt
½ cup dry white wine	¼ lb. butter, softened

Simmer liver in 2 cups of the water (or enough to cover) with the red wine, 1 garlic clove, 1 teaspoon salt, and ⅛ teaspoon pepper, covered, for about 25 minutes, or until tender. Remove liver and cool, then chill. Discard broth. Simmer pork in 3 cups water with the white wine, quartered onion, celery, parsley, bay leaf, MSG, 1 garlic clove, 1 teaspoon salt, and ⅛ teaspoon pepper, covered, for 1½ hours, or until tender. Remove meat, cool, then chill. Strain and reserve 1½ cups of the cooking broth.

Cut chilled meats into strips and run through the fine blade of a grinder with the small onion. Heat 1 cup of the reserved cooking broth. Add to the broth ½ teaspoon salt, ½ teaspoon pepper, the onion powder, and seasoned salt. Stir in the softened butter. Blend mixture well into the ground meats. Add ¼ to ½ cup of the remaining reserved broth, enough to make a smooth paste of the whole mixture. Add more salt if needed. Cover and chill.

MAKES 4 cups.

VENISON BONES

While it is true that bones take up a great deal of space in the freezer, also that they are best trimmed off the meat before packaging, certain bones are of value as a stock base (for gravies, sauces, and soups) and some are just plain good in themselves. It is always best to use bones quite soon; don't keep them frozen for more than a few weeks.

Marrow, a favorite dish in England, comes from the long bones. This is the "filling" of leg bones; even in an animal that has unpleasant body fat, marrow is an easily digestible and wholesome fat with a usually excellent flavor. The long bones are cut into about 2-inch sections and simmered or poached, or dry roasted in a 350° oven for about 1 hour. When they are cooked, the marrow slides out easily. (Old, very formal silver services frequently included "marrow spoons," long, curved spadelike instruments to remove the marrow in a genteel manner.) Marrow can be used alone as a spread (served piping hot) on appetizer crackers or toast, or can be used in other dishes.

IDAHO ELK RIBS (or caribou, antelope, moose, deer)

1 section of 4 ribs	1½ tsps. lemon juice
1 tbsp. sweet butter	1 tsp. onion salt
1 tsp. bacon fat	¼ tsp. pepper
2 tbsps. brown sugar	pinch of cayenne
⅓ cup vinegar	dash of Tabasco
2 tbsps. Worcestershire sauce	¼ cup chutney

Brown ribs in butter and bacon fat with brown sugar in a skillet over medium heat. Blend vinegar, Worcestershire, lemon juice, onion salt, pepper, cayenne, and Tabasco, and pour over ribs. Cover skillet and simmer slowly for 1¼ hours. About 5 minutes before serving, stir in the chutney.
SERVES 4.

NEVADA BARBECUED RIBS

2 to 3 lbs. venison spareribs	barbecue sauce

Roast in 300° oven until nearly done. Pour off fat from pan and pour on your choice of barbecue sauce. Bake very slowly for 2 more hours.
SERVES 1 or 2.

3½ SOUP (or base for soup and gravy)

3 lbs. meaty venison marrowbones	3 parsley sprigs
4 tbsps. sweet butter	½ tbsp. Kitchen Bouquet
3 qts. plus ½ cup cold water	3 peppercorns
½ cup minced onion	3 whole cloves
½ cup minced celery	1 tbsp. salt
½ cup minced carrot	½ large bay leaf
½ head cabbage, chopped	1 tbsp. beurre manié

Remove marrow from bones and set in a bowl over hot water to melt for marrow dumplings. Remove meat from bones, discard fat, and brown meat well in the sweet butter. Cover bones, meat, and butter with 3 quarts cold water. When boiling again, add onion, celery, carrot, cabbage, parsley, Kitchen Bouquet, peppercorns, cloves, salt, and bay leaf. Reduce to a simmer, cover, and cook for 3½ hours. Strain and chill. Remove fat and strain again. Reheat. Blend beurre manié with ½ cup cold water to make a paste. When soup is heated, add mixture to thicken. Serve as is or with marrow dumplings.

SERVES 8 to 12.

MARROW BALLS

2 cups marrow, melted over hot
   water and strained
1 cup dry bread crumbs
2 eggs, at room temperature

½ cup minced parsley
pinch each of salt, pepper, and
   cayenne

Mix half of the crumbs with the marrow. Add 1 egg and mix well; then add second egg and mix well. Add parsley and seasonings to remaining crumbs and add to marrow mix. Shape into quarter-sized balls and drop into the boiling soup. If the first dumpling disintegrates, add 1 tablespoon dry crumbs to mix. Repeat, adding crumbs as necessary until the marrow balls float in the soup. Simmer for 10 minutes and serve with 3½ Soup.

SERVES 8 to 12.

BIG-GAME STOCK (or base for soup and sauce)

1 hindleg shank
1 small turnip, quartered
½ head cabbage, quartered
4 carrots, cut lengthwise
4 onions, quartered
4 celery ribs with leaves, chopped

6 parsley sprigs
4 tsps. salt
5 whole peppercorns
4 qts. boiling water
beef consommé

Cut meat off bones, discard fat, cut meat into chunks. Crack the bones. Put bones, meat, and other ingredients into a heavy kettle and cover with the boiling water. Cover and simmer slowly for 6 hours, adding more boiling water as needed. Skim hourly. Strain through several thicknesses of cheesecloth until clear. Cool. Add enough beef consommé to make 4 quarts. Refrigerate or freeze.

MAKES 4 quarts.

GAME ESSENCE

meat from Game Stock
4 cups Game Stock

½ cup red wine
1 tbsp. red currant jelly

Purée in a blender the meat used to make Game Stock. Transfer to a soup kettle and add hot Game Stock, red wine, and red currant jelly. Simmer until heated through.

SERVES 6.

CLEAR VENISON SOUP

3 lbs. venison bones
1 lb. venison scrap meat
3 qts. water
2 onions, minced
2 carrots, minced
4 celery ribs with leaves, minced

4 parsley sprigs, minced
1 garlic clove, minced
1 tsp. salt
2 peppercorns
seasoned croutons for garnish

Combine all in a soup kettle, and bring to a boil. Reduce to simmer and cook, covered, for 2 to 2½ hours, or until liquid is reduced to 1 quart. Skim off fat. Strain soup through a cheesecloth-lined fine sieve, and chill. Remove any remaining layer of fat after chilling. Reheat, and garnish each serving with seasoned croutons.

SERVES 4 to 6.

NORWEGIAN GAME SOUP

2 qts. Game Stock
4 tbsps. butter
4 tbsps. flour
1 scant tbsp. sugar
1 tbsp. vinegar
1 tsp. salt
pinch of ground cloves

4 cooking apples
4 oz. drained, stewed prunes, chopped
2 small carrots, cooked and diced
2 small parsnips, boiled and sliced
pepper
Norwegian Dumplings

Melt butter, add flour, and stir until frothy to make a roux. Bring stock almost to a boil and stir slowly into roux. Add sugar, vinegar, salt, and cloves. Peel, core and slice apples, and stew in just enough water to prevent burning until mushy. Add to soup with prunes, carrots, and parsnips. Season with pepper to taste. Pour over Norwegian Dumplings in a heated tureen.

SERVES 6 to 7.

VEGETABLE SOUP CHASSEUR

6 cups Game Stock
2 cups spinach, washed and
　shredded
½ cup each of shredded scallions
　and mixed greens (kale, beet
　tops, watercress)
1 tsp. salt
dash of pepper

bouquet garni (5 parsley sprigs,
　1 celery rib, 1 rosemary sprig)
1 potato, diced
1 tsp. flour
½ cup sour cream
parsley, chervil, or chives for
　garnish

Bring stock to a boil; add spinach, scallions and mixed greens, salt, pepper, and bouquet garni. Reduce heat and simmer for 1 hour. Add potato and simmer for 20 minutes more, or until potato is tender. Remove bouquet garni and stir in flour mixed with sour cream until smooth. Garnish on serving.

SERVES 6.

VENISON LEFTOVERS

Leftovers are always convenient to have on hand; they make tasteful meals, generally quick and easy.

APPETIZERS

Serve very thin slices of rare roast or steak with dark bread and Mustard Sauce.

GAME PEA SOUP

Heat green split-pea soup (canned or homemade) or yellow pea soup with minced bits of leftover venison roast or boiled corned venison.

BROWN HASH

2 cups chopped cooked meat
2 cups chopped cooked potatoes
1 cup chopped onions
4 tbsps. butter, melted

1 tsp. salt
stock, hot
ground pepper and ginger

Combine meat, potatoes, and onions, and brown in melted butter. Add salt, and pour on barely enough stock to cover. Cover dish and simmer until liquid is absorbed. Season to taste with pepper and ginger.

SERVES 4.

RED FLANNEL HASH

1½ cups leftover meat (venison, bear, opossum), diced
6 beets, boiled and diced
4 potatoes, boiled and diced
3 onions, diced

1 tsp. salt
¼ tsp. pepper
4 tbsps. sweet butter
2 tbsps. heavy cream

Mix meat with beets, potatoes, onions, salt, and pepper. Melt 2 tablespoons of the butter and add meat mix. Allow to cook for 20 minutes to form a crust on the bottom; turn and sprinkle with a bit more butter. Brown the second side for 20 minutes or so without stirring. Blend in heavy cream and remaining butter. If too dry, add more cream.

SERVES 4.

ROCKY MOUNTAIN CURRY

4 cups diced cooked venison
1½ onions, minced
3 celery ribs, minced
2 apples, peeled, cored, and minced
¼ cup melted sweet butter
2½ tsps. curry powder
2 cups boiling stock
⅛ tsp. pepper
¼ tsp. ground ginger

⅛ tsp. Tabasco
2 tsps. Worcestershire sauce
2 tsps. salt
2 tbsps. flour
¼ cup cold water
½ cup seedless raisins
1 cup heavy cream
1 egg yolk, beaten
3 cups hot boiled rice

Plump raisins by soaking in hot water 10 to 15 minutes; drain. Sauté onions, celery, apples, and meat in butter until lightly browned. Stir in curry powder and simmer for 5 minutes. Add stock, pepper, ginger, Tabasco, Worcestershire, and salt, and cook, covered, for 20 minutes. Blend flour with cold water and add; cook, stirring, for 5 minutes to thicken. Remove and let stand for 1 hour. Reheat. Stir in raisins, then blend in cream and finally egg yolk just before serving on rice.

SERVES 4 to 6.

QUICK CURRY

2 cups diced, cooked meat
¼ cup seasoned flour
3 tbsps. bacon fat

1 onion, chopped
1½ tsps. curry powder
¾ cup brown gravy

Roll meat in seasoned flour and brown slowly in hot fat. Add onion and sauté slowly until soft. Blend in curry. Add gravy and cook slowly, covered, 15 to 20 minutes.

SERVES 2 to 3.

VENISON PASTIES

1 cup chopped cooked venison	3 oz. cream cheese
¼ cup minced onion	1½ cups all-purpose flour
butter	1½ sticks butter
¼ cup Brown Sauce, Béchamel	½ tsp. salt
Sauce, or gravy	1 egg beaten with 1 tbsp. water
salt, pepper, herbs	

Sauté onion in butter. Combine meat, onion, and sauce, and season to taste. Make pastry by combining cream cheese, flour, butter, and salt. Mix well and chill. Roll out thin and cut into 3- to 3½-inch circles or squares. Put on a spoonful of filling, and moisten edges of pastry. Top each round with another, or fold each round over to make a half-moon, and pinch sides together. Brush with egg wash. Bake at 375° for 15 minutes, or until browned. Serve hot or cold.

SERVES 4 to 6.

VENISON LYONNAISE

6 large slices leftover roast	1 to 2 tbsps. vinegar
butter	½ tsp. fresh tarragon, minced
2 or 3 onions, sliced	

Sauté meat slices quickly on both sides in butter; remove and keep warm. Add onions to skillet and sauté until lightly browned and separated into rings. Return meat if necessary to heat; sprinkle with vinegar. Mix 1 tablespoon butter and the tarragon and put on top before serving.

SERVES 6.

LEFTOVER SAUERBRATEN

6 slices leftover roast	8 gingersnaps, crushed
½ cup vinegar	10 whole cloves
3 bay leaves	1 tbsp. sugar
½ tsp. salt	a few drops of Worcestershire
2 cups water	sauce (optional)

Mix all but meat, and bring to a boil, stirring, until smooth. Add meat and heat gently. Remove meat, strain sauce, and return meat to heat before serving.

SERVES 4 to 6.

MEATBALL FRITTERS

1 cup leftover cooked meatballs or patties, broken up well
1 cup all-purpose flour
1 tsp. baking powder
¼ tsp. salt
1 cup milk
1 egg, beaten
fat for frying

Sift flour, baking powder, and salt together; add milk and egg, and stir until well mixed. Add meat; mix well and form into balls. Fry, either in shallow fat in a skillet, or in deep fat.

SERVES 4.

OZARK VENISON SALAD

4 cups cooked venison, cut into ¼-inch dice
½ cup French dressing
1 cup sliced celery
½ cup sliced stuffed olives
4 hard-cooked eggs, sliced
mayonnaise
pickles
salt and pepper

Marinate meat in French dressing for 1 hour, refrigerated, stirring occasionally. Drain off excess dressing. Combine meat with celery, olives, and eggs; serve topped with mayonnaise and garnished with pickles. Dust with salt and pepper.

SERVES 4 to 6.

VENISON VINAIGRETTE

5 cups julienne strips of cold cooked venison
1½ cups onion rings
½ cup olive oil
¼ cup white vinegar
2 tbsps. lemon juice
6 drops Tabasco
4 tsps. minced fresh chervil
1 tbsp. minced fresh summer savory
1 tbsp. minced chives
½ tsp. dry mustard
4 tbsps. capers
1½ tsps. salt
½ tsp. pepper

Combine meat and onion rings. Combine oil, vinegar, lemon juice, Tabasco, chervil, savory, chives, mustard, capers, salt, and pepper, and mix well. Pour over meat and onions, and toss gently. Marinate at room temperature for 3 hours, tossing occasionally. Cover and chill before serving.

SERVES 8.

SANDWICH FILLING OR PARTY SPREAD

Mix 1¼ cups minced cold cooked venison with 1 teaspoon salt, ½ tablespoon catsup, ½ teaspoon Worcestershire sauce, ½ teaspoon prepared horseradish, and 1 tablespoon melted butter. Chill.

MAKES 1½ cups.

VENISON, SALTED OR CURED

In this age of freezers, meat is rarely cured except for flavor. In the days before cold storage, pickling was frequently used as a preservative. Nowadays that method is used almost exclusively to make such dishes as German Sauerbraten and English Spiced Meat.

One of the still popular methods of preserving meat is salting or, as we usually call it, "corning." Corning is a method used for centuries all over the world as a preservative. Our word for the process is said to come from Anglo-Saxon England where grains of salt the size of an English grain they called "corn" (not the corn with which we are familiar) were used for the process.

Corning is an excellent treatment for any tough or strong-tasting meat. Cuts that are most generally corned are the plate, brisket, and flank, although any cut may be corned. Here are two different cornings that you might try. (The commercial cures put out by Morton's are excellent, of course, but there's no reason why you shouldn't do it yourself.)

Do not freeze after salting. Note that freezing tends to emphasize salt, but salted meat has a long life just refrigerated.

COLOMBIAN SALTING

3- to 4-lb. piece of bottom round roast
1 lb. salt, as pure as possible

Stand the roast on its side and make cuts about ½ inch apart, but not all the way through the roast. Stop 1 inch from the bottom so that the slices look like the pages of a book, still attached along one side. Pour the salt very thickly and carefully between the slices and over the top, making sure that the whole piece is very heavily salted. Re-form the roast to its original shape, and put it on a large platter. Cover it with cheesecloth and let it stand at room temperature in a cool room overnight. Pour off any liquid and add more salt if needed. Let stand as before for 24 more hours and drain again. Put meat on heavy foil or another large platter, cover again with clean cheesecloth, and dry in the sun (bringing it in at night and not putting it out on humid days) for 1 week, turning daily. Shake out loose salt, wrap in foil, and refrigerate.

COLOMBIAN SANCOCHO

1 lb. Colombian salted venison, well washed

1 lb. chuck, cut into 2-inch cubes

1 lb. lean pork, cut into 2-inch cubes

1½ qts. each of venison or beef stock, and chicken stock

1 lb. tomatoes, peeled, seeded, and chopped

2 large onions, sliced

1 cassava root (about 1 lb.), peeled and cut into thick slices

3 garlic cloves, minced

3½ lbs. chicken, cut into serving pieces

1 lb. sweet potatoes, peeled and sliced

1 lb. yams, peeled and sliced

1 lb. winter squash, peeled and cubed

1 lb. potatoes, peeled and quartered

2 ripe plantains, peeled and sliced

2 green plantains

3 ears of fresh corn, each cut into 3 pieces

salt and pepper

Combine the meats with stock, tomatoes, onions, cassava, and garlic. Bring to a boil, skim, and reduce to a slow simmer. Cover and cook for 1¼ hours. Add chicken, sweet potatoes, yams, squash, and potatoes. Cook until chicken is tender, about 30 minutes. Add the ripe plantains and simmer; liquid should barely move. Meanwhile, separately boil the green plantains in their skins for 30 minutes. Cool them, then peel and slice. Add to the pot and cook until all is done. Add the corn 5 minutes before serving, and adjust seasoning. Serve meat and vegetables separately, the broth in a tureen. Serve with limes and hot pepper sauce.

SERVES 6 to 8.

ENGLISH SALTED MEAT

4 to 5 lbs. bottom round or brisket, in one piece

4 qts. water

2 lbs. salt

2 oz. brown sugar

1 oz. saltpeter

1 sprig fresh thyme, or ½ tsp. dried

2 bay leaves

¼ tsp. ground cinnamon

Make a brine with water, salt, brown sugar, saltpeter, thyme, bay leaves, and cinnamon. Boil the mixture, then cool it. Completely cover the meat with the brine; weight if necessary to keep submerged. Keep in cool place, turning daily, and soak for 1 week. Remove meat and discard brine. Wash meat well before using for other recipes.

ENGLISH BOILED MEAT

1 piece English Salted Meat
bouquet garni of thyme, parsley,
   bay leaf, and 8 peppercorns
   tied in cheesecloth
12 small carrots

12 small white turnips
12 small white onions
Suet Dumplings
Horseradish Sauce

Cover a piece of English Salted Meat with water. Add bouquet garni. Bring to a gentle simmer and cook, covered, for 2½ to 2¾ hours, skimming from time to time. Add carrots, turnips, and onions, and cook for 45 minutes longer. Prepare Suet Dumplings. Remove meat and vegetables from broth, but keep warm. Bring liquid to a boil to cook dumplings. Serve all with Horseradish Sauce on the side.

SERVES 6 to 8.

SPICED CORNING

MARINADE

8 to 10 lbs. meat
1½ cups salt, as pure as possible
½ cup sugar
2 tbsps. pickling spices
1 tsp. whole cloves
1 tsp. peppercorns
3 bay leaves

3½ tsps. sodium nitrate (from
   the drugstore)
1 tsp. sodium nitrite (from the
   drugstore)
7 qts. warm water
1 tsp. minced onion
1 garlic clove, minced
1 lemon, sliced

In a glass, crockery, or unbroken porcelain container, mix salt, sugar, pickling spices, cloves, peppercorns, bay leaves, sodium nitrate, and sodium nitrite. Stir in warm water. When salt and sugar are dissolved, add onion, garlic, and lemon.

Add 8 to 12 pounds meat and be sure that it is completely submerged; weight if necessary. Cover and refrigerate. Turn every other day and stir the mixture daily for 15 days. To store, transfer the meat and some of the marinade to a plastic bag and tie tightly. Will keep for several weeks refrigerated.

TO COOK SPICED CORNED MEAT

Wash meat under running cold water, put in a deep, heavy pot, and cover with fresh water. Bring to a boil and skim. Reduce heat and simmer for 4 to 5 hours, until tender. Potatoes, carrots, onions, and cabbage wedges can be added during the final hour. Slice while hot across the grain in thin slices. Serve with mustard, horseradish, and/or a sauce of your choice.

CORNING ALTERNATE

5 lbs. brisket	1 tbsp. sugar
4 qts. water	½ oz. saltpeter
1½ cups salt	8 bay leaves
2 tbsps. pickling spices	8 garlic cloves

Make marinade with water, salt, pickling spices, sugar, saltpeter, and bay leaves. Bring to a boil and simmer for 5 minutes. Cool. Put brisket in a glass or crockery dish. Add garlic cloves and the cooled brine with spices. Put a weight on the meat to keep it submerged. Cover dish with several layers of cheesecloth, then with a lid. Put in a cool place for 12 days to pickle.

COOKED CORNED BRISKET

5 lbs. corned brisket

Remove meat from brine; rinse in fresh water. Put in a kettle with water to cover. Bring to a boil, skim as necessary, and simmer for about 3 hours, or until tender. Let cool in the broth for 1 hour. Drain meat and dry well. Slice thin; serve hot or cold.
  SERVES 12 to 14.

CORNED BRISKET REUBEN SANDWICHES

2 slices dark Russian rye bread	1 tbsp. mayonnaise
butter	1 tsp. chili sauce
2 oz. sliced, cooked corned brisket	2 oz. sliced Swiss cheese
¼ cup sauerkraut	

Butter bread. Layer 1 slice with meat, sauerkraut, and a mixture of mayonnaise and chili sauce. Cover with Swiss cheese and the other bread slice. Brown on a hot buttered grill; turn to toast other side.

SERVES 1.

DUTCH BOILED CORNED VENISON

1 corned brisket or boned shoulder	3 tbsps. minced watercress
4 qts. boiling water	1 tbsp. garlic salt
3 Bermuda onions, sliced thin	3 tbsps. minced chervil
3 tbsps. wine vinegar	3 tbsps. minced parsley
1 small head red cabbage, shredded	1 tbsp. ground allspice
	1 cup sorrel, minced

Add all but meat to water and return to a boil. Rinse meat under cold running water and add to pot; cover and cook slowly for 3½ to 4½ hours. If desired, 30 minutes before meat is finished, add a quartered head of cabbage, chunked turnips, carrots, onions, and/or potatoes. Do not thicken liquid.

BOILED CORNED VENISON À LA MAINE

1 corned venison shoulder	2 bay leaves
½ cup garlic vinegar	2 tsps. allspice berries
1 cup ginger ale	1 large onion, quartered

Soak meat in cold water to cover for 1 hour; drain and wipe dry. Put with remaining ingredients and water to cover in a kettle. Bring to a boil and simmer slowly for 35 minutes per pound. Let stand in cooking liquid for 30 minutes before serving. If desired, vegetables can be added for the last half hour of cooking time.

SERVES 4 to 6.

ENGLISH SPICED VENISON (a cold Christmas buffet dish)

8 to 10 lbs. flank	¼ tsp. grated mace
1 oz. each of saltpeter and ground ginger	6 tbsps. salt mixed with ½ cup sugar
2 tbsps. freshly ground black pepper	1 cup water
2 tbsps. ground allspice	½ lb. suet

Combine saltpeter, ginger, pepper, allspice, and mace, and rub well into meat on all sides. Put into a glass or crockery bowl and sprinkle with some of the salt and sugar. Keep in refrigerator for

2 weeks, turning and rubbing it daily with more salt and sugar mix. When ready to cook, roll and tie very tightly; put into roaster with the water and the suet larded over the top. Cover and cook at 325° for 6 hours. Remove and cool. Serve thinly sliced.

SERVES 16 to 20.

PASTRAMI

4 lbs. corned brisket, bottom or
   eye of round, in one piece
2 garlic cloves
1 tbsp. pickling spices

1 tbsp. cracked peppercorns
½ tsp. each of ground allspice,
   grated nutmeg, and paprika

Put meat in a large kettle, cover with cold water, and bring to a boil. Simmer for 10 minutes and drain. (This is to remove excess salt; it is not done commercially.) Cover with cold water again; add garlic and pickling spices tied in a cheesecloth bag (omit pickling spices if corning included them). Bring to a boil and simmer for about 1½ hours, or until about two-thirds done; fork test—it should resist the fork slightly. (Time will vary with shape of meat; a long slender piece will cook more quickly.) Drain off liquid.

Fold a double thickness of foil several inches larger than base of meat and put meat on it. Mix cracked peppercorns and ground allspice, grated nutmeg, and paprika. (This mix is flexible; you can adjust to suit your taste.) Press mixed spices into meat, coating all sides, then turn and coat under side. Smoke, either in a smoker or covered barbecue, over gray ash briquettes with small green oak, maple, ash, or madrone logs, about 3 inches in diameter; these make the most smoke. Try to maintain 300° in the fire; use a meat thermometer in meat. Put meat, on its foil, on the grill on the side away from coals. Cover grill and cook for about 1 hour, then smoke-cook for 4 hours more between 200° and 250°. The meat is done when the meat thermometer reads 155° to 160°. Remove and serve; or cool, wrap in foil, and refrigerate. Meat will shrink about 50%; a 4-pound piece will weigh about 2¼ pounds. Will keep in refrigerator for 2 weeks.

For sandwiches, slice across the grain, when cold, as thin as possible. If you want hot sandwiches, wrap slices in foil and heat at 350° for 15 minutes. You may want to scrape pepper coating off before serving.

For dinner, reheat piece, uncovered, at 325° for 35 to 40 minutes. Slice ½ inch thick.

CORNED VENISON LEFTOVERS

CORNED VENISON HASH

2½ cups diced, cooked corned
    venison
2 cups boiled and diced potatoes

1 tsp. minced parsley
¾ cup stock
4 tbsps. melted butter

Blend all ingredients and pat into a buttered baking dish. Bake at 350° for 30 minutes, or until browned on top.
SERVES 4.

CORNED VENISON HASHCAKE

2 cups ground, cooked corned
    venison
¼ cup ground lean salt pork
1 cup mashed potatoes
1 egg, beaten

1 tbsp. flour
½ tsp. onion salt
⅛ tsp. pepper
2 tbsps. sweet butter

Blend all but butter and form into cakes. Sauté in butter for 10 minutes per side.
SERVES 2.

YANKEE CORNED VENISON HASH

3 cups diced, cooked corned
    venison
4 tbsps. butter
⅔ cup boiling water

2 cups boiled and diced potatoes
¼ cup diced lean salt pork
⅛ tsp. pepper

Melt butter, add boiling water, then venison, potatoes, salt pork, and pepper, stirring thoroughly. Leave untouched over medium to low heat until bottom crusts. Gild the top quickly under a broiler before serving.
SERVES 4 or 5.

VENISON DRIED

Properly dried meat that is stored carefully has an exceptionally long storage life. If it is sealed in a container (tight jars or plastic bags are excellent), it will keep almost indefinitely. There is no need to refrigerate it if it has been thoroughly dried. Always dry fresh meat (hung but not frozen) since freezing breaks down the cell structure and destroys flavor.

    There are basically two forms of dried meat. One is "jerky," meat that is cut into thin strips and, in what is undoubtedly the authentic Indian method, simply air-dried. Thin, completely trimmed strips of venison were spread by early American Indians over handy bushes and shrubs to dry. The result was a greatly reduced weight of concentrated food value that supported tribes on long hunts and migrations. Jerky will be one-fifth to one-fourth of the weight of the original meat.

The second way to dry meat is in a large piece. When prepared like this, the chunk is thinly sliced before use. This method of drying is most familiar in markets in the form of chipped beef, and can, of course, be used for venison. Perhaps one of the easiest ways to dry-cure is simply to follow the directions on a package of Morton's Sugar Cure, which is available with or without hickory-smoke flavor. One old friend and guide in the high country of Wyoming simply hangs a treated venison ham from the outer rafter peak of his log cabin, cutting off what he needs through the long winter. This air-drying is similar to the process followed by the women of Grisons in the Swiss Alps who make a dried beef that commands a very high price. This system of drying in the sun and clear air is practical only in high country, however. Naturally while the meat is being dried it is brought indoors to avoid the evening and dawn dews.

One instrument that is most handy, whether for making jerky or for cutting slices from a dried ham or roast, is a mechanical slicer. Slices should always be very thin and as even as possible, and a machine makes the job easier. If you don't have a mechanical meat slicer or a friendly butcher who will run the meat through his machine, the best way is to use a very thin, extremely sharp knife. If you are slicing raw meat to make jerky, it is easiest to cut if the piece is first somewhat solidified in the freezer.

The raw meat for jerky can be sliced either with the grain or across it. If it is sliced with the grain, the resulting dried sheet will hold together and reconstitute into a thin slice when water is added. If, however, after making jerky you want to make the Indians' pemmican from it, slice the raw meat against the grain; this makes it much easier to pulverize the dried meat.

All the fat and tendons must be carefully trimmed from any cuts used for drying. Any fat that is left will spoil, in spite of the most complete drying, and ruin all your efforts. Tendons will become even more unpleasantly tough. If you want to dry a piece, be sure to pick a cut that is tendon free; hams and loins are the best choices.

102

The Indians sometimes smoked the thin strips of meat lightly over their campfires; this hastened the drying process when the weather was variable or they were about to move camp. Smoking also added flavor, of course. If your climate is not too humid, you can air-dry as the Indians did by stringing the meat over a clothes-line or spreading it out on a rack. Just be sure to cover it with cheesecloth (do not let it touch the meat) so that the birds won't get into it. It is easier, and quicker, however, to make jerky in your oven.

OVEN JERKY

Slice completely trimmed venison ⅛ inch thick. Spread the pieces, not overlapping, on cookie sheets, jelly-roll pans, or shallow baking dishes, or drape over oven rack wires. If you use the latter, line the bottom of the oven with foil to catch the drippings. Meat can be sprinkled with salt and pepper if you wish, but go easy with the salt, particularly if the jerky is to be used as a snack for hikers. The salt intensifies in the drying. Cook at the lowest possible heat for 5 to 6 hours, until the meat is completely dry. To be sure that it is properly crisp, leave it in the turned-off oven overnight, then seal in jars or bags.

Jerky that has been prepared with a minimum of seasoning, or none at all, can be seasoned before serving as a party snack. About 3 hours before serving, brush the pieces with catsup well seasoned with mustard, catsup thinned with vinegar, or barbecue sauce; or sprinkle it with lemon juice and season well with salt and pepper if they were not used in the drying.

Note: If you like your jerky just a bit moist, remove it from the drying process before it becomes brittle. Freeze it, since moist jerky will not keep well and is subject to mold.

QUICK JERKY

Cut 10 pounds of meat into ¼-inch strips. Boil in a mixture of 1 cup vinegar, 2 cups salt, 2 tablespoons pepper, and 2 quarts water for about 5 minutes. Drain the strips and roll them flat with a rolling pin. If the liquid that comes out is red, the meat hasn't been boiled long enough; the meat should be grayish brown and somewhat rubbery in texture. Spread the strips on oven racks, allowing space between for air circulation. Put into a 200° oven and cook, with the door slightly open, for about 1½ hours, or until the meat will crack but not break when bent.

Jerky, when prepared with seasonings, makes a different cocktail snack. The seasoning is very much a matter of taste, but here is one way that has proven popular.

SEASONED JERKY

3 to 5 lbs. meat strips
1 tbsp. onion powder
1 tsp. freshly ground black pepper
½ cup soy sauce
1 tbsp. seasoned salt
1 tsp. garlic powder
½ cup Worcestershire sauce

Make a marinade with the onion powder, pepper, soy sauce, salt, garlic powder, and Worcestershire. Soak the meat in it, refrigerated, overnight. Stir a couple of times while marinating. Drain meat and continue with drying.

Another way: brush with liquid smoke, then sprinkle with sugar. Let stand in layers, refrigerated, overnight.

PENNSYLVANIA SALTED SMOKE-CURED JERKY

7 oz. seasoned salt
1 oz. garlic salt
2 lbs. fine pure salt
1 oz. white pepper

Make a jerky salt of the ingredients. Sprinkle on only one side of meat strips. Put into a crock or enamelware dish with salted side up and let stand for 12 to 24 hours. Remove meat and *do not* rinse; put on trays and smoke in smoker at 150° to 180° with fruitwood fire for about 8 hours.

Mexico makes a dried meat, *carne seca*, that is just as flexible and easy to do.

MEXICAN CARNE SECA

2½ to 3 lbs. top round, cut 2 inches thick and sliced ⅛ inch thick across the grain
1 large onion, minced
2 tsps. dried oregano
2 garlic cloves, mashed
4 tsps. salt
½ tsp. coarsely ground pepper
¾ cup vinegar

Mix onion thoroughly with oregano, garlic, salt, pepper, and vinegar. Make layers of meat and onion in a deep glass, ceramic, or enamelware bowl, pouring the last of the onion mixture over the meat. Cover and chill overnight or up to 24 hours. Remove meat and shake off the onion and herb bits. Arrange meat for drying as in the recipe for Quick Jerky. This amount will fill 3 pans 15 x 10 inches. Dry at 200° for 6 to 7 hours, alternating pan positions in the oven every 1½ hours, until meat has turned brown, feels hard, and is dry to the touch. Remove, cool, and store airtight.

MAKES about ¾ pound, 3 to 4 cups loosely packed.

Jerky can of course be eaten out of hand, as it usually is by hikers and cocktail nibblers. Few people realize, however, that the dried meat can be reconstituted by returning water to it and result in more than just a snack. Jerky can be added to any liquid and simmered, in which case it will swell up almost to its original volume, making a satisfying meal for campers who do not have the facilities to care for fresh meat. There are other ways it can be used, too.

SEASONED JERKY SAUCE
(for scrambled eggs or omelet filling)

1½ oz. seasoned jerky, crumbled	3 tbsps. butter
3 onions, minced	1 tbsp. vinegar
¼ tsp. dried oregano	1 tsp. chile powder

Cook all ingredients over low heat until the onions just begin to brown, about 30 minutes. Enough for 4 to 6 two-egg omelets or 8 to 10 scrambled eggs (spoon over cooked eggs). Can be made ahead and reheated.

CARNE SECA SAUCE
(for a dip, or to be spooned on soft tortillas or rolls)

1 recipe Mexican Carne Seca
¾ cup hot water
1½ tbsps. salad oil
3 tomatoes, peeled and seeded
2 cups chopped green onions, including some tops
4 oz. canned green California chiles, membranes and seeds removed
3 cups venison, beef, or chicken stock

Pour hot water over *carne seca* and let stand for 30 minutes, stirring occasionally. Pound in a mortar with just a bit of the liquid until shredded into small pieces. Heat oil, add tomatoes, onions, and chiles. If you want to control the hotness, reserve some of the chiles and add later as desired.) Cook over medium heat, stirring, until onions begin to soften. Add stock and pounded meat and cook, uncovered, over medium heat, stirring from time to time, until the liquid is nearly absorbed, about 30 minutes.

MAKES 6 cups.

CAZUELA DE CARNE SECA (dried meat soup)

For each cup of Carne Seca Sauce, add 1 to 1½ cups venison, beef, or chicken broth and ¾ to 1 teaspoon minced fresh cilantro (coriander or Chinese parsley) or ¼ teaspoon dried. Bring to a boil and serve.

PEMMICAN

jerky
beef suet
bone marrow

salt and pepper
dried raisins, berries, or fruit
shelled, chopped nuts

Pound jerky in a mortar, or grind in a meat grinder, until reduced to a fine powder. Render enough beef suet and melt enough bone marrow (about half and half) to mix the powder to a thick paste. Season to taste with salt and pepper after mixing in dried raisins and dried berries or fruits and shelled, chopped nuts. Form into blocks, wrap tightly, and store airtight.

BLENDER PEMMICAN

8 oz. jerky
8 oz. dried raisins, berries, and
   fruits
8 oz. unroasted nuts

2 tsps. honey
4 tbsps. smooth peanut butter
¾ tsp. cayenne

Pulverize jerky in a blender. Add dried raisins, berries, fruits, and nuts. Heat honey with peanut butter to soften, and blend in. Thoroughly work in cayenne. Pack into sausage casings or bags and seal airtight. Keep in a cool dry place, or freeze.

Venison dried in the piece can be used in all the same ways as chipped beef, after carefully slicing very thin. These slices can be rolled around chilled sticks of cream cheese for "wheels" for cocktail snacks or used in many other ways.

CREAMED DRIED VENISON

1½ cups shredded dried venison
2 tbsps. flour seasoned with ½ tsp.
  paprika
2 tbsps. melted butter

1 cup milk, scalded
2 cups boiled and diced potatoes
2 hard-cooked eggs, chopped
¼ tsp. white pepper

Blend seasoned flour with butter; add milk and cook, stirring, until thickened. Add meat, potatoes, and eggs, in that order, stirring gently after each addition. If too thick, add more milk slowly, stirring. Season with pepper.

SERVES 2.

SYMPHONY VENISON

8 oz. dried venison, sliced thin and torn into bite-size pieces
2 tbsps. butter
1 tbsp. flour
1 pint sour cream
½ cup dry white wine
1½ tbsps. grated Parmesan cheese
1 can (10 oz.) artichoke hearts, sliced thin
buttered, toasted English muffins or buttered toast

Melt butter over low heat and cook meat until crinkled and crisp on the edges. Sprinkle on the flour and mix in, then add sour cream and wine. Stir thoroughly until smooth; sauce may be a bit grainy or lumpy at first. Add grated cheese and artichoke hearts and stir in very gently. Best done in an electric skillet at 180°, but can be done over very low heat. Serve on muffins or toast.

SERVES 4.

BEAR

The bears available to hunters on the North American continent range from the Alaskan Brown (averaging 800 pounds live weight, and they've been known to reach 1,600 pounds), through the Grizzly (which actually can be colored from light cream to black), to the smaller American Black Bear (which isn't really black but may be cinnamon, dark brown, blue-gray, or cream) and will range from 200 to 500 pounds live weight.

As with any game, the young animals are much more tender and, in the case of bears, much more tasty. While bears are still in

the juvenile stage their diet consists mainly of berries and roots. When bears reach 2 years, they turn omnivorous, eating fish from streams if available and even eating carrion. It's quite common for a bear to prefer a "high" garbage pail to a fresh meal. While the eviscerating of a bear is one of the most unpleasant chores in game cleaning, it is wise to check the stomach contents; if there is a sign that the bear has been eating fish, keep it in mind. That fish taste will be in the flesh when you eat it. Heavy seasonings and use of many herbs can help to some extent, as can marinating, but the fish taste is still there.

If you question the age of the animal, check the claws and teeth. Both are sharper in young animals. Since bears can be subject to the trichinosis parasite, the flesh should always be well cooked. This is not much of a disadvantage however, since even young bear is tough if cooked rare. Only young bear, incidentally, does not require moist cooking.

Bear should be hung for at least a week before cutting. The usual cuts are from the saddle, loin, haunch, and ribs. The paws of young bears are considered a delicacy by some. To skin bearpaw pads, hold over an open fire until the skin on the pads blisters, then peel off. Cut off nails.

The heavy body fat can be stripped off and rendered. This is a traditional dressing for leather goods, and many western cooks prefer to use bear fat in cake baking although personally I don't care to use it that way.

PENNSYLVANIA ROAST BEAR

1 young black bear haunch, all fat removed and wiped dry
salt and pepper
butter
mild mustard
flour

Dust well with salt and pepper, brush with melted butter. Spread with mild, prepared mustard, and coat with flour. Roast slowly at 300°, uncovered, for about 4 hours.

ROAST BLACK BEAR

3 to 4 lbs. bear roast, all fat removed	2 celery ribs, chopped
	1 small dry red pepper
½ cup flour seasoned with 1 tsp. salt and ½ tsp. pepper	1 small bay leaf
	1 pinch dried rosemary
4 to 8 tbsps. sweet butter	2 tbsps. catsup
4 cups boiling water	2 tbsps. Worcestershire sauce
1 garlic clove, minced	½ tsp. celery seeds
4 cubes beef extract	½ tsp. dry mustard
1 onion, chopped	2 tbsps. tart marmalade

Dry meat; dust with seasoned flour. Sear meat on all sides in hot butter in a Dutch oven. Add boiling water to come one-quarter way up the roast. Add garlic, beef extract, onion, celery, red pepper, bay leaf, rosemary, catsup, Worcestershire, celery seeds, and mustard. Cover and simmer, turning occasionally and adding water if needed. When very tender, about 3 hours, remove meat and thicken gravy with a paste of flour and water. Strain, add marmalade, and pour over thin slices of meat.

SERVES 8 to 10.

SPICED BEAR

3 to 4 lbs. fat-free bear roast,
    marinated (perhaps Cooked
    Marinade)
2 tbsps. honey
1 tsp. ground cinnamon

1 tsp. garlic juice
1 tsp. ground ginger
2 cups strained marinade
¼ lb. butter

Wipe meat dry and rub with mixture of honey, cinnamon, garlic juice, and ginger. Put in a roaster on a rack and dot with butter and baste with marinade every 30 minutes. Roast at 325° for 3 hours. If in a self-basting roaster, uncover for the last 30 minutes.
    SERVES 8 to 10.

HUDSON'S BAY BEAR POT ROAST

6 lbs. fat-free bear roast,
    marinated (perhaps Basic Red
    Wine)
4 tbsps. cider vinegar
1 tbsp. onion powder
1 tbsp. garlic powder
2 qts. water

egg-sized piece of beef suet
beef stock (if needed)
2 cups sliced mushrooms
2 cups halved seedless green
    raisins
1 cup thick tomato juice
6 oz. Burgundy wine

Pat meat dry, then pat with mixture of vinegar and onion and garlic powder. Put into a heavy Dutch oven with the water in the morning. Bring to a good boil, covered, and boil for 15 minutes. Discard liquid, wipe meat dry, and rinse pot. Score the suet and melt in the Dutch oven. Brown meat thoroughly, for 30 minutes at least, to make a thick crust. Roast at 325° until done (at least 2 hours for a young bear, 3 to 4 hours for an older one). Roast uncovered, basting often, using no salt; use beef stock if needed. Meat is ready when a fork draws clear, watery juice. At 15 minutes before meat is ready, add mushrooms and raisins and baste every 3 to 5 minutes. Just before serving stir in tomato juice and Burgundy.
    SERVES 12.

ROAST SADDLE OR HAUNCH OF YOUNG BEAR

1 saddle or haunch of young bear
12 strips salt pork, 1½ inches x
    ¼ inch
1 tsp. ground cinnamon
1 tsp. ground ginger
½ cup seasoned flour

2½ cups marinade, strained
    (perhaps Cooked Marinade)
2 cans (10¾ oz. each) cream of
    mushroom soup, undiluted
1 tbsp. sweet butter

Marinate the piece of meat for 48 hours. Drain and pat dry. Reserve and strain 2½ cups of the marinade. Roll room-temperature salt pork in mixed cinnamon and ginger; chill. Use these lardoons to lard the roast. Rub roast with seasoned flour and dust with remaining cinnamon and ginger. Put on a roaster rack and pour on 2 cups heated marinade and mushroom soup with butter. Roast, basting every 20 minutes, at 350° for 2½ to 3 hours. At 20 minutes before bear is done, add remaining seasoned flour mixed smooth with ½ cup cold marinade, and blend into pan juices.

PAN-FRIED BEAR STEAK

1 bear steak, 1 to 1½ inches thick, with fat removed	1 tsp. sage seasoning
¼ cup chili sauce	5 tbsps. cooking oil
1 tsp. ground ginger	salt and pepper
	1 cup sliced onion

Blend chili sauce, ginger, and sage seasoning, and spread thickly on both sides of the steak 3 hours before cooking. Let stand at room temperature. Heat oil; when it bubbles add steak and sizzle over high heat for 5 minutes per side. Reduce heat and remove steak. Sauté onion rings until golden in same pan. Return meat, cover pan, and cook over medium-low heat until tender. Season to taste.

KODIAK STEAKS

1-inch steaks or chops, cut into serving pieces	1 tsp. ground ginger
½ cup flour	1 tsp. onion salt
½ tsp. ground allspice	3 tbsps. sweet butter
½ tsp. pepper	salt and pepper

Marinate young steaks overnight, older ones longer, perhaps in Wine Vinegar Marinade. Mix flour with allspice, pepper, ground ginger, and onion salt. Pound flour mixture into meat. Brown in sweet butter over moderately hot heat. Season steaks with salt and pepper after browning. Cover and simmer until well done.

BEAR IN BURGUNDY

2 lbs. meat, cubed	1½ cups red Burgundy wine
½ cup seasoned flour	1 tbsp. grated nutmeg
4 tbsps. cooking oil	1 tsp. cinnamon

Dredge meat with seasoned flour and brown in the oil over medium-high heat. Add wine, nutmeg, and cinnamon, and cook in a pressure cooker according to manufacturer's instructions at 10 pounds pressure for 2 hours. Test for tenderness; if not as tender as desired, continue cooking without pressure, testing every 15 minutes. Canned or thawed frozen vegetables can be added to meat to make a stew.

SERVES 4 or more.

BISON OR BUFFALO

The bison, perhaps better known by the name of buffalo, has long been unavailable to hunters. However, with the herds increasing, one can sometimes buy a quarter when public herds are reduced. Bison or buffalo meat is also coming into the market. Commercial herds in several parts of the country—from Utah and Wyoming to Pennsylvania—are supplying restaurants and fancy markets. Yes, it can be bought, if you can afford the prices, which are considerably higher than those for the well-fed beef, to which a bison in top condition has been compared.

Roasts, steaks, and ground meat are the forms in which the meat goes to market. The meat is juicy and mild flavored. Traditionally, the hump has been the delicacy cut. This is fine grained; when salted and cut across the grain, it is considered almost as rich and tender as the tongue, which in its turn is a delicacy considered even better than an English tongue. The tongue of the bison was at one time as much of a single target for hunters as the robe (from the hide) or the hump; thousands of animals were slaughtered just for the tongue. These were smoke-cured, barreled, and shipped.

Bison meats should be well trimmed of fat; as with venison, the fat is not the best. The cuts are similar to venison or beef and are cooked the same way. As with venison, the meat is darker red than beef. Bison does tend to have a richer, fuller flavor and the gristle, unless removed, tends to be quite resistant to the teeth of the diner. Because the animal naturally has less marbling of fat through the meat than beef, buffalo roasts should be cooked at a lower temperature than beef: a standing rib roast is rare when the internal temperature reaches 135°. As with good beef and venison, roasts and steaks are best cooked to no more than medium-rare unless your family demands well-done meat; then it's a waste to serve them such good meat done that way.

If you think of ordering a quarter when the public herds of bison or buffalo are reduced, keep in mind that these are by nature some of the largest animals on the continent when full grown; a bull may well run 1,800 to 2,000 pounds and a cow (which also carries horns) will run about 800 pounds. I don't believe you can get specific about the size of the quarter you want.

JUGGED BUFFALO À LA PASS

1 family-sized buffalo roast, marinated (perhaps Wine Vinegar Marinade)
beef suet for larding
1 cup flour seasoned with 1 tsp. salt and ½ tsp. pepper
1 onion, diced
1 garlic clove, minced
¼ lb. sweet butter
4 cups water
4 cubes beef extract
3 cups tomato juice
12 whole white onions
6 carrots, cubed
6 tomatoes, peeled and quartered
1 cup sliced mushrooms
1 cup wine vinegar
juice of 1 lemon
2 tbsps. brandy
½ cup dry sherry

Drain the meat, lard with suet, and pat dry. Roll meat in seasoned flour. Brown diced onion, garlic, and floured meat in butter. Bring water to boil in a large casserole; add beef extract and tomato juice. Add browned onion and meat. Cover and cook for 1 hour. Add onions, carrots, tomatoes, mushrooms, vinegar, lemon, and brandy, and simmer, uncovered, for 1 hour. Skim off fat, add sherry, heat and serve. Can be thickened if desired.

SERVES about 6.

BUFFALO STEAK WITH WILD-RICE DRESSING

6 buffalo T-bone, rib, or chuck steaks
1 lb. ground buffalo, crumbled
1 cup raw wild rice
2 cups water
salt
½ cup minced onion
½ lb. mushrooms, sliced
2 tbsps. salad oil
3 cups cubed French bread, without crusts
1 cup beef broth, hot
¼ tsp. ground sage
dash of pepper

Wash rice, cover with water, and add ½ teaspoon salt. Bring to a boil, cover, and reduce heat; cook for about 30 minutes, or until tender. Drain well. Brown ground buffalo meat, onion, and mushrooms in oil, stirring often. Soak bread cubes in broth until soft. Stir in the rice, meat mixture, ½ teaspoon salt, the sage and pepper. Put into a greased 2-quart casserole, cover, and bake at 350° for 1 hour. About 15 minutes before serving, quickly broil or barbecue steaks to desired degree of doneness. Salt on both sides and put on a hot platter. Top with Herb Butter and serve with dressing.

SERVES 6.

BUFFALO STROGANOFF

2 lbs. buffalo top sirloin or top round, cut into ½-inch strips
⅓ cup flour seasoned with 1 tsp. salt
½ cup minced onion
½ lb. mushrooms, quartered

1 garlic clove, minced
2 tbsps. butter
6 tbsps. salad oil
1 cup beef broth
2 tbsps. Worcestershire sauce
1 cup sour cream

Shake meat pieces in a bag with salted flour. Sauté onion, mushrooms, and garlic in the butter and 2 tablespoons oil until soft. Remove from pan and add remaining oil. Brown meat quickly and remove. Combine leftover flour with pan drippings smoothly; gradually add the broth and Worcestershire and cook, stirring, until thickened. Blend in sour cream and heat slowly; do not let sauce boil. Return meat and onion mixture, and heat until steaming. (Also see Venison Stroganoff, pressure cooker.)

SERVES 4 to 6.

BAKED BUFFALO STEW

3 lbs. stew meat, cut into 1-inch cubes
2 cups minced onions
2 garlic cloves, minced
2 bay leaves
1½ tsps. salt
1½ tsps. MSG

¼ tsp. pepper
⅓ cup salad oil
½ cup flour
1½ cups dry red wine
1½ cups water
6 oz. tomato paste

Put meat, onions, garlic, and bay leaves in a shallow baking dish; sprinkle with mixture of salt, MSG, and pepper. Bake, uncovered, in 425° oven for 10 minutes. Reduce heat to 300° and bake for about 30 minutes longer, until the meat juices are released. Heat oil and stir in flour to make a smooth paste. Cook, stirring, until well browned. Remove from heat and gradually stir in wine, water, and tomato paste smoothly. Add meat with its juices. Cover and bake at 350° for about 2 hours, or until very tender.

SERVES 6.

114

QUICK STEW

2½ lbs. stew meat
1 onion, sliced and separated into
   rings
⅓ cup olive oil
1 cup red Burgundy wine
1 cup beef broth

1 cup tomato purée
1 bay leaf
1 tsp. salt
1 tsp. MSG
⅛ tsp. pepper

Sear meat on all sides in an oiled broiler. Remove, cool enough to handle, and cut into 1-inch cubes. Sauté onion rings in heated oil until soft but not browned; add meat. Blend in wine and cook quickly until wine is reduced by half. Stir in broth, tomato purée, bay leaf, salt, MSG, and pepper. Cover and simmer slowly for about 1 hour, or until very tender. Remove bay leaf before serving.
SERVES 4 to 6.

BAKED BUFFALO RIBS

4 lbs. buffalo ribs, cut into serving
   pieces

1 recipe Big Game Basting Sauce

Put ribs in a baking dish and bake at 350° until browned, about 30 minutes. Pour on Big Game Basting Sauce, cover, and bake for about 1½ hours longer, or until tender, basting occasionally.
SERVES 6.

BUFFALO LOAF

2 lbs. buffalo, ground
1 cup fine dry bread crumbs
1 tsp. salt
dash of pepper
½ tsp. *fines herbes*
¼ tsp. grated nutmeg

3 eggs
1 cup milk
1 cup shredded carrot
1 cup minced celery
1 cup minced onion
½ cup hickory catsup

Mix crumbs, salt, pepper, *fines herbes*, nutmeg, eggs, and milk, and beat well. Let stand for a few minutes. Gently blend in meat, carrot, celery, and onion. Spread evenly—don't mound—in a pan 13 x 9 inches and spread with catsup. Bake at 350° for about 1 hour. Let stand for 5 minutes to set before slicing.
SERVES 6 to 8.

BOAR

To be accurate, the boar is not a peccary or the javelina of the Southwest and Mexico. The wild boar was introduced to the United States (in the Great Smokies) earlier in this century from Europe or, some say, from Russia. The true wild boar ranges from 200 to 350 pounds and will grow a very respectable set of deadly tusks 3 to 6 ½ inches long. The boar is mainly a vegetarian although it will not turn down birds, particularly the young of ground-nesting species.

The razorback is a domestic pig that has gone wild through several generations. The peccary has 2 subspecies, the "collared," which is protected in the Southwest, and the "white-lipped," which is hunted in Mexico and South America. The peccary (which is the sportsman's javelina) is sometimes known as the "musk hog" for the strong scent that comes from the navellike gland on its back. It's a very strong gland and extremely smelly! In identifying the peccary, the hind foot has only three toes and the upper tusks turn downward. The "collared" peccary is the source of true pigskin, incidentally. Peccaries run about 50 to 70 pounds live weight.

While there are several species and subspecies of wild pig, all of them may be cooked in the same way.

There is no need to remove any wild pig fat. Since wild pigs are leaner than domestic pigs, you may even want to add some fresh pork fat from your butcher. This will depend, of course, on how much the carcass carries on it.

Naturally, wild pig makes excellent smoked hams and sausages.

TARHEEL ROAST LOIN

4 to 5 lbs. loin of young tusker, marinated (perhaps in Sangria)	1 tsp. or more dried oregano
3 juniper berries, ground	1 tsp. salt
1 tbsp. brown sugar	dash of pepper
1 cup juice of sour apples	dash of MSG
	2 or more garlic cloves, slivered

Blend juniper powder into brown sugar and dissolve in apple juice. Sprinkle loin with oregano, salt, pepper, and MSG. Gash the top of the loin on the fat side ½ inch deep and insert garlic slivers. Put meat on roaster rack. Roast uncovered, at 350°, basting freely every 15 minutes with apple juice, for 35 minutes per pound. Remove meat from pan, spoon out all fat, and make pan gravy.

SERVES 10 to 15.

ITALIAN HUNTER'S BOAR

leg of boar	1 celery rib, chopped
fat ham for larding	1 large parsley sprig, chopped
butter	salt and pepper
1 onion, sliced	1 cup white wine
1 carrot, chopped	1 cup stock

Lard a leg of boar with strips of fat ham. Brown in butter with onion, carrot, celery rib, parsley sprig, and salt and pepper. When browned, pour on white wine and cook for 2 minutes. Add stock. Cover and simmer very gently for 3 hours.

TARHEEL LOG CABIN ROAST LEG

1 large leg, boned and rolled	1 small bay leaf
5 garlic cloves, slivered	6 onions
½ cup flour seasoned with ½ tsp. paprika and ¼ tsp. pepper	6 potatoes, peeled
1 large carrot, sliced thin	½ cup applesauce
2 celery ribs, sliced thin	2 tbsps. applejack or hard cider
	1 tbsp. seasoned salt

Marinate the rolled leg for 12 to 24 hours, perhaps in Cooked Marinade. Drain and pat dry. Gash top (heavy meat) of leg and insert garlic slivers. Sift seasoned flour all over leg. On a rack in a self-basting roaster, put a bed of sliced carrots and celery. Put the meat on the vegetables, and put bay leaf on top. Roast at 325° for 40 minutes per pound. Add onions and potatoes 1 hour before meat is done. When done, remove meat and vegetables and pour off excess fat. Make gravy with 1 tablespoon seasoned flour to each cup of pan liquid remaining; strain gravy. Discard bay leaf. In top part of a double boiler heat applesauce and applejack; blend in strained gravy and seasoned salt and stir to heat. Thin if desired with boiling water. Serve apple-flavored gravy with the roast and vegetables.

WESTERN ROAST WILD PIG EN CROÛTE

Slice rib and tenderloin of wild pig, and slowly panfry. Re-assemble the slices. Prepare *croûte*: prepare enough dark-bread crumbs to make a ½-inch-thick layer all around the roast. Toast crumbs on a cookie sheet in a medium oven. Soak the toasted crumbs in enough red wine barely to cover for 2 minutes, then drain. Mix crumbs with 1 teaspoon ground cinnamon and 1 egg yolk, beaten, to each pound of bread crumbs. Form shell all around the reassembled meat slices with crumb mix. Bake at 350° until all is thoroughly heated, about 40 minutes. Serve with Cumberland Sauce. Scoring the crumb crust in line with the slice cuts before baking makes serving easier.

CREOLE ROAST PIG

Season well a roasting-sized wild pig, whole or in quarters, with salt, and red and black pepper. Put into a roaster with 4 to 5 cups water. Cover and cook on lower shelf of the oven at 350° until very tender, a matter of hours. This can be done early in the day; if so, reheat to continue. Uncover; increase heat to 450° to brown and crisp skin. Sweet potatoes and/or apples can be added to pan for the last 45 minutes.

TARHEEL BRAISED YOUNG WILD PIG LIVER

1 lb. wild pig liver, cut into ½-inch slices	6 potatoes, sliced
	2 carrots, diced
2 tbsps. flour seasoned with ¾ tsp. salt and ⅛ tsp. pepper	1 onion, sliced
	1 cup tomato juice
3 tbsps. pork drippings	1 cup boiling water

Cut liver slices into 2-inch squares and roll in seasoned flour. Brown in pork drippings and remove from skillet. Brown potatoes, carrots, and onion in remaining drippings. Return the liver, and add tomato juice and boiling water. Cover and simmer gently for 1¾ hours. Gravy can be thickened if desired.
SERVES 4.

Wild pig can be smoked just as fresh domestic hams can be. Again, Morton's curing aids and instructions are recommended.

TARHEEL WILD SHOAT HAM

1 country-cured ham of wild shoat
marinade in proportions of 3 cups
   red wine to 1 cup vinegar
2 tbsps. whole cloves
½ cup blackstrap molasses
½ cup brown sugar
cinnamon

Soak ham in marinade, covered, overnight. Drain. Reserve marinade. Put ham, rind up, on a roaster rack. Do not cover or add water. If ham is at room temperature, allow 30 minutes per pound at 325°, 10 minutes more per pound if refrigerated. Baste frequently with marinade. Meat is done when interior thermometer reads 175°. About 30 minutes before the ham is done, remove rind, score fat, and stud with cloves. Dribble on molasses and dust with brown sugar and cinnamon. Return to 450° oven for 15 minutes. Allow glaze to set for 20 minutes before carving.

BOAR SAUSAGES

Pork is the usual meat used in most commercial sausages, and wild pig can be used for the same purpose.

WISCONSIN LIVER SAUSAGE

1½ lbs. wild pig shoulder
½ lb. wild pig liver
1½ cups bread crumbs
1 onion, minced
1 tsp. salt
¼ tsp. pepper
½ tsp. dried thyme
½ tsp. dried marjoram

Cover shoulder with water and cook until tender; reserve liquid. Cover liver with water and cook until done through; discard liquid. Cool both meats. Grind meats several times with bread crumbs, onion, salt, pepper, dried thyme, and dried marjoram. Boil ground ingredients in the reserved shoulder cooking liquid for 10 minutes, stirring. Cold-pack in sterilized jars and cover tightly. Refrigerate. Use as a pâté or sandwich spread.

MAKES about 3½ pounds.

PENNSYLVANIA DUTCH SCRAPPLE

Use tongues, hearts, and liver as part of the meat. Cook meat in enough water to keep it covered; drain off and reserve liquid when meat separates readily. Run meat through the fine blade of a grinder. Measure ground meat and liquid; there should be about twice as much broth as cooked meat. Return meat to broth and bring to a boil. Soften the cereal used with some of the liquid; work it into a dough by hand, and then thin with more of the liquid to eliminate lumps. Pour the diluted cereal into the cooked meat and cook for another 30 minutes. Before the scrapple becomes too thick, season to taste. When scrapple has lost its raw cornmeal taste and is thick enough so that it piles up, it is ready to be spooned into loaf pans.

SCRAPPLE FORMULA

20 lbs. ground cooked meat
2¼ lbs. buckwheat or rye flour
7 lbs. fine-ground untoasted cornmeal
2 oz. black pepper
2 oz. salt

¼ oz. grated mace
¼ oz. grated nutmeg
¼ oz. ground sage or thyme
(liquid smoke can be added to taste)

Smooth scrapple in the loaf tins and set in a cool dry place to firm up. Remove loaves from the tins (dip tins briefly into hot water), slice and fry the scrapple; or overwrap and freeze.

ITALIAN SAUSAGE

35 lbs. lean wild pig, chopped fine
15 lbs. fatback meat from wild pig (or use domestic for enough fat), chopped fine
1¼ lbs. salt
2 oz. sugar

3 oz. white pepper
1 oz. ground coriander
1 oz. grated nutmeg
½ oz. paprika
¼ oz. garlic powder

Season meats with blended seasonings, mixing well. Stuff into casings. If your stuffer needs liquid, dissolve spices in 2 quarts water with ¾ ounce saltpeter and blend into meats. Can also be formed into patties.

MEXICAN CHORIZO (Sausage)

1 lb. fresh pig meat, including
   some fat, coarsely ground
1 tsp. salt

1 tbsp. chile powder (preferably
   Mexican with added spices)
1 garlic clove, mashed
1 tbsp. vinegar

Blend all ingredients well and pack into a crock; seal. Will keep for several weeks if refrigerated. Can also be packed into casings and smoked for flavor, or merely dried overnight between 60° and 70°.

FRENCH FRESH COUNTRY SAUSAGES

1 lb. lean pig meat
½ lb. hard fatback
¼ cup red wine
generous pinch of saltpeter

1 tbsp. salt
¼ tsp. sugar
¼ tsp. pepper
¼ tsp. *Quatre-Épices*

Work both meats through a coarse grinder. Mix well with wine, saltpeter, salt, sugar, pepper, and spices. Season to taste with savory, tarragon, thyme, chives, ground bay leaf, coriander, sage, marjoram, shallots, garlic, crushed juniper berries, parsley, and/or pimiento; the choice and possible combinations are individual to each maker. Stuff into casings (big ones) and hang to dry in an airy place at a temperature no higher than 60° for 5 days in cold weather, 3 days in cool weather, and 2 days in hot or very damp weather. Poach gently in simmering water or stock for 15 minutes to serve.

MAKES 1½ pounds.

GERMAN BRATWURST

1½ lbs. lean pig meat, put
   through fine grinder 3 times
1½ tsps. salt
⅛ tsp. ground sage

½ tsp. each of white pepper and
   ground allspice
1 cup (approx.) water

Mix seasonings with meat and enough water to give a consistency suitable for pressing into medium-sized casings. Scald. Brown in butter to serve hot; or scald, then dip into light cream, and broil about 6 inches from the source of heat, turning until evenly browned.

MAKES 1½ pounds.

121

TARHEEL LEFTOVER WILD HAM IN WINE

2-inch slice of cooked, cured wild pig ham	1 tbsp. butter
	1½ cups water
½ cup brown sugar	½ cup raisins
1 tbsp. cornstarch	½ cup dry red wine

Combine brown sugar and cornstarch; add butter and water. Cook, stirring, for 3 minutes until sugar and cornstarch are dissolved and mixture is smooth. Remove from heat and add raisins and wine. Put ham slice into greased baking dish and cover with sauce. Bake at 350° for 1 hour.

SERVES 4.

ROCKY MOUNTAIN GOAT

The mountain goat (which is not a goat, but a member of the ox family) is one of our animals that has dwindled drastically in number. Man again is the cause, but the goat has never been a source of income, except perhaps for the excellent goatskin rug. Because of man's impact, the Rocky Mountain goat has been pushed higher and higher and farther away from a goat's "good living." Cattle now graze the meadows and the goat doesn't like company of any kind.

It's obvious to anyone who's tried it that the Rocky Mountain goat is no particular prize on the table. The meat is strong and tough in an adult; the nannies and kids are the best eating. The billy may weigh between 150 and 250 pounds. The fine wool under the long hair would undoubtedly please someone who could spin it into yarn, but you'd need a lot to make much of anything out of it. The horns are considered only a minor trophy.

The goat has black glands which should be removed in cleaning. They are about 2½ inches in diameter and are located just behind the horns. The assumption is that this gland is important in the courting cycle, although little really is known about these shy, agile creatures.

Since the meat of an adult goat is dark and extremely tough, some make it a practice to pressure-cook it before continuing with recipes. Put rib, loin, and/or top round in soup stock to cover in a pressure cooker. Add 2 diced onions and cook following manufacturer's directions at 10 pounds pressure for 2½ to 3 hours. The dish can be finished by opening cooker and adding 1 cup diced potatoes, 1 cup chopped celery, and 1 cup canned tomatoes; cook at 10 pounds pressure for an additional 30 minutes.

As an alternative, pressure-cook the meat as above, then continue with marinating and cooking.

TEXAS ROAST KID

half of a young goat, including shoulder and breast, cut into serving pieces

salt and pepper
1 tbsp. dried oregano
5 cups Texas Salsa

Sprinkle meat generously with salt and pepper and put into a large roasting pan. Do *not* add any fat or liquid. Cover and bake at 450°, stirring pieces occasionally, for 2 hours. Sprinkle meat with oregano and bake, uncovered, for 20 minutes. Add the *salsa* and continue baking, uncovered, basting often, for 20 to 30 minutes.

SERVES 12.

MOUNTAIN SHEEP

The mountain sheep family, the Dall, Stone, and Bighorn, carry the most coveted of hunter's trophies in their curling horns. Members of the ox family like the goat, these animals are much better eating. In fact the Dall, which gets the highest rating, has been likened to the finest English mutton. The Bighorn ram, the largest of the subspecies, ranges from 250 to 300 pounds live weight; the ewes range from 125 to 175. The Stone (or black) is next smaller, with the Dall (or white) the smallest of the three, running around 200 pounds. All sheep have musk glands on all four feet which, if the legs are not removed, should be cut out.

A sheep with a full curl to the horns can be assumed to be an older animal. Some people feel that the creases that ring the horn are a means of counting the years, but there is not much to support the theory scientifically.

ROAST MOUNTAIN SHEEP

3 to 5 lbs. top round roast
2 tsps. garlic juice
2 tsps. onion juice
1½ cups tomato juice, warmed
4 tbsps. sweet butter

1½ tsps. brown sugar
salt and pepper
2 tbsps. flour
1 can (10¾ oz.) cream of
    mushroom soup, undiluted

Rub meat with garlic and onion juices. Put on a rack in a roaster and add 1 cup tomato juice with butter melted in it. Roast meat at 325° for 2½ to 3 hours, basting with tomato juice and butter at 20- to 30-minute intervals. During the last 30 minutes dissolve brown sugar in remaining ½ cup tomato juice and add to pan. Raise heat to 400° and baste every 5 to 10 minutes to brown. Season with salt and pepper before serving. Make a sauce by blending flour with soup, then stirring mixture into pan juices. SERVES 6 to 8.

RICE-STUFFED SHEEP BREAST

1 sheep breast, with pocket cut
   for stuffing
1 lb. venison, ground
3 tsps. garlic juice
1 cup raw converted rice
4 cups boiling water
3 tbsps. beef suet

2 tbsps. minced parsley
1 tsp. onion salt
½ tsp. minced fresh mint
¼ lb. butter, melted
¼ cup fine bread crumbs
2 cups boiling soup stock

Remove all fat from the breast. Rub the meat, inside and out, with 2 teaspoons of the garlic juice. Pour the rice into the boiling water and boil for 10 minutes; remove from heat and drain rice. Render the beef suet and add to rice. Stir in parsley, onion salt, mint, and remaining garlic juice. With a fork stir in the ground venison. Stuff the mixture loosely into the breast and skewer closed. Put the meat in a self-basting roaster; rub with the melted butter and sprinkle the crumbs through a sieve all over the top. Pour the boiling soup stock into the pan. Roast at 325° for 40 minutes per pound.
   SERVES 4 to 6.

ROAST RIBS

4 to 6 lbs. ribs (racks), cut into
   6-inch squares
2 tbsps. salt-pork drippings
¼ cup red wine

2 tbsps. pineapple juice
2 tbsps. vinegar
2 tbsps. soy sauce
1 tbsp. onion juice

Brown racks thoroughly in salt-pork drippings and put them in the bottom of a self-basting roaster. Blend remaining ingredients in a skillet, bring to a boil, and pour over meat. Cover and roast at 325° for 1¼ hours. Remove cover and baste at 10-minute intervals for 30 more minutes. Raise heat to 400° to finish, until crisp, brown, and aromatic.

SERVES 3 or 4.

PAN-BROILED MOUNTAIN SHEEP CHOPS

3 lbs. meat, from breast, chops, or shoulder, cut into 1½-inch cubes
4 tbsps. sweet butter
1 cup chopped onions
1 cup cut string beans
1 cup diced potatoes
½ cup diced celery
½ cup diced turnip
½ cup chopped carrots
2 tbsps. diced parsnips
2 tbsps. minced parsley
1 tsp. garlic salt
½ tsp. ground thyme

Melt butter in a Dutch oven and sauté meat and onions. Add remaining ingredients, cover, and roast at 300°, without removing the cover, for 3 hours.

SERVES 4 to 6.

SHEEP KEBABS

2 lbs. shoulder meat, cut into 1½-inch cubes
mint sauce
egg tomatoes
mushroom caps
small white onions

Marinate meat in commercial mint sauce to cover for 2 hours. Skewer meat cubes alternating with egg tomatoes, mushroom caps, small white onions. Broil, turning and basting with ½ cup mint sauce at 5-minute intervals, until brown on all sides.

PRONGHORN OR ANTELOPE

The pronghorn is another animal better known by another name, the antelope. Actually this is not a member of the antelope family, nor of the goat family, in spite of the similarity of the horns. This animal is unique; it has no relative anywhere in the world.

The pronghorn sheds its horns each year as do animals that wear antlers. When the horns are shed, however, the long, fibrous core remains. Both male and female carry horns. The doe runs around 65 pounds; her mate may average about 80. The larger and longer the horns, the older the animal is assumed to be.

125

The pronghorns' country is the sage desert, the wide open spaces of the "purple" rather than the culinary sage. Because the sage forms a fair part of their diet it does affect the flavor of the flesh. I personally rather like it and do not marinate the meat unless I know that the animal had been run in fright. The thing to keep in mind is that this sage does not blend well with culinary sage, so don't use any of that in your cooking.

People who find the wild sage taste in the meat not to their liking frequently soak the meat in milk for a few hours, then drain and continue with recipes. This does draw off some of the flavor and, of course, also takes some of the natural meat juices with it. Try it if you must, but do try the pronghorn plain first! The meat is fine-grained and there is little fat. Any that there is should be removed. Pronghorn meat lends itself well to recipes for veal.

ROAST SADDLE OF PRONGHORN

1 fat-free saddle
1 tsp. dried thyme
4 tbsps. butter

4 slices salt pork
2 tbsps. brown sugar
1 tsp. paprika

Blend thyme into 2 tablespoons of butter and rub well onto roast. Let stand for 3 hours. Put on a rack in a roaster. Pin on salt-pork slices so that pieces overlap. Use more if needed to cover. Roast at 300°, basting every 30 minutes. Cook for 30 minutes per pound. To brown, remove pork for the last 30 minutes and brush the saddle with a mixture of 2 tablespoons butter, brown sugar, and paprika. Increase heat to 400° and leave the door slightly ajar.
SERVES 4 to 6.

WYOMING MARINATED LEG

4 to 5 lbs. leg roast, boned
½ cup olive oil
2 cups red or white wine
juice of 2 lemons
2 tsps. salt

1 tsp. pepper
1 bay leaf
3 garlic cloves, minced
2 (or more) garlic cloves,
  slivered

Make a marinade with all ingredients except roast and slivered garlic. Soak meat in it for 24 hours, turning several times during marinating. Remove meat and drain. Stud with slivers of garlic to taste. Let stand for 1 to 2 hours at room temperature. Roast in

200° oven for 8 hours, basting with marinade from time to time. Serve well chilled for a cold buffet.

SERVES 8 to 10.

JACKSON ALTERNATIVE

10 to 12 lbs. antelope ham
bacon grease
salt and pepper
rosemary
tarragon
ginger

carrots, chopped
onion, chopped
consommé
butter
Worcestershire sauce
sherry (optional)

Trim ham and remove all fat and fibrous tissue. Smear with bacon grease. Dust leg with mixture to taste of salt, pepper, rosemary, tarragon, and ginger. Put into a covered roaster, and add chopped carrots and onion on top. Baste frequently with consommé, melted butter, and Worcestershire sauce; sherry can be added. Roast at 350° for about 10 minutes per pound for rare (preferably), or for up to 15 minutes per pound for well done.

SERVES 12 to 14.

BAKED PRONGHORN CARBONNADE

3 lbs. top sirloin or top round,
   cut 1 to 1½ inches thick
1 garlic clove, slivered
12 oz. bock beer or dark beer
¼ cup molasses

1 onion, sliced
1 tsp. grated orange rind
commercial Brown 'n' Season
2 tbsps. butter
2 tbsps. flour

Cut slits in the meat and insert garlic slivers. Put meat into a shallow pan and pour on a mixture of beer, molasses, onion, and orange rind. Let stand at room temperature for 2 hours, turning once. Remove meat and drain well; reserve marinade. Sprinkle both sides of meat evenly with Brown 'n' Season and put into a shallow baking pan. Bake at 425° for 25 minutes (medium rare) or to desired degree of doneness. Meanwhile, melt butter and blend in flour. Stir in strained marinade. Cook and stir over medium heat until sauce is thickened and smooth. Slice meat on an angle into ¼-inch slices. Pour some of the sauce over the slices; serve the rest separately.

SERVES 6 to 8.

ROLL-UPS

2 lbs. top round steaks, 1/4 inch
    thick
1/4 tsp. garlic salt
1 tsp. celery salt
1 tsp. paprika
1 tsp. dried parsley
4 to 6 carrots, cut into sticks
1/2 lb. loose pork sausage meat

1/2 cup flour
1 tsp. salt
1/4 tsp. pepper
1 tbsp. brown sugar
2 tbsps. sweet butter
1 tbsp. lard
2 cans (10¾ oz. each) cream of
    mushroom soup, undiluted

Pound the steaks to 1/8-inch thickness and cut into 4- to 5-inch squares. Mix garlic and celery salts, paprika and parsley, and rub well into both sides of meat. Put several carrot sticks on each piece, and spread with some sausage meat. Roll up and tie or skewer. Dust with flour mixed with salt and pepper, and sprinkle with brown sugar. Brown slowly in combined butter and lard. Pour on soup. Bake, covered, at 325° for 2¼ hours.

SERVES 6.

ANTELOPE CASSEROLE

1½ lbs. chuck, ground
4 tbsps. sweet butter
2 onions, minced
2 green peppers, minced
1/2 tsp. dried oregano
1/2 small bay leaf, broken
1/2 tsp. soy sauce

4 large potatoes, peeled and sliced
    1/8 inch thick
1 tsp. salt
1/4 tsp. pepper
2½ cups canned solid-pack peeled
    tomatoes
4 tbsps. salted butter

Melt half of the sweet butter. Brown the meat and remove. Add remaining sweet butter and sauté onions and green peppers until soft but not browned. Add oregano, bay leaf, and soy sauce; blend in meat. Put potatoes and meat mix in alternating layers in a greased casserole. Season each layer with salt and pepper. Heat tomatoes with salted butter and pour over casserole. Cover and bake at 350° for 1½ to 2 hours. (Can also be uncovered for the last 30 minutes, and topped with cottage cheese dusted with paprika or grated Parmesan cheese.)

SERVES 4 to 6.

HORSERADISH LOAF

2 cups ground pronghorn
¾ cup ground lean pork
¼ cup minced onion
⅓ cup milk
1 tsp. salt
2 tbsps. ground beef suet
⅓ cup grated fresh horseradish

2 eggs, beaten
⅓ cup catsup
1 cup cracker crumbs
⅛ tsp. pepper
1 tsp. mild prepared mustard
4 bacon strips

Blend all ingredients except bacon strips lightly but thoroughly; shape the loaf and place in a greased loaf pan. Bake at 350° for 1 hour. Top with bacon strips and cook for 30 minutes longer.
Serves 4.

PRONGHORN PATTIES

1 lb. pronghorn chuck, ground
½ lb. lean pork, ground
1 egg, beaten
1 onion, minced
1 tsp. mixed herbs
1 small bay leaf, crushed

½ cup flour seasoned with ½ tsp.
   salt and ¼ tsp. pepper
2 tbsps. sweet butter
1 tbsp. lard
1 can (10½ oz.) tomato sauce
½ cup sour cream

Blend meats; add egg, onion, and herbs, and mix well. Form into 2-inch balls, roll in seasoned flour, and flatten. Brown in butter and lard over medium heat for 5 minutes on each side. Add tomato sauce and simmer, covered, for 20 minutes. Remove patties and keep hot. Add sour cream to sauce, correct seasoning, bring to a quick boil, and pour over patties.
Serves 4 to 6.

CHAPTER 3

SMALL GAME

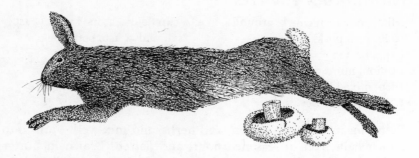

This country undoubtedly has more small-game hunters than any other kind; rabbit and squirrel hunters abound in almost every state. In many parts of the country a small-game hunter, going after a variety of targets, can hunt virtually every day of the year. If it's done with a small-bore rifle, incidentally, it's great practice for the big-game season, when the number of possible legal shots is greatly limited.

Small game, fur rather than hair bearers for the most part, are frequently the carriers and transmitters of tularemia. The germ of this disease is especially dangerous since it is one of the few that can apparently penetrate unbroken skin; it is not necessary to have an obvious bruise or cut for this organism to get into your blood and lymph channels. Because of this, many small-game hunters make it a practice *always* to put on a pair of unpunctured rubber or plastic gloves before handling the game. Others make it a practice not to take *any* game home until after the first good frost; cold seems to kill the bacterium.

There are two ways to tell whether the game should not be eaten. One of the first indications is that the game was too easy to take. If the animal is logy and doesn't seem to care if you shoot him or not, don't! That's a sick animal. Frequently, too, the coat is dull and scruffy looking. Some animals can be sick and not show it in actions; the only way to know about them is to open the abdominal cavity to eviscerate and look closely at the liver. If it is swollen and has light-colored lumps about the size of a matchhead, indicating tularemia, bury the carcass right there without further handling, even with gloves. Needless to say, do bury it well so that it won't be dug up by a dog, and certainly *don't* feed it to your hunting dog. Obviously, be sure to wash your gloves well after handling a diseased animal. Don't splash any of the wash or rinse water around; if it gets in your eyes you can still get the disease.

Small-game hunters, particularly those after the popular cottontail, should know that not all small white dots inside a rabbit mean that the meat is inedible for humans, although it *can* be bad for your dog. The cysts of the dog tapeworm show up in little jellylike sacs in the body cavity and sometimes on a normal-sized liver. While the white spots of tularemia are small and profuse, the white tapeworm cysts are scattered and about the size of a pencil tip.

FIELD NOTES

As with all game, immediate evisceration is of prime importance. Squirrel and rabbit are particularly easy to do. Make an abdominal slit, careful not to break the intestinal casing. Grasp the animal with a hand at each end and the slit away from you (and your hunting partner!) and give it a good snapping shake away from you; the entrails will fly out. (Many hunting dogs consider this their payment for hunting, but I don't allow my dogs to have it.) The same system works if you hold the animal with one hand at one end and give it a good sharp swing. After the entrails are out, remove the head and let the carcass drain for a few minutes. Wipe the cavity clean with grass, a clean cloth, or a few tissues.

Fur bearers, with the exception of rabbits and porcupines, bear musk glands which should be carefully and quickly cut out. Two are generally found under the foreleg (in the "armpit") and along the spine near the rump. These appear as nodules of a color different from the surrounding flesh. Unless these are removed they can impart a strong taste to the meat. To remove them means skinning on the spot, although many hunters don't skin out until arriving home. Carry the game in an *untied* plastic or paper bag in a game pocket, then transfer it to a cool thermal box for the ride home.

The young of any species is always the most delectable eating, but with small game the older adults of some species are just as good to eat. Others require precooking or marinating to tenderize them. The way to judge the relative age of the animals is to check their claws (which most of them carry) and their ears. The younger animals have sharper claws, and the ears are usually more pliable than in older ones. The teeth are cleaner and fewer of them are broken.

Small game, of course, is always skinned. Most of them skin out easily, needing no more than a cut large enough to get a grip on to pull the skin back and off. Those that need special handling are treated under their separate headings.

It is convenient to freeze small game whole, after skinning and careful cleaning at the sink. Freezing in one piece makes the choice of final preparation broader. On the other hand, keep in mind that badly shot-up areas should always be cut out at the final cleaning. A small animal that has taken a full shotgun charge dead center will not leave you with very much to eat. In the case of badly shot-up animals (and an active hunter in the family) it would be best to freeze the cut-up parts loose on a cookie sheet, then bag them. This way you can take out only what you want when you want it.

Small game presents no great butchering problems. They are easily cut into serving pieces with either a heavy kitchen knife or sturdy shears; I usually use a pair of heavy pruning shears which work very well. The only hard part of cutting (which need not necessarily be done) is to split the backbone lengthwise. If the back is large enough to require cutting, I simply cut it across with a hatchet on a board.

BEAVER

This is one of the true fur-bearing animals; prime skins bring a good price in the market. The meat is dark, rich, and delicious, but remember, the beaver can carry tularemia. This is also one of the animals that bears unpleasant glands which must be removed upon skinning. There is the "castor" gland near the tail under the belly and the usual musk glands in the small of the back and under the forelegs. These should be carefully cut out without damage and discarded. Also, remove all surface fat. Hang the carcass in a cool place for several days.

Beavers average about 45 inches in overall length, including the 10- to 12-inch-long tail, and weigh about 40 pounds. Some big ones, however, reach 60 pounds. Beaver is best, even with a young animal, if it is first poached in salted water for 1 hour. Instead of poaching beaver before cooking, some people marinate young ones overnight in water to cover with 1 tablespoon vinegar and 1 teaspoon salt per quart of water. Larger, older ones are sometimes parboiled in 2 baths of water to cover with 1 teaspoon onion juice to each gallon of water. This can be followed by braising (cooking slowly in moist heat in a covered pot such as a Dutch oven). There are many recipes for braised meat in Chapter 2 which are just as good for beaver as for venison.

Traditionally the beaver tail has been considered a delicacy. Some people parboil it first, but from what I've seen and friends' experiences it doesn't really need it. The trick to getting the rough skin off the tail before roasting over coals or grilling is to broil the tail over coals (or stove element), turning, for about 10 minutes, until the scaly hide blisters and scales off in sheets. The gelatinous meat is then roasted or boiled until tender. Since the taste is similar to pork, the tail is often cubed and baked with beans.

BASIC BEAVER TAIL

Roast prepared beaver tail over coals until done and tender. Or simmer in flavored liquid until tender.

BEAVER TAIL ROAST

beaver tail	1 egg
Basic Red-Wine Marinade	olive oil
½ cup vinegar	seasoned bread crumbs
1 tsp. salt	3 tbsps. melted butter
seasoned flour	

Marinate tail in Basic Red-Wine Marinade for 24 hours; dry. Simmer in water to cover with vinegar and salt until nearly done. Dry again and dust with seasoned flour, then dip into egg beaten with a little olive oil, then into seasoned crumbs. Put onto a greased rack and pour on 3 tablespoons melted butter. Roast at 350° until browned and done.

SERVES 2.

ROAST BEAVER TAIL (young beaver)

Put skinned tail in a roasting pan, season well with salt and pepper, and top with a thin layer of minced onions. Lard top with slices of bacon and roast at 350° until tender.

PENNSYLVANIA ROAST BEAVER

1 young beaver, prepared for
  baking
baking soda
black pepper

salt and pepper
onions, sliced
salt-pork or bacon strips

Parboil beaver gently for 10 minutes in water, with 1 teaspoon baking soda and 1 teaspoon black pepper to each quart of water; drain. Put meat in roasting pan. Sprinkle with salt and pepper inside and out. Cover with sliced onions and strips of salt pork or bacon. Roast at 350° until the meat almost falls off the bones.

MISSISSIPPI PIONEER BAKED BEAVER

8 to 10 lbs. beaver, fat removed,
  and cut into parts
1 bay leaf
2 medium-sized onions, chopped
1 or 2 garlic cloves, minced

½ cup chopped celery tops
flour
suet
salt and pepper

Soak the meat in salted water overnight. Parboil in the same water with bay leaf, onions, garlic, and celery leaves until half done.

134

Drain and roll in flour, then brown in rendered suet. Season with a dusting of salt and pepper. Bake in a covered pan at 350° until tender.

SERVES 12.

HOME-FRIED BEAVER

1 beaver, disjointed, with fat
    removed
1 tbsp. salt
1 tbsp. vinegar
1 cube of beef extract
2 cubes of vegetable extract
1 tsp. pickling spices
1 tsp. onion salt

1 tsp. garlic salt
1 bay leaf, broken up
1 tbsp. flour seasoned with ½ tsp.
    pepper and 1 tsp. salt
4 tbsps. lard, melted
2 cups brown gravy
1 tsp. apricot jelly

Marinate meat in enough water to cover, with salt and vinegar, overnight. Remove meat from the marinade and put in a kettle with fresh water to cover; add extracts, pickling spices, onion and garlic salts, and bay leaf, and simmer gently, covered, for 2½ to 3 hours. Rinse meat under hot water and dry well with paper towels. Dust with seasoned flour and brown in melted lard in a baking dish to form a crust. Cover dish and bake at 350° for 30 to 45 minutes. Pour lard off. Heat gravy, melt jelly in it, and pour over meat. Let heat gently for 10 minutes.

FUR TRAPPER'S BEAVER

1 beaver, cut into serving pieces
1 tbsp. celery seeds
1 tbsp. garlic juice
1 bay leaf
1 tbsp. onion salt

1 cup seasoned flour
½ cup melted lard
1 cup red wine
2 cups medium cream sauce

Parboil beaver in water seasoned with celery seeds, garlic juice, bay leaf, and onion salt. When nearly tender, remove and pat dry. Dust with seasoned flour and brown in melted lard. Add red wine, bake at 350°, covered, for 1 hour or until completely tender. Pour on cream sauce and broil briefly until golden brown.

FROGS' LEGS

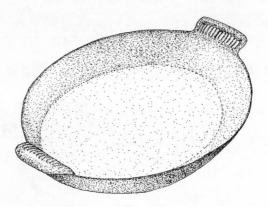

While people who are familiar with frogs' legs only on high-priced menus or in specialty markets may not think of getting them as sport, there's little doubt that a "leg man"—or woman—considers them good eating. Getting them in the wild is great sport, as anyone knows who has gone out with a gig and tried spearing them! Some people do it bare-handed at night using a light; that way they do absolute minimum damage to the edible meat, which includes the body meat of large frogs—just as good as the legs.

Assuming you have the whole, undamaged animal, the first thing is to kill it by slapping its head sharply on something hard. The head is then cut off; this is best done by holding the forelegs back along the body, putting the blade of a hatchet on the spot to be cut, then hitting the hatchet with a hammer—a two-man job. The feet are cut off in the same way, with a heavy blade and a hammer. With a knife or scissors slit the belly open and remove the viscera. Peel the skin off, using pliers or pincers. The back legs are cut off above the joint with hatchet and hammer.

Frogs' legs are usually served by the pair, but there's no reason why they should not be cut apart if so desired. The size of the legs —jumbos, small, or in between—will determine how many you will need for a meal for your family.

Frogs' legs freeze well, but even commercially frozen ones have a spooky tendency to twitch when they're in a hot pan. Let nervous cooks be forewarned!

FRIED FROGS' LEGS

16 pair small frogs' legs	1 or 2 eggs, lightly beaten
salt	1 cup fine bread crumbs
seasoned flour	4 tbsps. butter

Wash and drain the legs, and sprinkle with salt 1 hour before cooking. Dust with flour, roll in eggs, then in crumbs. Fry in hot butter, turning once, until golden.
    SERVES 4.

POLISH RAGOUT

10 pair medium-sized frogs' legs	½ cup white wine
salt	¼ cup bouillon
flour	salt and pepper
3 tbsps. butter	3 egg yolks, lightly beaten
4 mushrooms, sliced	lemon slices
¼ lb. sweetbreads, blanched and diced	

Wash, dry, and salt legs as in recipe for Fried Frogs' Legs. Roll in flour and fry in half of the butter until light golden. Arrange in a close-fitting pan; add mushrooms, sweetbreads, remaining butter, wine, and bouillon. Season, cover, and simmer for 30 minutes. Remove legs and keep warm. Combine a bit of the sauce with egg yolks, then return yolks to sauce to thicken. Serve with lemon slices.
    SERVES 4 or 5.

WESTERN STYLE FROGS' LEGS

18 to 24 pair frogs' legs	¼ tsp. dried savory
½ cup vinegar	½ tsp. pepper
cooking oil	1 tsp. salt
2 tbsps. ice water	¼ tsp. ground ginger
2 eggs, beaten	½ tsp. garlic powder
1 tsp. paprika	1 cup (approx.) cracker dust

Marinate frogs' legs in water to cover (about 3½ cups), with the vinegar, overnight. Drain. Pour enough oil into a skillet to reach a depth of ¼ inch. Heat oil to 375°. Blend ice water and eggs.

Blend paprika, savory, pepper, salt, ginger, garlic powder, and cracker dust. Dip legs into eggs, then into cracker mix; repeat egg and cracker layers. Fry for about 5 minutes on each side, turning once. Legs can be cooked in a deep-fryer if preferred.

SERVES 6 to 8.

NEW ORLEANS FROGS' LEGS

18 to 24 pair frogs' legs
marinade (⅓ water, ⅓ vinegar,
⅓ white wine)
2 garlic cloves, minced

½ cup flour seasoned with ½ tsp.
salt and ¼ tsp. pepper
¼ lb. sweet butter
pinch of cayenne
1 cup dry white wine

Soak frogs' legs in enough marinade to cover, with 1 minced garlic clove, overnight. Dry well; dredge with seasoned flour. Melt butter and add cayenne. When butter simmers, add legs; cook, turning frequently, to brown. After 5 minutes add remaining minced garlic. After 3 minutes more, add 1 cup white wine and cook until alcohol is boiled away, about 5 minutes.

SERVES 6 to 8.

SAUTÉED FROGS' LEGS

4 pair frogs' legs
1 egg, beaten
½ cup fine dry bread crumbs
2 tbsps. salad oil

2 tbsps. butter
1 garlic clove, mashed
parsley sprigs
lemon wedges

Dry legs thoroughly with paper towels; dip into beaten egg and let drain. Dip into crumbs and shake off excess. Heat oil and butter and add garlic; cook for 1 minute to season oil; add legs. Sauté over high heat until lightly browned on both sides, a total of 8 to 10 minutes. Serve with parsley and lemon wedges.

SERVES 2.

DEVILED FROGS' LEGS

4 pair frogs' legs
2 tbsps. salad oil
2 tbsps. butter

1 tsp. prepared mustard
1 tsp. Worcestershire sauce
2 tbsps. dry white wine

Dry legs well with paper towels and sauté in combined oil and butter over high heat until lightly browned, about 4 minutes. Remove from heat and drain off fat. Mix remaining ingredients

138

and pour over legs. Return to heat and boil rapidly for 2 or 3 minutes. Serve with reduced sauce.

SERVES 2.

CURRIED FROGS' LEGS

4 pair frogs' legs	dash of salt
2 tbsps. salad oil	dash of pepper
2 tbsps. butter	¼ cup heavy cream
2 tbsps. dry white wine	chutney
2 tsps. curry powder	

Dry legs well with paper towels and sauté in oil and butter over high heat for about 5 minutes. Pour off fat and add wine. Cover skillet and cook over high heat for about 3 minutes, shaking pan occasionally. Mix remaining ingredients and pour over legs; heat to simmering. Serve with chutney.

SERVES 2.

FROGS' LEGS PROVENÇALE

12 large or 24 small pair of frogs' legs	salt and pepper
	½ cup salad oil
1 cup milk	½ lb. butter
1 cup (approx.) flour seasoned with salt and pepper	1 tbsp. minced garlic
	¼ cup minced parsley
2 cups peeled tomatoes	

Soak legs in milk for about 15 to 20 minutes. Drain but do not dry. Coat with seasoned flour. Simmer tomatoes until thickened, 20 to 30 minutes. Season to taste. Heat oil and 4 tablespoons butter; cook legs until golden on both sides, turning once. Butter a heatproof serving dish lightly and arrange the legs in it in a single layer. Spoon the tomato sauce over the centers of the legs. Pour fat from skillet and wipe it dry with a paper towel. Add remaining butter to skillet and add garlic; do not brown the garlic, but when the butter is hot and foamy pour over legs. Sprinkle with parsley upon serving.

SERVES 4 to 6.

FROGS' LEGS WITH RICE

1 lb. frogs' legs	4 oz. dry sauterne
2 tbsps. butter	½ cup light cream sauce
4 shallots, minced	2 cups hot cooked rice

Melt butter until sizzling but not brown. Add legs and sauté briskly until tender. Sprinkle with shallots and add wine and light cream sauce. Simmer for 5 minutes to reduce sauce. Serve on cooked rice with sauce over all.

SERVES 4.

MUSKRAT

Another true fur-bearer, the muskrat (also known in restaurants and in some areas as "marsh rabbit," although there is a true swamp or marsh rabbit) is noted for its clean food habits. It's a vegetarian and as such seldom eats anything to give an off-flavor to its dark meat, but it can carry tularemia. The fat is unpleasant and should be removed. This is most easily done if the skinned and cleaned carcass (it has musk glands, too, which should be removed) is refrigerated overnight. This hardens the fat and makes it easier to peel off.

The muskrat, even a young one that will weigh about 1 pound and serve 2 people, should be soaked overnight at least, in 2 or 3 baths of water with 1 tablespoon salt per quart, or use 1 cup vinegar to each quart of water. Older, larger specimens will reach 3 pounds in weight and require longer soaking. Incidentally, the muskrat fur, after the long guard hairs were plucked off, was at one time called "Hudson seal"—a favorite fur of fashionable women earlier in the century.

ALLEGHENY BAKED MARSH HARE

1 muskrat	1 tsp. dried summer savory
salt	1 cup minced celery
3 medium-sized potatoes	2 large carrots, cut into quarters
2 tbsps. butter	3 slices bacon
pepper	

Soak muskrat in water to cover, with 1 tablespoon salt per quart of water, overnight. Cook potatoes and mash with butter, ½ tablespoon salt, ¼ teaspoon pepper, the savory and celery. Stuff muskrat with potato stuffing, and sew up or truss. Rub with 1 teaspoon salt and ⅛ teaspoon pepper. Put on a rack in roaster, with legs tied to body. Arrange carrot quarters around the muskrat and the bacon on top. Bake at 400° for 10 minutes. Pour 2 cups hot water over the meat and cook for an additional 35 minutes. Remove bacon and cook for 10 minutes more.

SERVES 2 to 4.

MOUNTAIN FRIED MUSKRAT

1 muskrat	1 tsp. salt
1 egg yolk	½ cup flour
½ cup milk	3 tbsps. fat

Soak muskrat as described in basic information, then drain and cut into pieces. Parboil meat pieces for 20 minutes, drain, and wipe with a damp cloth. Make a batter of egg yolk, milk, salt, and flour. Dip meat pieces into batter and brown in hot fat. Reduce heat, cover, and cook slowly for 1½ hours, turning a few times.

SERVES 2 to 4.

MICHIGAN SPECIAL HARE

1 young muskrat	½ medium-sized onion, sliced
4 cups water	½ cup melted butter
1 tsp. salt	1 cup catsup
⅛ tsp. pepper	½ tsp. Worcestershire sauce

Soak muskrat overnight, then drain and cut into pieces. Put meat in a deep pan with the 4 cups water, salt, pepper, and onion, and cook, covered, slowly for 1 hour. Remove and dry meat pieces, and brown them on one side in melted butter. Turn and add mixed catsup and Worcestershire. Almost cover meat with water, about 1 cup, and simmer until sauce is thickened, about 30 minutes.

SERVES 2.

PENNSYLVANIA STEWED MARSH RABBIT

4 young muskrats, cut into serving pieces	1 cup sliced carrots
salt, pepper, paprika, and red pepper	¼ lb. salt pork, diced and rendered
2 cups sliced onions	2 tbsps. flour

Soak saddles and hind legs in salt water for 24 hours. Dry with paper towels. Season meat, onions, and carrots well. Put in a Dutch oven with salt pork and simmer, covered, with just enough water to prevent scorching. Just before serving, thicken pan juices with flour.

SERVES 8.

PENNSYLVANIA MUSKRAT FRICASSEE

1½ to 2 lbs. dressed muskrat	dash of red pepper
water	¼ tsp. paprika
salt	¼ cup bacon fat
¼ cup flour	1 cup sliced onions
¼ tsp. pepper	

Soak muskrat in brine of four cups water and 1 tablespoon salt, refrigerated, overnight. Drain, rinse thoroughly in fresh water, and drain again. Cut into serving pieces. Shake with flour, 2 teaspoons salt, pepper, red pepper, and paprika to coat well. Brown meat slowly on all sides in bacon fat; add onions and cook until onions are soft. Add ½ cup water. Reduce heat, cover, and simmer gently for 20 to 30 minutes, adding more water if needed. Thicken gravy with leftover seasoned flour if desired.

SERVES 3 or 4.

CREOLE MARSH RABBIT

1 muskrat, cut into serving pieces	½ tsp. salt
vinegar	⅛ tsp. pepper
water	3 tbsps. bacon drippings
4 onion slices	1 cup sour cream
4 bay leaves	½ cup stewed prunes, diced
12 whole cloves	

Marinate meat in equal amounts of water and vinegar to cover, with onion, bay leaves, cloves, salt, and pepper, refrigerated, for two days. Be sure the meat is always covered with liquid. Drain meat and pat dry; reserve the marinade. Sear meat on all sides in hot fat. Drain off fat and add enough marinade to cover pieces of meat. Cover skillet and simmer until tender, about 30 minutes. Just before serving add sour cream and prunes. Bring to a rapid boil; discard bay leaves. Serve with fried bread triangles and the sauce poured over.

SERVES 3 or 4.

ALLEGHENY MARSH HARE LOAF

1½ lbs. soaked muskrat, boned and ground once	¼ onion, grated
	¼ tsp. dried thyme
2 eggs, beaten	1 tsp. salt
1 cup evaporated milk	¼ tsp. pepper
⅓ cup fine dry bread crumbs	1 tsp. Worcestershire sauce

Mix all together as for a standard meat loaf. Put in a loaf pan, then set the pan in another pan of water. Bake at 350° for 1½ to 2 hours.
SERVES 6.

NUTRIA

The nutria is unfamiliar to most of us, but it is so prevalent it is considered a pest in some parts of the country, particularly Texas and Louisiana. The pelt is soft and deep and enjoys popularity as a fur for coats and coat collars. With this animal also, glands must be removed before preparing. Also, beware of tularemia.

BAYOU ROASTED NUTRIA

nutria	salt and pepper
onions, sliced	cayenne
cooking oil	parsley

Boil nutria in water for 15 minutes. Meanwhile fry desired amount of sliced onions in oil in a Dutch oven. Add nutria, cut into serving pieces or whole, and cook slowly, brushing from time to time with oil seasoned with salt, pepper, cayenne, and parsley.

Nutria can be cooked by muskrat recipes.

OPOSSUM

This animal, too, has musk glands which must be removed when it is cleaned. It does not, however, have strong flavored or smelly fat, although most cooks remove all the body fat. This is best done by chilling first.
The meat is light and fine-grained. Some people like to marinate it before cooking for 4 to 6 hours (in ½ teaspoon ground sage, 2 tablespoons sugar, 1 tablespoon salt, and ¼ cup vinegar to 2 cups water or cider to cover); but this is not really necessary. The 'possum can reach 9 pounds, serving a family generously.

DIXIE ROAST OPOSSUM

1 8-lb. opossum, fat removed
1 opossum liver
salt and pepper
butter
1 medium-sized onion, chopped
1 cup cracker crumbs

½ tsp. soy sauce
1 hard-cooked egg, chopped
½ tsp. celery salt
5 cups boiling water
8 cubes beef extract
4 to 6 strips salt pork

Rub opossum inside and out with salt and pepper. Fry liver in hot butter until well done. Remove liver and brown onion; remove onion. Chop liver and blend with onion, crumbs, soy sauce, chopped egg, celery salt, and 1 cup boiling water with 2 beef extract cubes. Stuff opossum with this mixture and truss. Put in a roaster, back up, and pin on salt pork. Dissolve 6 beef cubes in remaining boiling water and pour around opossum. Roast at 350° for 2½ to 3 hours, basting frequently.
Serves 6 to 8.

ROAST OPOSSUM

5 lbs. opossum, fat removed
3 green peppers, chopped
2 onions, chopped

¼ cup flour seasoned with ½ tsp.
 salt and ¼ tsp. pepper
4 yams, peeled

Cover opossum with boiling water, add green peppers and onions, and parboil until tender, about 1½ hours. Remove and pat dry. Dust with seasoned flour. Roast on a rack surrounded by yams at 325° until golden, basting every 15 minutes with cooking liquid. Serve with Pepper Sauce or Poivrade Sauce.
Serves 4.

ALLEGHENY ROAST 'POSSUM

2 to 2½ lbs. 'possum, fat removed
Apple and Raisin Stuffing
3 sweet potatoes

2 tbsps. brown sugar
¼ to ⅓ cup flour

Stuff with Apple and Raisin Stuffing, and truss. Dust with salt and pepper; put on a roaster rack. Roast at 325° for 1 to 1½ hours (30 to 35 minutes per pound). For the last 30 minutes, put peeled and parboiled sweet potatoes around the meat. Dust meat with brown sugar mixed with ¼ to ⅓ cup flour. Baste with juices 3 times during the last 30 minutes.
Serves 4.

STUFFED 'POSSUM

1 8-lb. 'possum
2 cups bread cubes
1 onion, chopped
1 can (2 oz.) anchovy filets,
    chopped
2 tbsps. minced parsley
1 garlic clove, mashed
1 tsp. caraway seeds

¼ tsp. paprika
2 eggs, beaten
1 can (10¾ oz.) consommé,
    undiluted
2 tbsps. butter
1 cup water
1 tbsp. Worcestershire sauce

Parboil 'possum in salted water. Make a stuffing of bread cubes, onion, anchovy, parsley, garlic, caraway, paprika, eggs, and consommé; mix well. Cook in the butter in a skillet until mixture is stiff. Stuff 'possum; put in a roaster. Add water and Worcestershire sauce. Roast at 450° until brown. Reduce heat to 350° and continue until well done, basting often, 2 to 2½ hours.

SERVES 6 to 8.

Alternate Stuffing

Mix equal proportions of chestnuts, applesauce, and bread cubes; stuff 'possum. Cover stuffed 'possum with slices of sweet potato, and pour on 1 cup boiling water mixed with ½ cup lemon juice. Baste often while baking at 350° until tender, 2½ to 3 hours.

PORCUPINE

The porcupine is rarely an intentional hunter's target, but many hunters take a whack at one when they come across it inadvertently. Some people encourage this, particularly foresters who resent the porky's habit of "ringing" trees, leading to the tree's eventual death. Others insist that porcupines should be killed only in dire emergency; they have been called a "walking lunchbox." Since porcupines are very slow-moving, anyone lost in woods where porcupines live can always eat. The animal can be easily killed with a club for a source of food.

Whatever your particular attitude is, should you want to try a porcupine, go right ahead. It is not necessarily true that they taste like kerosene! The porcupine cleans out easily. Much as you would proceed with a rabbit, slit the belly area, thus avoiding the quills. Naturally, remove the stomach. The hide peels off easily, as does the rabbit's, right down to the feet and there you are with lean, dark meat. (In Pennsylvania, if the quills aren't to be saved, they are first singed off, then the skin is cut off.) Porkies can range from 9 to 40 pounds.

NEBRASKA PORKY

1 porcupine, skinned
parsley flakes
lemon juice

garlic powder
orange peel

Boil gently in water to cover to remove excess fat; skim fat as it renders out. (This is a good practice, but if the animal is not fatty, it can perhaps be skipped.) Drain, and re-cover with water to which a sprinkling of parsley flakes, a good dash of lemon juice, a dash of garlic powder, and some orange peel have been added. Simmer for about 1 hour. Remove, dry, and grill, seasoned only with freshly ground black pepper.

PENNSYLVANIA ROAST PORKY

Singe and skin 1 porcupine. Rub inside and out with plenty of salt, pepper, and bacon fat. Roast over campfire coals.

NEW ENGLAND BROILED PORCUPINE LIVER

Since the porky is a sedentary animal, the liver is relatively large. The liver is very sweet and is considered one of the finest of game livers.

Soak the whole liver in salted water for 15 minutes. Remove, drain, and wipe dry. Cut liver into ¾-inch-thick slices. Drop slices into boiling water for 1 minute. Remove, drain, and cool. Remove thin membrane from the edges and all of the gristle and tubes. Wrap each slice with a slice of bacon and broil for 5 minutes.

Porcupine is also good dipped into beaten egg, then into corn-meal, and deep-fried. Small pieces of liver and meat can also be used with bacon, tomato, and mushrooms for shish kebabs.

RABBIT AND HARE

The rabbit and hare family is a relatively large one, which is just as well. Perhaps more weight in rabbits is shot as game than in all other species of animals combined. There is the cottontail (2 to 3 pounds), found all over the country. The swamp or marsh rabbit of the Southeast has webbed hind feet and is an excellent swimmer; it can weigh 3 pounds. The snowshoe rabbit (called varying hare because of its seasonal color changes) and the jackrabbit are also popularly hunted species (ranging from 4 to 10 pounds). The arctic, at 12 pounds, is the largest.

Rabbits are generally good eating, but they are notoriously susceptible to becoming hosts for tularemia.

Young specimens are always the best eating, although the snowshoe does not get worse with age. On the other hand, both the snowshoe and jackrabbit are a bit sinewy to start with, even at an early age. Moist cooking is the best treatment for these. Cottontails, particularly young ones, have moist white meat and are excellent fried. They can be used in chicken or pheasant recipes.

PROVENCE STUFFED RABBIT

2 lbs. young rabbit	salt and pepper
rabbit liver	6 small carrots, halved
2 tbsps. butter	1 onion, chopped
chopped cooked veal or ham	a few parsley sprigs
1 tbsp. blanched, chopped salt	1 bay leaf, crumbled
pork	thin strips of bacon
1 tsp. dried thyme	1 cup (approx.) white wine

Sauté liver in butter until cooked through; chop, and combine with an equal amount of chopped cooked veal or ham and the salt pork. Mix in ½ teaspoon of the thyme and salt and pepper to taste. Stuff rabbit with this mixture; skewer opening. Put in a roaster just large enough to hold it. Add carrots, onion, parsley, bay leaf, and remaining thyme. Top with bacon strips and roast at 325° for about 1 hour, or until tender, basting occasionally with pan juices and a bit of white wine if needed. Transfer meat to a hot platter, surround with the carrots, and keep warm. Strain pan juices and return to roaster; stir in 1 cup white wine and bring to a boil. Cook, stirring, to deglaze until well blended. Serve sauce separately.

SERVES 3.

POLISH ROAST HARE

2 young hare, about 3 lbs. each	2 cups vegetables: sliced onion,
6 oz. larding pork	chopped carrots, chopped
juice of 1 lemon	celery, and parsley roots
2 tsps. ground pepper	1 tsp. salt
1 tsp. ground thyme	3 tbsps. butter
1 tsp. ground juniper	flour

Lard the whole hare. Sprinkle with lemon juice, rub with mixed pepper, thyme, and juniper, and cover with vegetables; refrigerate for several hours. Add salt for the last 30 minutes. Discard vegetables. Put meat in a shallow dish and dot with butter. Roast at 450° to 500° for 1 to 1½ hours, basting often. When nearly done, dust with flour and continue basting until browned.

SERVES 6 to 8.

POLISH HARE WITH SOUR CREAM

2 young hare, about 3 lb. each   3 tbsps. flour
2 cups sour cream

Marinate as in recipe for Polish Roast Hare for 2 days. Wipe and proceed as in that recipe. When nearly done, add sour cream blended with flour; blend into drippings; baste again several times.

SERVES 6 to 8.

NEW ENGLAND BAKED RABBIT

Rub a young rabbit inside and out with seasoned flour. Lay breast side up on a rack in a roaster; dot with butter. Bake at 350° for 40 minutes, or until tender. Turn, baste with pan drippings, and broil to brown. Thicken drippings as desired.

HOME-BAKED RABBIT

Stuff rabbit with well-seasoned bread and mushroom stuffing; truss. Place rabbit in roaster and cover top of rabbit with bacon slices. Dice rabbit heart and liver and add to pan. Pour over rabbit 1 cup of chicken bouillon, then 1 cup of sherry mixed with a pinch of basil. Bake 10 minutes at 400°, then at 350° for 60 to 70 minutes.

SERVES 4.

CIVET OF RABBIT IN WINE

2 young rabbits, 2½ to 3 lbs. each,   1½ tbsps. flour
   cut into serving pieces   3 cups beef bouillon
¾ lb. salt pork (pour on boiling   ¾ cup dry white wine
   water, let stand 5 minutes,   1 bay leaf
   drain and dice)   2 tsps. chopped parsley
3 tbsps. butter   2 tsps. minced thyme
¾ lb. very small white onions   salt and pepper

Try out salt pork bits until golden, remove from pan. Add butter and sauté onions, covered, until brown, about 15 minutes. Remove

148

onions and keep hot. Fry rabbit pieces golden; remove and keep hot. Blend flour and bouillon, wine, herbs, and seasonings into pan. Add rabbit and simmer, covered, until tender, 1½ to 2 hours. Serve with browned onions.

SERVES 6 to 8.

ITALIAN HUNTER'S RABBIT

2½ to 3 lbs. rabbit, cut into
   serving pieces
seasoned flour
4 tbsps. olive oil
2 tbsps. butter
1 onion, chopped
1 garlic clove, minced
1 celery rib, minced

1 carrot, shredded
¼ lb. mushrooms, sliced
1 can (1 lb.) tomatoes with liquid
⅓ cup dry red wine
¼ cup chopped parsley
½ tsp. dried rosemary
¼ tsp. dried basil
¼ tsp. oregano

Dust rabbit with seasoned flour. Heat oil in a Dutch oven and brown meat well on all sides. Remove meat and add butter to pan. Add onion, garlic, celery, carrot, and mushrooms, and cook, stirring occasionally, until onion is lightly browned, about 10 minutes. Return meat to pan. Cut tomatoes into wedges and add. Add wine, parsley, rosemary, basil, and oregano. Stir to blend, cover, and simmer gently for about 1 hour. Remove meat, and keep warm. Cook sauce, uncovered, to thicken to taste. Correct seasonings; return meat. Serve on cooked pasta.

SERVES 4 or 5.

FRENCH-STYLE RABBIT

2½ to 3 lbs. rabbit, cut into
   serving pieces
seasoned flour
4 tbsps. olive oil
2 tbsps. butter
1 onion, chopped
1 garlic clove, minced
½ lb. mushrooms, sliced
1 cup chopped cooked ham
1 tomato, peeled, seeded, and
   chopped
2 tbsps. chopped parsley

¾ tsp. paprika
½ tsp. sugar
½ tsp. dried basil
½ tsp. coarsely crushed juniper
   berries
⅛ tsp. dried thyme
½ cup dry white wine
1½ tsps. cornstarch, dissolved in
   1 tbsp. water
salt
¾ cup sour cream

Dust rabbit with seasoned flour. Heat oil in a Dutch oven and brown meat well. Remove meat. Add butter to pan with onion, garlic, and mushrooms. Sauté, stirring, until onion is soft, about 4 minutes. Return meat to pan, and add ham, tomato, parsley, paprika, sugar, basil, juniper, thyme, and wine; stir to blend. Cover and simmer gently for 50 minutes, or until tender. Remove meat and keep warm. Reduce sauce until slightly thickened. Add dissolved cornstarch and cook, stirring, until thickened. Remove pan from heat. Correct seasoning with salt and stir in sour cream just until blended, then spoon sauce over meat.

SERVES 4 or 5.

HARE IN BEER

5 to 6 lbs. hare, cut into serving pieces
2 cups light beer
2 cups thin-sliced onions
1 cup grated carrot
1 tsp. salt
¼ tsp. pepper
¼ tsp. grated nutmeg

1 bay leaf, crumbled
¼ lb. smoked bacon or salt pork, blanched and cut into strips ½ x ¼ inch
3 tbsps. butter
seasoned flour
1 lb. small potatoes, peeled and sliced thin

Make a marinade of the beer, onions, carrot, salt, pepper, nutmeg, and bay leaf. Marinate meat, refrigerated, for 24 hours, turning occasionally. In a heavy skillet sauté the bacon or salt pork in the butter until crisp. Remove, drain, and reserve strips. Drain and dry meat; reserve marinade. Dust meat with seasoned flour and brown in fat remaining in pan. Add unstrained marinade and bring to a boil. Cover and simmer for 1¼ hours. Add the potatoes and fried pork strips and simmer, covered, for 30 minutes more. Skim off fat.

SERVES 6 to 8.

POLISH HARE PÂTÉ

shoulder, neck, forepaws, liver, and heart of large hare
1 cup chopped onion, carrot, and celery, mixed
3 or 4 slices bacon or salt pork
pinch of dried marjoram
pinch of dried thyme
pinch of ground juniper

1 cup bouillon
2 tbsps. sweet cream
2 egg yolks, lightly beaten
salt and pepper
thin toast
2 to 3 tbsps. butter
2 tbsps. bread crumbs

150

Combine meat, vegetables, bacon or salt pork, marjoram, thyme, juniper, and bouillon; simmer until meat falls from the bone. Drain and bone meat; put meat, liver, and bacon through a grinder twice. Add cream, lightly beaten egg yolks, and salt and pepper to taste; mix well. Spread toast thinly with pâté. Brown butter, add crumbs, and pour over pâté.

BRAISED RABBIT AND GRAVY

2 rabbits, 2½ lbs. each, cut into
   serving pieces
½ cup seasoned flour

3 tbsps. butter
¼ cup hot water
2 cups milk

Roll rabbit pieces in seasoned flour; shake off excess and reserve. Brown pieces slowly in hot butter, then add water and cover. Reduce heat and cook slowly until tender, about 1 to 1½ hours, adding water if needed. Uncover and cook 5 minutes to crisp. Remove from heat and keep warm; remove all but 2 tablespoons of pan juices. Stir in 2 tablespoons of reserved flour, add milk and heat, stirring, until thickened. Season to taste with salt and pepper.
   SERVES 6 to 8.

SPANISH-STYLE RABBIT

1 frying rabbit, cut into serving
   pieces
2 tbsps. butter
1 tbsp. olive oil
1 pork chop, boned and minced
1 onion, minced
1 small can (4 oz.) pimientos,
   drained and minced
½ cup dry white wine

½ cup chicken broth
1 tbsp. tomato purée
pinch of dried marjoram
pinch of dried thyme
pinch of dried fennel
salt and pepper
1 small jar (6 oz.) marinated
   artichoke hearts, drained

Sauté rabbit in butter and oil until golden. Remove meat and reserve. Sauté chop meat until brown; remove and reserve. Cook onion and pimientos until onion is soft, adding more butter and oil if needed. Stir in wine, broth, tomato purée, marjoram, thyme, fennel, and salt and pepper to taste. Cook, stirring, over low heat until well blended. Return rabbit and pork, add artichoke hearts, and simmer for 15 minutes, or until tender.
   SERVES 4.

CANADIAN JUGGED HARE IN WINE

1 hare, 4 to 5 lbs., or 2 rabbits,
   2 to 3 lbs. each, cut into serving
   pieces, reserving blood and
   juices
port wine
1 tsp. whole cloves
1 tsp. peppercorns

2 medium-sized bay leaves
1 tsp. ground marjoram
½ cup flour seasoned with ½ tsp.
   salt and ¼ tsp. pepper
¼ lb. (approx.) sweet butter
½ cup lean salt pork, cubed
1 cup small white onions, peeled

Marinate meat in port wine barely to cover, with cloves, pepper-corns, bay leaves, and marjoram, covered and refrigerated, for 2 to 3 days. Remove meat and bring marinade near to boiling point; strain. Roll dried meat in seasoned flour and brown in butter. Put into a greased casserole in layers with salt pork and onions. Pour on hot marinade; add boiling water to cover. Cover dish and bake at 325° for 3 hours. About 30 minutes before dish is finished, thicken as desired.

SERVES 6 to 8.

BELGIAN RABBIT IN WINE

2 rabbits, 2½ lbs. each, or 1 hare,
   cut into serving pieces
livers
2 large onions
1 bay leaf
2½ cups red Burgundy wine
1 tbsp. red-wine vinegar
juice of 1 lemon
pinch of dried thyme
½ tsp. salt

¼ tsp. pepper
5½ tbsps. butter
1 tart apple, peeled, cored, and
   chopped
2 shallots, minced
2 cups beef broth
2 tsps. cornstarch, dissolved in
   1 tbsp. water
1 tsp. Kitchen Bouquet

Slice 1 onion thin and break into rings. Put onion rings, rabbit, and bay leaf in a shallow bowl. Pour on a mixture of wine, vinegar, lemon juice, thyme, salt, and pepper. Cover and refrigerate for 24 to 36 hours; less time for young rabbits. Drain rabbit. Reserve marinade and onion rings but discard bay leaf. Chop livers and sauté in 2 tablespoons of the butter. Chop remaining onion and add with apple to livers. Sauté until onion is soft. Add 1 cup of the reserved marinade and simmer, covered, for 1 hour. Melt remaining butter and brown rabbit well on all sides. Add shallots, reserved onion rings, rest of marinade, and beef broth. Simmer, covered, for about 1 hour, or until tender. Remove rabbit and keep warm. Purée liver mixture in a blender. Stir liver purée, cornstarch mix, and Kitchen Bouquet into pan liquid. Cook, stirring, until smooth and thickened. Simmer, covered, for 10 minutes more. Serve the sauce with the rabbit.

SERVES 6 to 8.

LOUISIANA FRIED RABBIT

1 young rabbit, cut into pieces
½ cup flour seasoned with 2 tsps. salt, ⅛ tsp. paprika and dash of cayenne

½ cup bacon drippings

Dredge meat with seasoned flour. Cook in hot but not smoking fat until golden brown on all sides. Reduce heat and cook slowly for about 30 to 45 minutes, until tender, depending on size. Serve with Cream Gravy if desired.

SERVES 4.

GERMAN HASENPFEFFER

legs and saddles of 2 hares, cut into serving pieces
1 cup dry red wine
½ cup vinegar
½ cup water
1 large onion, sliced
5 peppercorns, crushed
4 juniper berries, crushed
1 tsp. dried thyme

4 whole cloves
1 bay leaf
flour
4 tbsps. butter
¼ cup Cognac, warmed
12 small white onions
1 tsp. arrowroot or cornstarch
salt and pepper

Combine wine, vinegar, and water with onion, peppercorns, juniper, thyme, cloves, and bay leaf, and simmer for about 15 minutes. Let cool, and pour over meat. Marinate, refrigerated, for 24 to 36 hours, turning occasionally. Remove meat and pat dry with paper towels. Strain and reserve marinade.

Dust meat lightly with flour and brown in butter. Transfer meat to a casserole; pour on Cognac and ignite. Allow flames to die out. Add white onions and enough of the reserved marinade barely to cover the meat. Bake at 325° for 1½ hours, or until fork-tender. Mix arrowroot or cornstarch with a bit of pan liquid, stir smooth, and use to thicken sauce. Season with salt and pepper to taste.

SERVES 6 to 8.

VIENNESE RABBIT

4 rabbits, 2½ lbs. each, dressed
    weight, each cut into 6 pieces
¼ lb. butter
4 large onions, diced
2 tbsps. paprika
1 tbsp. salt
2½ lbs. tomatoes, peeled, seeded,
    and chopped

1 green pepper, cut into halves
    and seeded
4 cups dry white wine
2 tbsps. flour
3 tbsps. catsup
¾ cup sour cream

Melt butter in a Dutch oven; add diced onions. Cover pan and cook slowly for 30 minutes without letting onions color. Arrange rabbit pieces on bed of onions; sprinkle with paprika and salt. Add tomatoes, green pepper, and white wine. Cover and simmer for 2 hours, or until tender, adding water if needed to maintain liquid level. Discard green pepper. Freeze half of the mixture. Continue with the rest. Mix flour with the catsup and sour cream, then mix with a bit of hot sauce from the pot. Stir into pot and cook, stirring, until thickened. Adjust seasonings.

    To serve the frozen part, thaw first, then finish in the same way with flour, catsup, and sour cream.

    SERVES 12; each half serves 6.

GYPSY RABBIT DINNER

3 lbs. rabbit, cut into pieces
bouquet garni of 1 large bay leaf,
    3 sprigs thyme, 2 whole cloves
5 onions, minced
chicken fat, size of small egg
6 peppercorns, crushed
salt

equal water and red wine to cover
1½ cups diced carrots
12 small white onions
12 mushroom caps
18 small potatoes
2 tbsps. beurre manié
1 tbsp. minced parsley

Put rabbit, bouquet garni, minced onion, chicken fat, peppercorns, and salt in large kettle. Cover with water and wine. Bring to boil, lower heat, and simmer gently 2½ hours without stirring. Add carrots, onions, mushrooms, and potatoes and cook, covered, until vegetables are tender, about 25 to 30 minutes. Remove bouquet garni and thicken with beurre manié; add parsley and simmer 5 minutes more.

    SERVES 6.

POLISH HUNTER'S HARE

2 hares, about 3 lbs. each, cut into serving pieces and marinated as in Polish Roast Hare for 2 days
6 to 8 oz. sliced bacon or salt pork
¼ cup bread crumbs

10 to 12 shallots, minced
2 tsps. paprika, ground juniper, or thyme
2 cups dry red wine
salt and pepper

Line a large casserole with some of the bacon or salt pork and sprinkle with the bread crumbs, then half of the shallots. Dust with paprika, juniper, or thyme. Arrange half the meat in a layer and top with the remaining shallots and then the rest of the bacon or salt pork. Pour on the wine and dust with salt and pepper. Cover casserole and bake at 350° for 3 hours. (If made in 2 casseroles, one may be frozen and reheated at 350° just until heated through.)
SERVES 6 to 8.

SOURED RABBIT

1 rabbit, 2½ to 3 lbs., cut into serving pieces
1 cup garlic vinegar
1 onion, grated
6 peppercorns
1 tsp. seasoned salt

1 small bay leaf
1 cup water
½ cup flour seasoned with ½ tsp. salt and ¼ tsp. paprika
3 tbsps. sweet butter
½ cup milk

Make a marinade of vinegar, onion, peppercorns, seasoned salt, bay leaf, and water. Marinate rabbit pieces 48 hours. Drain and reserve the marinade. Roll meat in seasoned flour; shake off and reserve excess. Sauté meat in butter in a Dutch oven until brown. Add marinade to the depth of ¼ inch. Bring to a boil, cover, and simmer for 1 hour. Thicken gravy with the remaining flour blended smooth with the milk.
SERVES 2 to 4.

RABBIT IN BARBECUE SAUCE

3 lbs. rabbit, cut into serving pieces

seasoned flour
3 tbsps. cooking oil

Roll meat in seasoned flour, brown in cooking oil in Dutch oven. Pour on Small Game Barbecue Sauce. Cover and bake at 325° for 45 minutes or until tender. Uncover and put under the broiler for 15 minutes or until browned.
SERVES 6.

FRENCH COLONIAL CIVET OF HARE

6 lbs. hare, cut into serving pieces
liver and blood of hare
½ cup red wine
4 tbsps. cooking oil
1 onion, minced
1 small bay leaf, broken
¼ tsp. dried thyme
¼ tsp. pepper

½ lb. salt pork, diced
2 onions, quartered
2 tbsps. flour seasoned with ½ tsp.
    salt and ¼ tsp. pepper
1 tbsp. minced celery leaf
2 garlic cloves, minced
¼ cup heavy cream

Marinate meat in wine, oil, minced onion, bay leaf, thyme, and pepper, refrigerated, for 8 to 12 hours. Drain, but reserve and strain the marinade. Render salt pork in a Dutch oven; add quartered onions and seasoned flour and cook, stirring, until light brown. Add and sear the meat. Add water to cover, celery leaf, and garlic. Cover and cook over medium heat for about 1 hour, or until tender. At 20 minutes before the meat is done, add the strained marinade, chopped hare liver, and blood and cream mixed. Stir and heat but do not let boil.

SERVES 6 to 8.

PENNSYLVANIA RABBIT PIE

1 large dressed cottontail, cut into
    serving pieces
2 tbsps. minced parsley
2 tbsps. salt
¼ tsp. pepper

¼ tsp. paprika
½ cup canned mushrooms
2½ cups stock
uncooked pastry for 1-crust pie
    (top)

Put rabbit in a kettle with 1 tablespoon parsley, 1 tablespoon salt, and ⅛ teaspoon pepper, cover with boiling water, and cover the kettle tightly. Simmer for 3 hours, or until tender; or bake in a 300° oven. Keep at least 3 cups liquid in the kettle. Put meat pieces in a greased 4-quart baking dish, season with remaining salt and pepper and the paprika. Add mushrooms and 1 tablespoon parsley. Pour on stock but not enough to touch pastry crust. Top with pastry. Bake at 425° for 20 minutes, then at 350° for 30 minutes. Heat remaining stock to serve with pie. Serve with Mulled Cider Applesauce.

SERVES 2.

MANDARIN GAMEBURGER

1 small rabbit, boned and ground
1 onion, minced
1 egg, beaten
1/2 cup bread crumbs

1 1/2 tsps. ground ginger
1/2 cup flour seasoned with 1 tsp.
    salt and 1/2 tsp. paprika
4 tbsps. sweet butter

Blend rabbit, onion, egg, bread crumbs, and ginger into 4 patties. Dredge patties with seasoned flour and brown quickly in butter to form a crust on both sides. Pour on your choice of sauce, cover, and bake at 350° for 45 minutes. Raise heat to 400° to brown for 15 minutes.
SERVES 2.

RABBIT LEFTOVERS

SCALLOPED RABBIT

2 cups diced, cooked rabbit
2 cups rabbit gravy or 2 cups rich
    stock thickened with 2 tbsps.
    each butter and cornstarch
salt, pepper, and paprika

2/3 cup soft bread crumbs
2 cups sliced, cooked potatoes
seasoned dry bread crumbs
6 tsps. melted butter

Mix the cooked rabbit and gravy and season well to taste with salt, pepper, and paprika. Generously grease a 2-quart casserole or 6 individual large custard cups and fill with alternating layers of meat and gravy, soft bread crumbs and potatoes. Top with seasoned bread crumbs and drizzle on the melted butter. Bake at 350° for 30 minutes for the casserole, about 15 to 20 minutes for the individual custard cups.
SERVES 6.

RABBIT CHOP SUEY

1 cup shredded, cooked rabbit
1 1/2 tbsps. butter
1/2 cup green pepper, cut into thin
    slivers
1/2 cup onion, cut into thin strips
1 cup slivered celery
1 can (1 lb.) bean sprouts,
    drained and rinsed
1 can (8 oz.) bamboo shoots,
    drained, rinsed, and chopped

1 can (8 oz.) water chestnuts,
    drained, rinsed, and cut into
    thin slivers
1/2 cup water
2 tbsps. cornstarch
1/4 cup saki or dry sherry
2 tbsps. soy sauce
1 can (4 oz.) mushroom pieces,
    drained, reserving liquid

Melt the butter and sauté the green pepper, onion, and celery for just 2 minutes. Add and cook the meat for 3 minutes. Add the bean sprouts, bamboo shoots, water chestnuts, and water. Make a paste of the cornstarch and saki or sherry and add. Cook, stirring, until the liquid is thickened, then add soy sauce and mushrooms. If a bit more liquid is needed, use the mushroom liquid.

SERVES 6 to 8.

RABBIT SALAD

2 cups chopped cooked rabbit
¼ cup chopped pickle
¼ cup chopped celery
1 tbsp. chopped onion
½ cup diced cooked potatoes

½ tsp. salt
1 tbsp. pickle liquid
½ tbsp. lemon juice
¼ cup mayonnaise

Mix rabbit, pickle, celery, onion, potatoes, and salt lightly. Mix pickle liquid, lemon juice, and mayonnaise, and pour on. Chill for 1 hour.

SERVES 4 to 6.

RABBIT COCKTAIL OR SANDWICH SPREAD

¾ cup minced cold cooked rabbit
3 pimiento-stuffed green olives,
    minced
1 strip green pepper, minced

1 hard-boiled egg, minced
2 tsps. Mustard Sauce
3 tbsps. mayonnaise
a few drops Worcestershire sauce

Blend all ingredients thoroughly. This may be served cold or spread on one side of a slice of bread and then lightly toasted under a broiler.

MAKES about 1 cup.

RABBIT PIE

3 cups chopped cooked rabbit
1 cup diced cooked potato
1 cup diced cooked carrot
¼ cup diced green pepper
¼ cup chopped onion

rich rabbit or chicken stock
Worcestershire sauce
salt and pepper
baking powder biscuit dough for
    the top crust

Blend rabbit, potato, carrot, pepper, and onion, and put into a 6-quart casserole. Pour on enough stock to almost cover and season

158

to taste with Worcestershire, salt, and pepper. (Stock can be lightly thickened with cornstarch if desired.) Heat thoroughly at 350° then top with biscuit dough in a single sheet and bake at 450° for 10 minutes, then at 350° for 15 minutes.

SERVES 4 to 6.

RACCOON

Raccoons should have all the fat, inside and out, removed, as well as the glands that are under the legs, along the spine, and in the small of the back. The meat is very dark, long-fibered, and somewhat coarse; it is improved by an hour's parboiling before continuing with a recipe. Young ones, 7 to 8 pounds, can be marinated overnight in 1 tablespoon salt per quart of water. Older ones, up to 13 or 14 pounds, should be marinated for 24 hours.

ALLEGHENY ROAST COON

7 to 8 lbs. coon, fat removed
water
2 tbsps. salt

½ tsp. pepper
1 onion, sliced
3 carrots, cut into chunks

Parboil the raccoon in water to cover with salt, pepper, onion, and carrots for 3 hours. Put in a roaster, and add 1 cup of the parboiling broth, strained. Roast uncovered at 375° for 2 hours.

SERVES 10 to 12.

CANADIAN ROAST YOUNG COON

2 young 7-lb. coons, cut across the   water
    back behind the ribs, with hind   2 tsps. baking soda
    legs attached   stuffing of your choice

Soak coons in a strong brine solution overnight. Pour off the water
and scrape off the fat inside and out. Put into boiling water to
cover and simmer for 45 minutes. Add baking soda to the water
and boil, uncovered, for 5 minutes. Wash in warm water and cook
again in boiling water to cover for 15 minutes. Scrape again inside
and out to remove scum. Cover one cavity with your choice of
stuffing, tie the other cavity on top as a lid. Roast, covered, at 350°
for 45 minutes; uncover and brown for 15 minutes.
    SERVES 10 to 12.

STUFFED ROAST COON

8 lbs. coon   apple-raisin stuffing (see page 272)
water   4 slices salt pork
salt

Soak coon in salted water to cover for 18 hours, changing salted
water once. Fill with apple-raisin stuffing; skewer closed. Put in a
roaster with 1 cup water. Sprinkle lightly with salt and cover with
4 slices of salt pork. Roast at 350° for 1½ to 2 hours, or until
tender. When the coon browns on top, turn it. Baste frequently
to prevent drying.
    SERVES 4 to 6.

COON WITH GRAVY

7 lbs. coon, cut up, or 2 young   salt and black pepper
    3-lb. rabbits   1 can (14 oz.) evaporated milk
4 slices bacon   flour
1 medium-sized onion, chopped   cayenne
½ cup vinegar (use water for
    rabbit)

Combine bacon and onion, and sauté in a Dutch oven. Add meat,
vinegar or water, and salt and black pepper to taste. Cover and
simmer until tender, adding water as needed to keep meat moist.
Add evaporated milk thickened with flour and seasoned with a
dash of cayenne for gravy.
    SERVES 6 to 8.

FRICASSEED COON

7 lbs. coon, fat removed, cut into
   8 to 10 pieces
1 cup flour seasoned with 2 tbsps.
   salt and ½ tsp. pepper

4 tbsps. butter
2 cups broth

Roll meat in seasoned flour, and brown in hot butter in a heavy Dutch oven. Add broth, cover, and simmer for 2 hours, or until tender.

SERVES 8 to 10.

COON GOULASH

8 lbs. coon, fat removed, with
   meat cut into 1½-inch cubes
6 tbsps. butter
3 cups broth
2 garlic cloves, minced

2 bay leaves
1 tsp. salt
¼ tsp. cayenne
3 tbsps. flour
1 cup tomatoes

Brown meat cubes in 3 tablespoons butter. Add broth, garlic, bay leaves, salt, and cayenne; simmer, covered, for 2½ hours. Cream remaining 3 tablespoons butter and the flour together, add a bit of liquid, and then return to the pot. Cook, stirring, to thicken. Add tomatoes and cook gently, covered, for 30 minutes, stirring from time to time.

SERVES 8 to 10.

COON LOAF

2 lbs. fat-free meat from coon,
   ground
½ cup cracker crumbs
½ cup ground onion
1⅓ tsps. salt

½ tsp. pepper
2 eggs, lightly beaten
¼ tsp. ground thyme
1 cup evaporated milk

Mix all together well and form into a loaf; place in a greased loaf pan. Set loaf pan in another pan of hot water, and bake at 350° for 1¾ hours.

SERVES 6 to 8.

CORNBELT COONBURGERS

1 lb. coon, fat removed
1 oz. salt pork
½ medium-sized onion
1 celery rib
½-inch-wide strip of green pepper
½ cup fresh bread crumbs, soaked
  in ¼ cup milk

½ tsp. salt
⅛ tsp. pepper
dash of cayenne
½ tsp. ground thyme
fat for cooking
½ cup catsup with 1 tsp.
  Worcestershire sauce

Grind meat, salt pork, onion, celery, and green pepper together. Mix with soaked crumbs, salt, pepper, cayenne, and thyme. Mix well and form into cakes. Brown well in fat on both sides. Pour on catsup with Worcestershire. Cover and simmer for 30 minutes; or bake in 350° oven.

SERVES 4.

PENNSYLVANIA COON SOUP

2 lbs. bony coon meat
½ cup celery, diced
1 small carrot, diced
1 small onion, sliced
6 cups cold water
2 tsps. salt

⅛ tsp. pepper
¼ cup raw long-grain rice
1 tsp. dried herbs of your choice
1 pinch dried rosemary
2 tbsps. chopped parsley
2 tbsps. butter

Put meat, celery, carrot, onion, and water in a large soup kettle. Heat to boiling point, reduce heat, cover tightly, and simmer for 2 hours. Add salt and pepper and simmer for 30 minutes more. Strain. Bring the strained broth to a boil and add rice slowly; let cook for 20 minutes. Remove meat from bones, chop, and add to soup. Add herbs and butter. Serve as soon as heated.

MAKES 4 to 5 cups.

SQUIRREL

Squirrel, along with rabbit, is one of the most popular of small game, but it is much more varied when it comes to edibility. If the squirrels have been eating acorns, which can be judged by the area in which they are taken, they should be soaked in 1 tablespoon vinegar per quart of water overnight before cooking.

Squirrels have scent glands in the small of the back as well as under all four legs. These, of course, should be removed. Do not remove all of the body fat; some should be left for flavor. A young squirrel's meat is pink to rosy in color while raw; it turns a darker red as the animal ages. If you think you have an old, tough animal, soak it in ¾ cup salad oil with ¼ cup lemon juice for 1 hour before cooking. Many people use squirrel to stretch upland game-bird recipes, and squirrel is frequently substituted in chicken recipes.

Gray squirrels dress out at about ½ pound, fox squirrels around ¾ pound.

Some people tell the age of a squirrel by checking the underside of the tail in a good light. If there are two or three dark bands running the length of the fur on either side, it's a young one. Older squirrels have only one such band.

BROILED SQUIRREL

1 squirrel, split to lay flat	⅛ tsp. pepper
1 tsp. salt	1 tbsp. melted butter

Rub squirrel with salt and pepper; brush with melted butter. Put on a greased rack and broil for 40 minutes, basting every 10 minutes.

SERVES 1 or 2.

ALLEGHENY ROAST SQUIRREL

1 squirrel	1 cup fresh bread crumbs soaked
1½ tsps. salt	in ¼ cup light cream
¼ tsp. pepper	1 tsp. onion juice
1½ tbsps. lemon juice or tarragon	1 tbsp. melted butter
vinegar	2 cups brown meat broth
1 cup chopped mushrooms	

Mix 1 teaspoon salt, ⅛ teaspoon pepper, and the lemon juice or vinegar. Rub squirrel with the mixture. Add mushrooms to crumbs with remaining salt and pepper and the onion juice. Stuff squirrel with this mixture and truss. Brush squirrel with melted butter and put on a rack. Partly cover with broth and water. Roast for 1½ hours. Use pan drippings for gravy.

SERVES 1 or 2.

SMOKY JOE SQUIRREL

2 medium-sized squirrels	1 tbsp. commercial barbecue
1 tsp. celery salt	smoke liquid
½ tsp. white pepper	4 tbsps. butter
	½ cup consommé

Rub squirrels inside and out with mixture of celery salt, white pepper, and barbecue smoke liquid. Let stand for 15 minutes. Rub with soft butter and put under a broiler. Heat ½ cup consommé and melt any remaining butter in it; use for basting while broiling. Broil under highest heat for 20 minutes per side, just enough below the source of heat to prevent burning.

SERVES 2 to 4.

ALLEGHENY SMOTHERED SQUIRREL

2 squirrels (if older, cut into serving pieces)

½ cup flour seasoned with 1 tsp. salt, ⅛ tsp. pepper, and ½ tsp. paprika

¼ cup bacon drippings

¼ to ½ cup sliced onion

1 parsley sprig, minced

1 cup light cream

Dredge meat with seasoned flour; brown in drippings. Sprinkle on onion and parsley. Add cream and cover pan. Simmer over low heat, or in 300° oven, for 1 to 1½ hours. Thicken gravy if desired. Sprinkle with more paprika.

SERVES 2 to 4.

ALLEGHENY SQUIRREL PIE

1 squirrel, cut into 2 or 3 pieces

3 tbsps. flour

½ tbsp. minced parsley

1 tsp. salt

⅛ tsp. pepper

½ cup sliced mushrooms

2 cups stock or milk

prepared biscuit mix

Cover meat with water and cook for 1 hour. Remove and bone. Add flour, parsley, salt, pepper, and mushrooms to stock. Cook to thicken, 5 to 10 minutes. Add meat and pour into 2-quart baking dish. Top with biscuit mix topping. Bake at 350° until golden, 30 to 40 minutes.

SERVES 1 or 2.

ALLEGHENY SQUIRREL WITH DUMPLINGS

2 squirrels, cut into serving pieces

3 tbsps. butter

3 cups water

1 tsp. salt

⅛ tsp. pepper

⅓ cup sliced onion

½ cup diced celery

1 cup carrot, cut into sticks

2 to 3 tbsps. flour

prepared dumpling dough

Brown meat in butter. Cover with water, season, and simmer for 1 hour. Add onion, celery, and carrot, and more water if needed, and cook for 15 minutes. Thicken with flour dissolved in ¼ cup water. Drop in dumpling dough, cover, and steam for 12 to 15 minutes.

SERVES 4.

SOUTHERN SQUIRREL CASSEROLE

2 squirrels, cut into serving pieces	1 small onion, minced
seasoned flour	½ cup chopped celery
¼ cup rice	1 cup diced tart apple
1 green pepper, minced	boiling water

Roll the pieces of meat in seasoned flour and put into a well-greased, large shallow casserole. Sprinkle on the rice, green pepper, onion, celery, and apple. Barely cover with boiling water. Cover the dish tightly with a double thickness of foil and bake at 300° for about 1 hour, or until tender.

SERVES 4.

STEWED SQUIRREL WITH SOUR CREAM

2 squirrels, cut into serving pieces	4 strips bacon, minced
1 cup minced onions	3½ cups beef broth
2 tbsps. butter	⅛ tsp. pepper
½ cup quartered mushrooms	¼ tsp. salt
½ cup flour	1 cup sour cream
1 tbsp. minced parsley	water

Brown onions in butter in a Dutch oven. Add squirrels and mushrooms and brown lightly. Add flour and brown it. Add parsley and bacon, and cook until bacon is half done. Add broth, season to taste, and stew slowly for 45 minutes. For the gravy, combine sour cream and some water. Stir into squirrel broth; heat, but do not boil after adding sour cream.

SERVES 2 to 4.

SQUIRREL POT PIE WITH DUMPLINGS

2 to 3 lbs. dressed squirrel, cut into serving pieces	½ tsp. pepper
	2 tbsps. butter
2½ cups water	New England Dumplings
1½ tsps. salt	

Put meat in a kettle with water, add salt, and bring to a boil. Reduce heat to a simmer, cover tightly, and simmer for 2½ to 3 hours, or until meat is tender enough to fall off the bone. Bone the meat and return meat to kettle. Add pepper and butter. Bring liquid to a boil. Lay on the dumplings and continue until done.

SERVES 4 to 6.

FRIED SQUIRREL

1 squirrel, cut into pieces	½ cup sour cream
flour	½ cup canned mushrooms
butter	¼ cup sherry

Roll meat in flour and fry in butter. Make gravy of pan drippings. Remove from heat and add sour cream, mushrooms, and sherry.

SERVES 2.

CREOLE SQUIRREL PIE

1½ to 2 lbs. squirrel, or other small game	4 tbsps. flour
2 tbsps. minced onion	½ cup chopped onion
1 green pepper, minced	1 tbsp. minced parsley
1 celery rib, minced	pastry for 2-crust deep-dish pie, unbaked
4 tbsps. butter	

Boil meat in water to cover, with minced onion, green pepper, and celery, until tender. Remove meat, bone, and chop. Strain broth. Melt butter, stir in flour to make roux, and add chopped onion and parsley. Add meat and pour in strained broth; cook, stirring, until smooth. Cook over low heat for about 20 minutes. Turn into pastry-lined, deep 6-cup pie pan, top with pastry, and bake until crust is done.

SERVES 4 to 6.

WOODCHUCK

'Chucks, groundhogs, whistle pigs, pasture pigs—whatever you call them—have dark meat with a mild flavor and adapt readily to any squirrel or rabbit recipe. The fat is unobjectionable, but generally removed anyway. The 'chuck has scent glands high on the inside of the forelegs and in the small of the back, which must be removed. Generally only the older animals are parboiled or soaked before cooking, although some cooks soak woodchucks as a matter of course in cold salted water for 6 to 12 hours. Older 'chucks (worn teeth and claws are a good indication of age) benefit from parboiling in water to which ½ teaspoon or more of baking soda has been added. An adult will weigh 6 to 8 pounds.

FRIED 'CHUCK

Cut meat into strips, and dry. Dip into beaten egg, then into cornmeal. Fry in butter or bacon drippings until tender and browned.

BAKED 'CHUCK

Cut 'chuck into serving pieces, and roll in seasoned flour. Put into a greased pan and brown in a hot oven. When browned, add a chip of garlic to each piece, pour on some water, and simmer until water has boiled away. Continue to bake at 350° until tender.

WOODCHUCK PIE

6 lbs. chuck, cut into 2 or 3 pieces	⅛ tsp. pepper
¼ cup chopped onion	4½ tbsps. flour
¼ cup chopped green pepper	12 small uncooked biscuits or
½ tbsp. minced parsley	biscuit topping
1 tbsp. salt	

Parboil 'chuck in water for 1 hour, drain, reserving the broth. Bone the meat. Add onion, green pepper, parsley, salt, pepper, and flour to the cooking broth and cook, stirring, until thickened. Measure 3 cups; add water if needed. Add the meat and put into a 2-quart deep baking dish. Top with biscuits or biscuit topping. Bake at 400° for 30 to 40 minutes.

SERVES 4 to 6.

MOHAWK VALLEY 'CHUCK

8 lbs. woodchuck, cut into serving pieces	3 tbsps. bacon drippings
water	2 cups (approx.) boiling broth or stock
vinegar	1 cup chopped celery
1 onion, chopped	1 onion, in rings
1 tsp. garlic salt	3 whole cloves
½ cup flour seasoned with ½ tsp. salt and ¼ tsp. pepper	1 tsp. Kitchen Bouquet

167

Marinate the woodchuck in equal amounts of water and vinegar to cover, with the chopped onion and garlic salt, for 12 to 15 hours. Drain and reserve marinade. Dry meat. Dredge with seasoned flour and lightly brown in drippings in a heavy skillet. Parboil in marinade for 20 minutes; drain again. Cover meat with boiling broth or stock; add celery, onion rings, and cloves. Cover and simmer until tender, about 2 hours. Color with Kitchen Bouquet, and thicken with remaining seasoned flour.

SERVES 6 to 8.

WOODCHUCK MEAT LOAF

1 lb. 'chuck meat, ground	½ cup dry bread crumbs
1 lb. pork, ground	1½ tsps. salt
1 egg, lightly beaten	⅛ tsp. pepper
1 cup milk	1 tbsp. minced onion

Mix meats completely; add egg, milk, crumbs, seasoning, and onion. Mix well and put into a greased loaf pan. Bake at 350° for 1 hour. Let set for 5 minutes before slicing.

SERVES 6 to 8.

WOODCHUCK PATTIES

Make like Cornbelt Coonburgers.

'CHUCK BURGERS

'chuck meat, parboiled and ground	salt and pepper
bread or cracker crumbs	egg, beaten
onion, chopped	fat
	apple or currant jelly

Grind parboiled meat, add crumbs or crackers, and blend with chopped onion to burger consistency. Season with salt and pepper. Form into patties. Dip into beaten egg, roll in more crumbs, and fry in hot fat. Spread with apple or currant jelly and bake at 350° for 1 hour.

MIXED SMALL GAME

Certain species of small game are particularly compatible and can be blended in the same dish. For instance, there is a close relationship between squirrel and rabbit and they make a nice combination. Frogs' legs, if they are young and tender, can also be added to the dish. Darker meats such as muskrat and woodchuck can also be combined. Since these animals are larger, the blendings are more apt to occur in dishes using leftovers.

TARHEEL KEBAB

2 lbs. tender young game, boned and cut into 1½-inch cubes
¼ cup melted bacon drippings and butter mixed
2 tbsps. lemon juice
¼ lb. salt pork or bacon, cubed

1 medium-sized onion, cut into thick slices
2 tomatoes, cut into thick slices
12 mushroom caps
barbecue sauce

Brush game cubes well with melted drippings and butter, then with lemon juice. Let stand for 30 minutes. Partially fry salt-pork pieces. Thread meat cubes, salt pork, onion, tomato, and mushrooms onto skewers. Brush with your choice of barbecue sauce, and broil under medium-hot broiler, basting and turning, for 30 to 35 minutes.
SERVES 6.

TARHEEL OVEN-GRILLED SMALL GAME

2 or 3 young, tender, small game animals cut into serving pieces
garlic cloves

lemon or lime juice
butter
bacon drippings

Rub meat with garlic cloves and lemon or lime juice 30 minutes before cooking. Cover bottom of heavy skillet with ½ to 1 inch of half butter and half bacon drippings and heat in 475° oven for 10 minutes. Put meat in hot fat and roast for 25 to 30 minutes, basting every 5 minutes with hot fat. Remove, drain on paper towels, and season.
SERVES 2 or 3.

BRUNSWICK STEW

2 young squirrels, or equivalent amount of small game
1 large onion, sliced
½ lb. lean ham, diced
3 qts. water
6 cups tomatoes
2 cups lima beans

4 large potatoes, diced
2 cups grated corn
1 tbsp. salt
¼ tsp. black pepper
1 small pod of hot red pepper
6 tbsps. butter

Simmer squirrels, onion, and ham gently in the water for 2 hours. Add tomatoes, limas, potatoes, corn, salt, black pepper, and hot pepper pod; cover and simmer gently for 1 hour, stirring occasionally. Add butter and serve as soon as it melts.

SERVES 2.

TARHEEL JUGGED SMALL GAME

2 to 3 lbs. older small game, cut into serving pieces	2 to 3 cups water
2 tsps. paprika	6 whole cloves
½ cup flour seasoned with 1½ tsps. salt and ⅛ tsp. pepper	3 onions
	½ tsp. dried thyme
⅓ to ½ cup lard	½ bay leaf
½ cup chopped celery	2 tbsps. catsup
¼ cup chopped parsley	½ lemon, sliced thin
½ cup raw long-grain rice	2 tbsps. butter

Dust meat with paprika, then dredge with seasoned flour. Fry in hot lard for 10 to 15 minutes, turning the pieces. Remove to jug, crock, or casserole. Sauté celery, parsley, and rice in drippings, stirring, until rice is browned. Add 2 cups water and boil for 10 minutes; pour over meat. Add cloves, onions, thyme, bay leaf, catsup, and lemon, and add enough more water to cover meat. Cover dish and bake at 275° for 3 hours, or until very tender. Thicken sauce with flour as desired; add butter and correct seasonings.

SERVES 4 to 6.

TARHEEL RING OF SMALL GAME

1½ lbs. older small game, boned	1 tsp. salt
2 oz. salt pork	⅛ tsp. pepper
1 small onion, chopped	dash of cayenne
2 celery ribs, chopped	½ tsp. ground sage
1½ cups bread cubes, or 1 cup cooked rice	1 tsp. Worcestershire sauce
1 egg, beaten	¼ to ½ cup milk

Grind game and salt pork fine, add remaining ingredients, and mix well. Pack into a greased 6-cup ring mold and bake at 300° for 1½ hours, or until browned and shrunken somewhat from sides. For highly flavored game, brush top with mix of ¼ cup catsup and ½ teaspoon dry mustard before baking.

SERVES 4 to 6.

TARHEEL SMALL-GAME PIE

2 to 3 lbs. older, tougher small
   game

Brown in fat, add water to cover, and season as desired. Cover and simmer for 1 to 2 hours. Bone meat. Make a pie with choice of cooked or canned vegetables, game meat, and seasonings. Moisten with choice of gravy or sauce. Top with pastry or biscuit dough, and bake at 425° for 30 minutes to brown topping.

SERVES 4 to 6.

LEFTOVER SMALL GAME

RAILROAD HASH-HOUSE HASH

1 cup diced cooked small game	½ tsp. pepper
1 tbsp. vinegar	3 strips bacon
3 tbsps. melted butter	½ cup diced cooked potatoes, cold
1 small bay leaf, crushed	½ cup chopped onion
1 tsp. salt	

Put meat in a glass bowl and mix in vinegar with a wooden spoon. Let stand for 2 hours. Then work in melted butter, bay leaf, salt, and pepper, again with a wooden spoon. Fry bacon in a skillet, remove and crumble, and add to potatoes. Sauté onion in bacon fat until brown; remove. Increase heat to high and put the meat in the skillet in a flat layer. Brown and turn and brown; if the pan is too dry, add more butter. When meat is browned on both sides, add potatoes and fold in. Reduce heat to low and sauté, uncovered, for 1 hour, turning at 20-minute intervals.

SERVES 4.

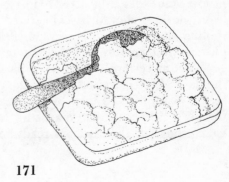

171

CHAPTER 4

GAME BIRDS

FIELD NOTES

Whether a game bird is taken from the woods or the wetlands, it is important that it be attended to as soon as possible. At the very least, the bird should be eviscerated at once. Quick cleaning and cooling of game birds gives the flesh a flavor and texture that pleases most palates, yet the system followed by the English for generations certainly does have its followers. Particularly before the days of refrigeration, it was the custom to hang an uneviscerated and unplucked bird by the head in a cool, airy place until the neck simply pulled apart and broke. This was the point at which they felt the bird was ready to eat. To me this comes close

172

to being tainted meat, if not actually beyond the point of safe edibility. On the other hand, hanging for perhaps 1 or 2 days in such a cool, airy place—be sure it's really cool and not humid—does heighten the flavor. It may be worth your trying, at least once when conditions permit. The English also consider certain small game birds, particularly woodcock, most delectable when un-eviscerated and they often serve them that way.

Since all birds are structurally the same they can be cleaned the same way. Some hunters are talented with a forked stick. They break one arm of the fork off short and use it rather like a buttonhook, inserting it in the vent and twisting it; upon withdrawing it, the entrails come out. Another, and perhaps surer, method is to make a slit from in back of the breastbone and around the vent. When this is done you can reach inside and easily remove all the entrails. Of course, save the heart, liver, and gizzard for stuffing or gravies. Discard the rest, including the red, spongy lung material.

The head, unless it is to be left attached during transportation for identification, can be cut off close to the breastbone, and the crop can be removed. If the head is to be left on, the crop can still be removed in the field; the crop is a saclike enlargement of the gullet in which the bird's food is softened for digestion. Slit this and the contents can be removed. Lungs and windpipe can be removed through the same slit extending to the breast. The wing is usually cut off at the second joint and the legs at the first feathered joint. Note that sometimes one or more of these must be left on for identification in transit.

Skinning is undoubtedly easier than plucking and less time-consuming, but the cooked bird will be dry. If you do want to skin the bird (the flytiers will be grateful for the skin with feathers intact), most birds can be skinned without using a knife. Cut or tear through the skin at the belly (if the bird is not first eviscerated), then pull the skin from the slit, pulling in opposite directions with both hands. Pull the bottom half of the skin to the tail and cut off the nub to leave a bare, tidy carcass. Intestines can now be removed (if not done previously) by cutting below the breastbone and scooping out the innards from both ends.

The internal cavity should be wiped clean before transporting. If possible, cool the bird before packing it loosely into a plastic bag or a game pocket; as with all game, birds should be cooled as quickly as possible.

Depending on the hunting method (and of course game regulations), the bird may sometimes be plucked when it is eviscerated. Birds are much easier to pluck while they still contain body heat; the feathers come free much more easily and the skin is less apt to be torn in the process. Except with certain waterfowl, leaving the skin on and intact makes for a moister, more flavorful bird. In plucking a bird, do not try to take great handfuls of feathers. The job goes more quickly if you grasp only what you can comfortably control between your thumb and the inside edge of your hand. Be sure to pull the feathers toward the head of the bird, against the direction of the feather. (See Waterfowl for the wax technique.)

After birds are drawn and plucked, most of them should be singed. (See Waterfowl for handling down.) This can be done carefully over any open flame. Birds that are not singed should be gone over carefully with tweezers to remove the tiny pinfeathers. Tweezers are also helpful (along with a sharp-pointed kitchen knife) to remove stray shotgun pellets if they can't be popped out with the fingers. Any badly shot-up areas should be cut away.

After careful washing, it is best to pack birds for freezing whole, unless members have been so badly shot up that they have to be removed. Again, as with small game, the choice of recipes is broader if birds are left whole. If the birds are badly shot up, it is sometimes wise to freeze meaty parts—breasts and thighs—loose and use the smaller, less meaty parts for stock. Pruning shears are handy to dismember all except the biggest birds.

The age of a game bird generally dictates the cooking method to be used. Young birds are much more tender and can be delicious cooked quickly and simply. Older birds in general need longer, slower, moist cooking. There are several ways of judging the age of birds. The young of a species will have a soft, resilient breastbone tip; the claws will be sharp (as will spurs, if the bird carries them), and the lower bill will generally be less rigid than the upper. If you can pick up a bird by its lower jaw without its breaking, that is a young bird.

While it is something that few nongame cooks consider, I most sincerely urge you to try *rare* roasted game birds. When the flesh is still a bit pink (some people like it even bloody rare, as with beef), it's at its moistest and most flavorful. This cooking is done with high heat, and the test is the color of the fluid from a fork-poke in the meaty part. Depending on the degree of rareness desired, the liquid that flows out of the holes will be moderately or lightly pink or almost clear. Please, *never* cook a bird so well-done that nothing flows from the holes!

One of the most impressive ways to serve guests any of the medium to large birds is boned. (Small birds that have only a bite of meat on them are really best as "finger food" so that all the good can be enjoyed.) A boned bird is easy to carve, and many butchers will bone one for you if you ask and pay a small fee. However, it is not difficult to do at home, and practice makes each one easier and quicker to do than the one before.

In boning a bird, the point is to keep the skin intact as an envelope, hence it makes sense to attempt boning only a bird that was neatly head-shot. There is no point in trying it, or having it done professionally, if the bird is not pretty well untouched. All that is needed to bone a bird is a small, sharp knife and a pair of shears.

Cut a deep slit to the bone from the neck of the bird down the back to the tail, exposing the backbone. With the small knife, with the edge always cutting against the bone, scrape and cut the flesh from the frame down one side of the bird, pulling the flesh away from the bones with your fingers. When you come to the ball joints connecting the wing and the second joint of the leg to the carcass, cut through the joints with the shears and continue down the frame until you get close to the ridge of the breastbone where the skin and bone meet. Be very careful at this point as the skin is thin and easily slit. Repeat this with the other side of the bird. Turn the bird so that you can cut very closely against the ridge of breastbone to free it without cutting the skin. Chop off wings at the elbow, leaving just the upper wing attached.

At this point you have a skin with the wing and legs still attached. To continue boning, find a pair of ball joints for the wings and a pair for the legs at the second joint. Remove the second-joint bones by detaching the meat from around the exposed joint, scraping the meat free while holding the end of the joint. When you get to the end of the bone, cut it free from the ball joint of the drumstick.

The bird can be used at this stage, stuffing it and re-forming it with the legs and wings. Shape the body with stuffing to make it look "natural" and skewer and lace the long back cut together. Cook as required.

If you wish to remove the remaining bones, chop off the outside ball joints of the drumsticks and wings and scrape the meat off the bone from inside the bird, pulling the skin inside out (you will wind up with folds where these limbs were). With pliers, pull out any tendons in the drumsticks.

The skin can now be stuffed, rolled, and tied, forming something like a long sausage. Small scraps of flesh can be used to level off the flesh layer before stuffing so that it is closer to the thickness of the breast. The carcass should be used for stock.

In the following sections (Upland Birds and Waterfowl), species are arranged in order of descending size.

Bobwhites, grouse, and turkeys, birds that scratch for feed as do barnyard fowl (order Galliformes), are the game birds *par excellence* both as sport and as food. These birds (except the sage grouse) all have crops in which bolted food is moistened for digestion. The breast is usually well rounded and particularly meaty, making that the choice part for eating. The columbine birds (order Columbiformes) are the pigeons and doves (including the now extinct passenger pigeon), also with meaty breasts.

UPLAND BIRDS

Upland birds generally need some additional fat in cooking, even though they have not been skinned. If the birds have been skinned, add more fat than is called for in the following recipes. Each recipe assumes (unless noted differently) that the bird is unskinned.

Medium and large birds, incidentally, are excellent smoked, either cold-smoked for flavor and then cooked, or hot-smoked and eaten hot or cold. Do try them, following your smoker's directions.

WILD TURKEY

The wild turkey, which some years ago was endangered, has made a great comeback. The Commonwealth of Pennsylvania has, not far from my home, one of the largest wild-turkey farms in the country from which it has not only rejuvenated the stock which the Indians and early settlers knew here, but supplied many other states with stock for their own introduction or reintroduction programs.

The wild turkey, the ancestor of our domestic bird, is similar to it, discounting the modern addition of extra-heavy breast meat and injection-induced fat. After adding additional fat, any favorite turkey recipe can be followed. The wild turkey is generally more slender-bodied and longer-legged than its domestic counterpart and its feathers are dark chestnut-tipped rather than white. The tail feathers, incidentally, are an excellent gauge as to the bird's age and tenderness. Fan the tail feathers before plucking; if the tips are all even, it's an older bird; if the two central feathers are obviously longer than the rest, it's that year's bird and prime eating.

As a general rule, turkey should be cooked thoroughly but not dried out.

The largest of our game birds, a fully mature tom turkey may weigh 30 pounds or a bit more. He'll need a lot of gentling to make good eating.

OLD VIRGINIA TURKEY

If you have an old bird, wash the inside well with 1 cup of water in which 1 tablespoon baking soda has been dissolved; rinse and plunge into boiling water for 5 minutes. Stuff bird with mixture of bits of cold cooked meat (pork, beef, or other), chopped celery, minced stewed giblets, chopped hard-cooked eggs, crushed soda crackers, salt and pepper to taste, and 1 tablespoon melted butter to blend all together. Rub the bird well with butter; season generously with salt and pepper. Put in a roasting pan with 2 cups chicken broth, and bake in a 400° oven. When the bird begins to brown, dust lightly with flour and baste. Cook, turning bird often, until done, 35 to 45 minutes per pound. If the breast browns too much, cover with a buttered sheet of brown paper to keep it moist.

NEW ENGLAND ROAST TURKEY

Put bird on a V-rack in a roaster, breast down or on its side on a flat rack. If the latter, turn halfway through cooking. Cover bird with cheesecloth dipped into melted butter, remoistening the cloth as it dries. Turn breast up for last 45 minutes or 1 hour. Cook at 350° for 30 to 40 minutes per pound, depending on age, with an additional 5 minutes per pound if stuffed.

LATINO TURKEY

5-lb. bird, cut into serving pieces	18 small white onions
4 cups sweet sherry	3½ cups canned tomatoes
1 tbsp. salt	2 bay leaves
½ tsp. pepper	⅛ tsp. ground basil
¼ lb. butter	1 cup sliced stuffed olives

Combine sherry, salt, and pepper in a glass bowl; add turkey and marinate, refrigerated, for 18 to 24 hours, turning from time to time. Drain, reserving marinade. Melt butter in a heavy Dutch

oven and brown turkey pieces and onions. Add tomatoes, bay leaves, basil, and marinade and cover; bake at 350° for 1½ hours. Add olives and bake, uncovered, for 30 minutes more. Discard bay leaves; season with the additional salt and pepper to taste.
SERVES 8.

ALLEGHENY OVEN-FRIED TURKEY

10 lbs. turkey, cut into serving pieces
½ cup flour seasoned with ½ tsp. salt and ¼ tsp. pepper
melted butter
chicken or turkey broth

Dredge turkey pieces with flour; shake off excess. Brown pieces in hot butter. Remove, and place in a single layer in a greased baking dish. For each 2 pounds, mix 2 tablespoons melted butter and 2 tablespoons broth and pour over. Cover dish and bake at 325° until tender, 2½ to 3 hours. Uncover for last 30 minutes to crisp skin.
SERVES 6 to 8.

MOCK SMOKED TURKEY

1 or 2 legs with thighs
½ cup flour seasoned with 1 tsp. smoky salt and ¼ tsp. white pepper
1 to 2 tbsps. bacon fat

Rub seasoned flour well into skin; refrigerate for 3 hours. Brown in hot fat, turning often, for 20 minutes. Add barely enough water to cover bottom of skillet; cover skillet and bake at 350° until joints move easily, about 2½ hours.
SERVES 1 or 2.

TEXAS TURKEY BARBECUE

1 young bird, about 4 lbs., split and cut into serving pieces	2 tbsps. Worcestershire sauce
	2 cups tomato juice
1 or 2 garlic cloves, minced	½ cup lemon juice or vinegar
1 tsp. sugar	4 tbsps. butter
¼ tsp. dry mustard	1 tsp. chile powder
2 tsps. salt	½ tsp. oregano
¼ tsp. pepper	

Put meat skin side down in a shallow pan with garlic. Pour water up to three-quarters of the depth of meat. Cook at 375° for 1 hour, turning occasionally; water should reduce barely to cover the bottom of the pan. Mix sugar, mustard, salt, and pepper; add Worcestershire, tomato and lemon juices, butter, chile powder, and oregano; heat. When hot, pour over bird. Cook, basting frequently, for 1 to 1½ hours, or until tender. If the sauce is too thick, add some boiling water. Brown under the broiler, skin side up, for 3 minutes, to form a crisp crust.

SERVES 4.

TURKEY TARRAGON SCALLOPINI

1½ lbs. boneless raw breast from young bird	1 tbsp. minced parsley
¼ cup flour	½ tsp. salt
5 tbsps. butter	½ tsp. crushed tarragon
¼ lb. mushrooms, sliced	⅛ tsp. pepper
	⅓ cup dry vermouth

Slice turkey across the grain into ½-inch-thick slices. Lay slices between sheets of wax paper and pound with a meat mallet until uniformly ¼ inch thick. Dredge with flour, coating all over; shake off excess. Melt about half of the butter and add meat slices without crowding. Cook until slices are just lightly browned on each side, about 4 minutes total. As the pieces are cooked, transfer to a serving dish and keep warm. Melt remaining butter, reduce heat to a minimum, add mushrooms and cook until limp, about 5 minutes. Stir in parsley, salt, tarragon, pepper, and vermouth, and boil for about 2 minutes, stirring to deglaze pan. Pour over meat and serve.

SERVES 4 to 6.

SPICED TURKEY HAITIAN STYLE

6 to 7 lbs. turkey, in parts and boned	1 garlic clove, crushed
½ cup light rum	1 tsp. salt
juice of 1 lemon	¼ tsp. pepper
3 dried hot peppers, seeded and crushed	4 cups water
	vegetable oil
1 tbsp. white vinegar	1 onion, sliced into rings
	crushed dried hot red peppers

Marinate turkey meat for 2 hours in mixture of rum, lemon juice, hot peppers, vinegar, garlic, salt, and pepper. Add with marinade to the water and simmer gently, covered, for about 30 minutes, or until tender. Remove meat from liquid and dice. Sauté meat in least possible amount of oil until well browned on all sides. Add

179

the onion rings and additional dried red peppers to taste. Cook until onion is soft. Serve dry, without sauce.

SERVES 6 to 8.

TURKEY LEFTOVERS

MEXICAN MOLE DE GUAJOLOTE

meat from 10 to 12 lbs. simmered or stewed turkey, boned, in large pieces
2 tbsps. toasted sesame seeds
2 tbsps. peanuts
½ cup water
2 green peppers, chopped
2 tomatoes, peeled and seeded
2 green chile peppers
½ tsp. garlic powder
dash of ground cloves
½ tsp. ground cinnamon

⅛ tsp. pepper
½ tsp. crushed red pepper
1 tbsp. chile powder
1 onion, minced
¼ tsp. salt
2 tsps. sugar
3 oz. (squares) semisweet chocolate
2 tbsps. hydrogenated vegetable shortening
2 cups turkey or chicken stock
¼ cup cornmeal

In a blender make a smooth paste of sesame seeds, peanuts, and ½ cup water. Add green peppers, tomatoes, chile peppers, garlic powder, cloves, cinnamon, pepper, red pepper, chile powder, onion, salt, sugar, and chocolate. Mix well in blender. Pour into hot shortening in a 2-quart saucepan, and cook until bubbly. Stir in stock and cornmeal (moisten cornmeal well first in stock to prevent lumping), and simmer for 45 minutes. Mix until smooth in blender, pour over meat, and simmer until thoroughly heated. For a darker sauce, use unsweetened chocolate with ¼ cup sugar.

SERVES 8 to 10.

MEXICAN MOLE VERDE (Green Tomatillo Sauce)

3 to 4 cups cooked turkey, sliced
1 onion, minced
¼ cup ground blanched almonds
2 tbsps. salad oil
2 cans (10 oz. each) tomatillos (Mexican green tomatoes)
1 tbsp. minced fresh coriander, or 1 tsp. dry

3 tbsps. (approx.) canned California chiles, minced, seeded, and trimmed
2 cups turkey broth
salt and pepper
1 cup (approx.) sour cream

Combine onion, almonds, and oil; cook, stirring, over moderate heat until onion is soft and almonds lightly browned. Whirl tomatillos with liquid in a blender until fairly smooth; add to onion. Stir in coriander and chiles; taste for hotness; it should be fairly mild. Add broth and simmer fairly rapidly, uncovered, until reduced to 2½ cups; stir occasionally. Can now be covered and chilled for several days or frozen. Arrange the turkey slices in a wide heat-proof dish and pour on the sauce. Cover and warm gently over low heat; when sauce begins to bubble slightly, simmer for 5 to 10 minutes. Add seasoning to taste. Serve with sour cream garnish.

SERVES 4 to 6.

MONTE CRISTO SANDWICH

4 slices cooked turkey	½ cup milk
4 slices cooked ham, tongue, or roast meat	½ tsp. salt
8 slices day-old white bread	4 slices Swiss cheese
2 eggs	1 tbsp. vegetable oil
	2 tbsps. butter

Trim crusts from bread. Dip slices into eggs beaten with milk and salt; soak thoroughly. Make sandwiches with 1 slice each of turkey, meat, and cheese. Melt oil and butter and brown sandwiches on both sides. Serve hot.

MAKES 4 sandwiches.

PINEHURST SOUP

2 cups cooked turkey, cut into julienne strips	5 cups turkey broth
2 tbsps. butter	1 cup tart red apple, cut into julienne strips
1 tbsp. curry powder	1 tbsp. lemon juice
½ cup chopped onion	¼ tsp. pepper

Melt butter and add curry powder; cook for 1 or 2 minutes, and add onion. Cook for about 4 minutes longer to soften but not brown the onion. Add broth, turkey, and apple. Cover and cook for about 8 minutes, or until apple is tender. Season to taste with lemon juice and pepper.

SERVES 6.

TURKEY CROQUETTES

3 cups minced cooked turkey
3 hard-cooked eggs, minced
1 cup minced fresh mushrooms
¾ tsp. salt
¼ tsp. pepper
¼ tsp. grated nutmeg

¼ tsp. poultry seasoning
2 eggs
¼ cup flour
2 tbsps. milk
¾ cup dry bread crumbs
2 cups cooking oil

Combine meat, hard-cooked eggs, mushrooms, salt, pepper, nutmeg, and poultry seasoning; stir in 1 egg, beaten. Form mixture into 12 balls of ½ cup mix each. Sprinkle with flour. Dip in the second egg beaten with the milk. Roll in crumbs, cover, and refrigerate for at least 30 minutes. Heat oil in a deep pan to 375°. Slide balls, two or three at a time, into the oil and cook for 3 or 4 minutes, or until golden brown. Drain on paper towels. Serve with mushroom sauce or a brown gravy seasoned with Madeira or sherry.
SERVES 6.

TURKEY À LA KING

3 cups cubed cooked turkey
2 cups sliced mushrooms
¼ cup chopped green pepper
4 tbsps. butter
2 cups medium-thick white sauce
2 egg yolks, beaten

2 tbsps. sherry
1 tbsp. minced pimiento
1 tsp. salt
½ tsp. paprika
¼ tsp. pepper

Sauté mushrooms and green pepper in butter for 4 minutes, or until tender. Add a little hot white sauce to egg yolks and then, off the heat, add yolks to balance of sauce. Add mushrooms and peppers, and sherry, pimiento, salt, paprika, and pepper. Heat only long enough to heat through, about 3 minutes.
SERVES 6.

TURKEY DIVAN

4 cups cubed cooked turkey, or
  1 to 1¼ lbs. turkey slices
1 bunch broccoli (1½ lbs.)
1 cup shredded Parmesan cheese
6 tbsps. butter

½ cup flour
2 cups concentrated turkey stock
salt and pepper
½ cup heavy cream, whipped

Cook broccoli until just tender; drain. Arrange in a shallow 1½-quart casserole or 6 individual ramekins. Sprinkle with half of the cheese. Distribute the turkey evenly on top. Melt butter, stir in flour, and cook until bubbly. Remove from heat and slowly add stock. Heat, stirring, until sauce is thickened; season to taste. Whip cream, fold into sauce, and spoon sauce over turkey. Use a fork to help the sauce get down through the mixture. Sprinkle with rest of the cheese. Bake, uncovered, at 400° for 15 minutes. Put 5 inches from the source of heat in a broiler, until mixture is bubbly and lightly browned.

SERVES 6.

WILD RICE AND TURKEY CASSEROLE

3 cups diced cooked turkey
3 cups turkey broth
1 cup raw wild rice
1 lb. mushrooms, sliced
1 onion, sliced
6 tbsps. butter

2 tsps. salt
¼ tsp. pepper
½ cup sliced blanched almonds
1½ cups heavy cream
3 tbsps. grated Parmesan cheese

Wash rice, cover with boiling water, and let stand for 1 hour. Drain. Sauté mushrooms and onion in 1 tablespoon of the butter over low heat for 10 minutes, to soften. Combine drained rice, turkey, vegetables, salt, pepper, and almonds in a greased 4-quart baking dish. Add turkey broth and cream and mix lightly. Cover and bake at 350° for 1½ hours. Remove cover, sprinkle with cheese, and dot with remaining butter. Bake at 450° for 5 minutes to crisp top.

SERVES 6 to 8.

TURKEY DUMPLINGS

2½ cups ground cooked turkey
1½ cups sifted all-purpose flour
4 tsps. baking powder
1 tsp. salt

1 cup milk
1 egg, beaten
about 3 cups thin turkey gravy or
  broth

Sift together flour, baking powder, and salt. Add turkey meat and mix well. Add milk to egg and stir into turkey mix. Heat gravy or broth in a deep pan. When it boils, drop in mounded tablespoons of the turkey mixture to make dumplings. Cover pan at once and cook for about 15 minutes.

MAKES about 10 medium-sized dumplings.

TURKEY PATTIES

2 cups ground or minced cooked
   turkey
⅔ cup mayonnaise
1 tbsp. grated onion

½ tsp. salt
⅛ tsp. pepper
1 cup fine dry bread crumbs

Combine well all but crumbs. Shape into 8 patties 1 inch thick. Roll in dry crumbs. Put about ½ inch apart on brown paper on a cookie sheet. Bake at 425° until golden, about 15 minutes.
    SERVES 4.

PHEASANT

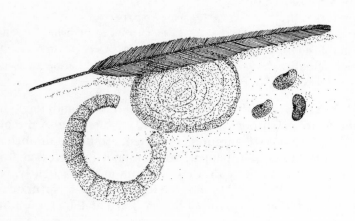

The most popular and available game bird in the country is the ringneck pheasant, an alien introduced into this country, in the Northwest, only at the end of the last century. Also known as the Chinese, China, Mongolian, and Oregon pheasant, this bird has several cousins which are slowly being introduced in a few isolated areas on an experimental basis—the Lady Amherst, English Green, and Golden.

    The reasons for the ringneck's popularity are obvious. It's a good dog bird and it can also be successfully walk-up hunted. It's a bird large enough (a cock may weigh 2¾ to 3½ pounds) for the shotgunner to feel it's worth the expenditure of a shell, and the meat (all white and very similar to chicken) is approved of by anyone who likes chicken. This similarity to chicken means that any of your favorite chicken recipes can be used for pheasant. However, keep in mind that the wild bird, or even a bird from a game farm, needs a bit of additional fat.

If you want to crisp-fry pheasant according to your favorite recipe and it has to wait a bit before serving, drain the pieces as soon as they are fried, put them into a brown paper bag, and keep in a warm oven. This works with any young, tender bird.

An additional way of telling the age of a pheasant (aside from the breastbone and lower bill test) is by the feathers at the leading edge of the wings. If the last, outermost feathers are softer and noticeably shorter than the remainder, it is a young bird that has just finished moulting. A pheasant can have a long life; not long ago a banded bird was live-trapped and the banding date was 17 years before; so it's wise to judge the age accurately. With that banded bird, which was released to continue living, chances are you wouldn't be able to get a fork in the gravy!

BASIC ROAST PHEASANT (young bird)

Put 1 small onion, 1 celery rib, and 1 parsley sprig in the cavity of the bird. Lay strips of bacon over the breast. Roast at 350° for 45 to 60 minutes, until done, basting frequently.

ALLEGHENY ROAST PHEASANT

1 older bird, cleaned	1 tsp. salt
5 cups water	⅛ tsp. pepper
1 onion	4 strips bacon
3 celery ribs	

Pour 4 cups of the water, boiling, over and into bird. Drain after 5 minutes. Put onion and celery into cavity but do not sew or skewer closed. Rub bird with salt and pepper. Put in roaster with bacon strips on top and remaining 1 cup water in the pan. Roast, uncovered, at 350° for 2 hours, or until tender.

SERVES 2.

FRUITED PHEASANT

3 pheasants, 1½ lbs. each	juice of 3 oranges
½ lemon	1 tsp. grated lemon rind
salt and pepper	1 cup pheasant or chicken stock
5½ tbsps. butter	⅓ cup muscatel wine
1 cup white raisins	

Rub birds inside with cut side of lemon. Season well with salt and pepper. Put in a baking dish, breast up, and spread with butter. Add remaining ingredients to the dish. Bake uncovered at 350°, basting every 10 minutes, for about 45 minutes.

SERVES 6.

PHEASANT WITH SAUERKRAUT

2 pheasants	1½ lbs. sauerkraut
1 tsp. salt	½ cup dry white wine
pinch of pepper	1 cup diced pineapple
4 slices bacon	1 tbsp. flour
3 tbsps. butter	

Sprinkle birds inside and out with salt and pepper. Put 2 slices of bacon across each breast and tie in place. Brown birds in butter in a Dutch oven for 15 minutes. Drain sauerkraut, mix with wine and pineapple, and use to surround birds. Cover and cook slowly on top of stove for about 1 hour, or until birds are tender. When done, remove birds to a platter and remove bacon. Stir flour into sauerkraut and bring to a boil, stirring. Arrange around birds.

SERVES 4.

BREADED PHEASANT CUTLETS

boned breast and thigh meat of 1 pheasant, flattened well
1 egg, beaten with 1 tbsp. chopped chives
½ cup fine dry bread crumbs, seasoned with ½ tsp. salt and ¼ tsp.
   white pepper
4 tbsps. sweet butter

Dip meat into egg, then roll in crumbs. Sauté in melted butter in a heavy skillet until brown.

SERVES 2.

BREAST OF PHEASANT SMETANE

2 to 4 breasts of pheasant, partridge, or grouse, boned	1 large onion, minced
4 tbsps. salt butter	2 tbsps. sweet butter
½ tsp. salt	⅔ cup dry white wine
¼ tsp. pepper	1 cup sour cream
1½ tsps. paprika	1 tbsp. lemon juice

Melt the salt butter. Dust the breasts with salt, pepper, and paprika, and sauté over low heat for 20 minutes. Keep warm. In another skillet sauté onion in sweet butter until golden; add wine and cook until nearly evaporated. Add sour cream, mix until smooth, and simmer for 5 minutes. Remove from heat and blend in lemon juice slowly. Pour over meat.

SERVES 2 to 4.

PHEASANT KIEV

6 large breasts, skinned, boned, and halved
seasoned butter
salt and pepper
2 eggs

¼ cup milk
2 cups fine dry bread crumbs
cooking oil
lemon wedges
watercress

Pound breasts between sheets of wax paper until very thin. Put a lump (about 1½ teaspoons) of well-chilled seasoned butter (garlic butter, chive butter, anchovy butter, or plain butter) in the middle. Season as desired with salt and pepper. Fold in sides and roll to enclose butter completely; skewer. Dip into eggs beaten with milk, drain, and roll in bread crumbs. Carefully shake off excess. Let dry for at least 5 minutes, then chill for 30 minutes. Heat cooking oil about 1½ inches deep to 375°, and fry breasts 2 at a time until golden; or bake at 400° for 15 minutes. If frying, drain on paper towels. Garnish with lemon wedges and watercress.

SERVES 6.

SCOTTISH JELLIED PHEASANT PIE

breasts from 2 pheasants
½ lb. lean pork
1 onion

salt and pepper
bacon
rich pheasant stock

Skin and bone breasts and remove membranes. Cut into small thick slices. Reserve giblets and trimmings for stock. Pound pheasant slices well between sheets of wax paper. Grind pork with onion and season highly with salt and pepper. Spread pheasant with ⅛-inch-thick layer of pork mix. Line a shallow baking dish with bacon and cover with pheasant slices. Cover top with more bacon slices, and pour in enough stock to fill the dish halfway. Cover dish and set in another pan half filled with hot water. Cook at 300° for 2 hours, adding water to outer pan as needed. Reduce about 3 cups stock by half and add to fill the baking dish. Cool the pheasant. Cover dish with wax paper and weight lightly. Chill until firm. Remove wax paper and carefully remove any fat from the top before serving as a jellied "pie."

SERVES 6.

SOUTH DAKOTA PHEASANT STEAKS

4 boned breasts, or 8 boned thighs	2 tbsps. sweet butter
½ cup seasoned flour	1 small onion, minced
1 tsp. paprika	1½ cups light cream
1 tbsp. lard	1 tsp. minced chives

Flatten meat between sheets of wax paper. Dredge with seasoned flour and dust with paprika. Melt lard and butter; sauté meat in mixture for 10 minutes per side; remove and keep warm. Sauté onion in saucepan; blend in 1 tablespoon seasoned flour and stir in cream. Cook, stirring, until smooth and thickened. Return meat pieces to sauce and cook at a low simmer for 10 minutes. Add chives and serve.

SERVES 4.

CORNED PHEASANT

1 pheasant, cut into serving pieces	½ cup onion vinegar
½ cup salt	6 peppercorns
½ cup brown sugar	½ tsp. grated nutmeg
1 bay leaf	

Mix all ingredients but pheasant. If the mixture is not strong enough to float a small raw potato, add enough salt to do so. Bring to a boil, then chill. Place the bird pieces in a crock, weight them to keep submerged, and pour on brine to cover. Cover crock and keep in cool place for 12 days. Wash in three changes of cold water on removal. To serve, cook slowly in skimmed milk, covered, for 2 hours, or bake in 300° oven for 2½ hours. Excellent for pheasant pie.

SERVES 2.

PHEASANT SAUSAGE

7 birds, boned and skinned	1 tbsp. ground sage
4 to 5 lbs. fat pork	½ tsp. white pepper
1 tsp. onion juice	

Grind all ingredients together and form into cakes or put into casings. Can be smoked.

MAKES about 12 pounds.

BROILED PHEASANTS

6 birds, 1¼ to 1½ lbs. each, split, backbones and breastbones removed

salt and pepper
melted butter
1½ cups fine bread crumbs

Flatten boned meat lightly between sheets of wax paper. Season with salt and pepper and brush with melted butter. Put breast down on broiler rack and broil about 5 inches from the source of heat for 8 or 9 minutes. Turn, brush again with melted butter, and broil for 8 or 9 minutes longer. Turn birds again, brush with melted butter, and sprinkle each one with 2 tablespoons crumbs, and dribble on a little melted butter. Broil for 2 or 3 minutes more, or until crumbs are browned. Turn again, sprinkle each bird again with 2 tablespoons crumbs, drizzle on a little more butter, and broil for 2 minutes more. Serve with deviled butter.

SERVES 6.

CREAM OF PHEASANT SOUP

1 medium-sized pheasant, cut into pieces
3 lbs. chicken bones
butter
1 onion
1 carrot, diced
1 leek, diced
1 celery rib, diced
3 tbsps. tomato purée
2 bay leaves
½ tsp. dried thyme

½ tsp. pepper
2 tsps. juniper berries
3 whole cloves
6 tbsps. flour
2 cups red Burgundy wine
4 qts. pheasant or chicken stock
3 tbsps. currant jelly
2 cups heavy cream
1 cup sherry
salt

Sauté pheasant and chicken bones in least possible amount of butter until golden brown. Add onion, carrot, leek, and celery, and sauté for 5 minutes. Add tomato purée and all herbs and spices, and cook slowly for a few minutes. Sprinkle with flour and stir in thoroughly. Transfer to a stockpot. Put Burgundy, a little of the stock, and the jelly into a skillet and simmer for a few minutes; stir into stockpot. Add remaining stock. Simmer for 1½ hours. Remove pheasant from soup; cut breast meat into julienne strips as garnish. Strain soup; add cream, sherry, and salt to taste; adjust seasonings. Freeze without cream and sherry if desired; add when heating. Serve with some strips of pheasant in each serving. SERVES 18.

PHEASANT CACCIATORE

2½ lbs. pheasant, cut into serving pieces
½ cup olive oil
3 cups canned plum tomatoes
2 tbsps. tomato paste

1 onion, chopped
2 garlic cloves, minced
pinch of hot red pepper
1 tsp. dried oregano
2 tbsps. minced parsley

Sauté bird in oil in a Dutch oven until brown. Put tomatoes through a sieve and add with remaining ingredients; stir in well. Simmer slowly, covered, until bird is tender, about 30 minutes for a young one. Remove meat from pan and reserve. Simmer sauce for an additional hour, covered. Return meat and freeze or reheat. Serve with spaghetti. SERVES 3.

PHEASANT SALTIMBOCCA

12 breasts, 6 to 8 oz. each, split, boned, and skinned
12 paper-thin slices of prosciutto or boiled ham
¼ lb. Swiss cheese, sliced thin
¼ cup flour
1 egg, lightly beaten
¼ cup fine dry bread crumbs

2 tbsps. shredded Parmesan cheese
¼ tsp. garlic salt
¼ tsp. crumbled dried tarragon
4 tbsps. butter
½ cup pheasant or chicken broth
½ cup dry sherry
1 tbsp. cornstarch, blended with 1 tbsp. water

Put 1 slice of ham and 1 slice of Swiss cheese on underside of each breast, roll up lengthwise, and skewer. Dip rolls into flour, shake off excess, and dip into egg. Drain briefly and roll in crumbs mixed with Parmesan, garlic salt, and tarragon. Brown in butter on all sides. Transfer to a baking dish and pour on broth and sherry. Freeze; or continue by baking uncovered in 350° oven for 30 minutes (40 if refrigerated), or until meat is done. Remove to a warm platter. Drain juices into small pan, bring to a boil, and stir in cornstarch to thicken. Spoon sauce over meat before serving.

SERVES 12.

SCOTTISH PHEASANT STOCK

giblets, trimmings, and frame of
  2 or 3 small pheasants,
  including blanched and skinned
  feet
2 qts. water
1½ tsps. salt

a few peppercorns
3 small leeks
2 celery ribs
1 onion, stuck with cloves
½ bay leaf
thyme

Simmer birds in water with salt for 1 hour, skimming. Add remaining ingredients and simmer for 1 hour longer. Strain. Cool.

MAKES 6 cups.

PHEASANT LEFTOVERS

PHEASANT TETRAZZINI

1 pheasant, 3 to 4 lbs., or 1½ lbs.
  cooked pheasant, boned and
  diced
¼ lb. fresh mushrooms
¼ lb. butter

2 tbsps. flour
1 cup heavy cream
¼ cup dry sherry
8 oz. spaghetti, cooked and
  drained, hot
½ lb. grated Parmesan cheese

Simmer pheasant in water to cover until done. Cool in the broth for 3 hours; strain and reserve broth. Bone pheasant and cut meat into chunks; reserve skin and bones. Return bird skin and bones to broth; bring to a boil, reduce heat, and simmer, covered, for 45 minutes. Remove cover, and boil to reduce broth to 2 cups. Strain and reserve broth. Sauté mushrooms in butter; remove mushrooms and blend flour into butter. Stir in the broth and simmer, stirring, for 2 minutes. Remove from heat and stir in cream and sherry. Add half of the sauce to the meat. Mix half of the sauce with spaghetti and mushrooms. Line a greased casserole with spaghetti and pour the meat into the center. Sprinkle with the grated cheese. Bake at 350° until browned, about 20 minutes.

SERVES 4 to 6.

PHEASANT STROGANOFF

3 lbs. cooked pheasant, boned and diced
⅔ cup flour
¼ lb. butter, melted
4 cups pheasant broth
1 can (6 oz.) mushrooms, drained

1 can (4 oz.) pimientos, drained and minced
3 tbsps. chopped chives
2 cups sour cream
salt, pepper, Tabasco
10 cups cooked spinach noodles, hot

Stir flour gradually into melted butter; slowly stir in broth. Cook, stirring, over low heat until thickened and bubbly. Add mushrooms, pimientos, chives, and pheasant. Simmer until bubbly. Remove from heat and stir in sour cream. Reheat but do not boil. Season with salt, pepper, and Tabasco to taste. Serve in a ring of hot green noodles. Garnish if desired with minced parsley and minced crystallized ginger root.

SERVES 8 to 10.

PHEASANT ROLL-UPS

2 cups coarsely chopped cooked pheasant
8 oz. tomato sauce
¼ cup water
½ cup chopped onion
¼ cup chopped green pepper

1 small garlic clove, minced
a few drops of liquid pepper
shortening
6 corn tortillas or crêpes
½ cup grated Cheddar cheese

Combine tomato sauce, water, onion, green pepper, garlic, and liquid pepper; bring to a boil and reduce to a simmer for 5 minutes. Heat enough shortening to be ½ inch deep in a skillet; heat tortillas on both sides until limp, or use warm crêpes. Drain tortillas on paper toweling. Fill each with one-sixth of the meat, softened if desired with a bit of sauce. Fold over and arrange in a baking dish. Top with rest of sauce. Bake at 375° for 10 to 15 minutes. Sprinkle with cheese and return to oven until cheese melts.

SERVES 6.

PHEASANT SPREAD

2 cups boned cooked pheasant
2 cups diced salami
½ cup diced carrots
1 tsp. salt

¼ tsp. pepper
½ cup grated Swiss or Parmesan cheese
12 stuffed green olives

Grind pheasant, salami, and carrots with seasonings into a paste. Spread on buttered bread, sprinkle with cheese, and decorate with olives. Or use browned bacon bits instead of salami, or use Cheddar slices instead of grated cheese. Season. Brown in broiler.

Also see Turkey and Partridge Leftovers.

GROUSE

The grouse family is a rather broad one and includes many names, with the ruffed grouse probably being the most popular, certainly the best known. Among the subspecies, perhaps the "fool hen" is the most common local name; it is applied to at least three subspecies that I know of. The sage cock or hen is actually a sage grouse, and the name prairie chicken is applied to at least two subspecies. Since the ruffed grouse is sometimes also called pheasant or partridge, it shows how interchangeable, and perhaps useless, names can be.

The grouse family ranges from the smallest, the ptarmigan (a close relative of Scotland's red grouse) at 24 ounces, through the ruffed grouse, which will weigh 24 to 30 ounces, to the dusky which may grow to as much as 3½ pounds. As always, the young are the better eating. Some species, whose diets affect their flavor, are better treated with a marinade for 4 to 8 hours, even though young. This is a matter of taste, however. As with all game, try the meat first in the simplest way, then you will know how to correct seasonings in the future.

One of the best ways to judge a grouse's age is by the main wing feathers. The tips of the two outmost (leading) feathers on each wing are obviously more pointed than the rest in young birds.

RHODE ISLAND STUFFED GROUSE

whole birds	mushrooms
white wine	¾ lb. butter, melted
egg	2 tbsps. paprika
milk	1 tsp. poultry seasoning
chestnuts	

Make a moist bread stuffing with wine, egg, milk, chestnuts, and mushrooms. Loosely stuff and truss birds; wrap birds twice around, firmly, with cheesecloth that has been moistened in ½ to ¾ pound butter, melted and seasoned with paprika and poultry seasoning.

Baste with this mix every 15 to 20 minutes while roasting at 325° for 2 to 2½ hours.

EACH grouse serves 1 or 2.

POLISH GROUSE IN SOUR CREAM

6 whole birds, marinated (perhaps
   a White Wine Marinade)

2 cups sour cream
1 tsp. flour

Roast on a spit or in a 400° oven until almost done, about 40 minutes; then baste for remaining time, another 10 to 20 minutes, with sour cream blended smooth with flour.

SERVES 6 to 8.

DANISH GROUSE

1 bird per person
1 fat bacon slice per bird
1 tbsp. butter per bird

2 tbsps. light cream per bird
2 or 3 mushrooms per bird, sliced

Tie bacon onto bird breast. Fry bird in melted butter, turning frequently, until browned. Cover and simmer gently until tender. Remove bird and keep warm. Add cream and mushrooms to pan and simmer for 1 or 2 minutes. Pour over birds on serving.

SERVES 1.

DANISH STUFFED GROUSE

2 ptarmigan
10 oz. boiled potatoes, mashed
   with 4 tbsps. butter

½ cup flour seasoned with ½ tsp.
   salt and ¼ tsp. white pepper
4 oz. bacon fat
¾ cup brown stock, boiling

Stuff birds with potatoes. Dip into seasoned flour and brown in bacon fat. Drain off all but 1 tablespoon fat. Baste birds with some of the stock, cover, and simmer slowly, basting every 15 minutes until all the stock is used. Thicken sauce as desired.

SERVES 2.

POLISH GROUSE WITH MADEIRA

6 whole birds, marinated (perhaps
   a White Wine Marinade)
bacon slices
1 tbsp. juniper berries, crushed
salt

flour
½ cup Madeira
6 medium-sized mushrooms,
   quartered
12 shallots

Line a casserole dish with bacon slices. Cut marinated birds into quarters, rub with crushed berries, and dust with salt. Put birds on bacon strips in the casserole, skin side up. Simmer, covered, until bacon begins to brown. Dust birds with flour. Add wine, mushrooms, and shallots, and simmer until tender, about 1 hour.

SERVES 6.

GROUSE WITH RED CABBAGE

6 birds, marinated (perhaps Basic Red Wine Marinade)
1 medium-sized head of red cabbage
salt and pepper
juice of ½ lemon

2 to 3 oz. salt pork, diced
½ large onion, chopped
2 tsps. flour
1 cup dry red wine
1 tsp. sugar

Quarter the grouse and brown as described in Polish Grouse with Madeira. Shred cabbage, blanch, and drain. Season cabbage and sprinkle with lemon juice. Brown salt pork and onion in a casserole, stir in flour. Add cabbage, wine, and sugar, and simmer covered for 15 minutes. Add browned bird quarters, and simmer for 1½ hours.

SERVES 6.

BAKED GROUSE

1 bird per person
apple, sliced and pared

onion, sliced
¾ cup orange juice

Stuff whole grouse with equal parts of sliced, pared apple and sliced onion, and pour on about ¾ cup orange juice. Cover tightly or seal with foil, and bake at 400° for 1 hour. Or use stuffing as a bed for parts of birds.

SERVES 1.

SCOTTISH GROUSE

2 young grouse, hung unplucked and uneviscerated for 3 to 5 days
butter seasoned with salt, pepper, and lemon juice, or cranberries
bacon

salt
cayenne
2 slices bread, crusts removed
flour
concentrated chicken stock

Pluck and clean birds, taking care not to pierce skin. Reserve livers. Wipe inside and out with a damp cloth but do not wash birds. Put a large lump of seasoned butter (or some cranberries) in each cavity; truss the birds. Tie strips of bacon around birds and roast at 325° for 15 to 25 minutes for rare, basting frequently with pan juices and a little melted butter. Parboil livers for 1 minute, then chop and mash with a fork; season highly with salt and cayenne. Toast bread slices and spread with livers. Remove bacon from birds; put birds on prepared toast. Dust with flour. Remove to a clean pan and roast at 500° for 10 minutes, or until breasts are brown. Combine pan juices with a little stock and serve on the side.

SERVES 2.

BACK BAY GROUSE

4 breasts
5½ tbsps. sweet butter
⅔ cup dry sherry
⅓ cup black-currant jelly

½ cup seedless grapes, halved
salt and white pepper
½ cup whipped heavy cream

Melt butter in top part of a double boiler and sauté breasts for 18 to 20 minutes, until tender. Remove breasts, and make a sauce by adding sherry, jelly, and grapes. When hot and smooth, return the breasts and simmer very slowly, uncovered for 15 minutes. Remove meat again; season with salt and white pepper and stir in whipped cream gently. Return meat and cook slowly for 5 minutes.

SERVES 4.

LOON BAY BEAN-BAKED GROUSE

Bake cleaned grouse, cut into serving pieces or halved, in a crock with old-fashioned New England baked beans until tender.

PTARMIGAN BREASTS

1 breast per person
salt and pepper
garlic salt
a few drops of soy sauce

½ tbsp. butter, melted, per breast
flour and cracker crumbs, or
    cornmeal and dry cereal crumbs
bacon fat

Dust breasts with salt, pepper and garlic salt. Add 2 or 3 drops of soy sauce to ½ tablespoon melted butter per breast, and spread on the breasts. Let stand at room temperature for 1 hour. Dip breasts into a mixture of flour and cracker crumbs, or cornmeal and dry cereal crumbs. Brown in hot bacon fat. Add a little water, cover, and steam for about 30 minutes, or until tender.

SERVES 1.

BROILED PTARMIGAN

1 bird per person
cooking oil

salt and pepper
1 lean bacon slice per bird

Split birds down the back and press flat. Brush with cooking oil and sprinkle with salt and pepper. Put in a preheated broiler skin side down. Broil for 15 minutes, turning once. Top each with a lean bacon slice and broil until bacon is done. Can also be basted with barbecue sauce.

SERVES 1.

FRIED PRAIRIE CHICKEN

1 whole bird
½ cup flour seasoned with ¼ tsp.
white pepper, ½ tsp. savory
and ½ tsp. salt

pinch of dried thyme
pinch of dried basil
1 slice bacon
4 tbsps. sweet butter

Dust bird with seasoned flour, reserving extra. Put thyme and basil on the bacon slice and roll it up; put it in the cavity and truss bird. Melt butter and brown bird on all sides. Cover and bake at 350° for 50 to 60 minutes. Blend reserved flour into pan juices before serving.

SERVES 2 to 4.

PRAIRIE CHICKEN PAPRIKA

2 birds, cut into serving pieces
½ cup flour seasoned with ½ tsp.
salt and ¼ tsp. pepper
2 tbsps. sweet butter
½ cup chopped onion
1 tbsp. paprika

3 tbsps. hot water
2 tbsps. flour
1 cup sour cream
1 tbsp. lemon juice
salt and pepper

Dredge pieces with seasoned flour and brown in sweet butter. Remove birds and soften onion in butter. Return birds and sprinkle with leftover seasoned flour and paprika. Add hot water and cook, covered, for 30 minutes to 1 hour, until tender, adding 1 tablespoon hot water at a time if needed. Remove pieces and keep hot. Add 2 tablespoons flour to pan smoothly, then the sour cream; cook slowly, stirring until thick. Cover and cook for 10 minutes. Add lemon juice and season to taste. Return bird to sauce and reheat.

SERVES 2 to 4.

PARTRIDGE

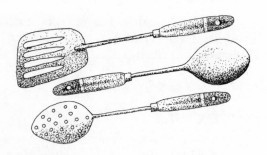

The redleg, chukar, and hun (Hungarian) partridges range in size between a large quail and a small ruffed grouse. The hun will weigh about 12 to 13 ounces and will usually serve 1 person. It's a good game species, and excellent eating when young and tender. As with grouse, in young birds the tips of the two outermost, leading, wing feathers are more pointed than the rest.

ROAST PARTRIDGE INDIANA

2 whole birds
2 egg-sized pieces of salt pork
1 tsp. ground sage
1/4 lb. butter, softened

1 tbsp. flour seasoned with 1/2 tsp. salt and 1/4 tsp. white pepper
4 slices bacon
1/4 cup tomato sauce
3/4 cup sour cream

Roll salt-pork pieces in sage and put into cavities of birds. Truss birds. Rub with soft butter, dust with seasoned flour, and top with bacon slices. Put into an open pan in a 350° oven for 30 minutes. When birds test done, add tomato sauce blended with sour cream, and serve.

SERVES 4.

ROAST PARTRIDGE WITH RAISINS

2 whole birds
1 cup white bread crumbs
1½ cups scalded milk seasoned
  with ½ tsp. salt, ¼ tsp. white
  pepper

4 tbsps. butter, melted
1 cup seedless raisins
½ cup flour seasoned with 1 tsp.
  salt and ¼ tsp. pepper
4 strips bacon

Plump raisins by soaking in hot water 10 to 15 minutes; drain. Soak crumbs briefly in milk and squeeze until only moist. Add melted butter and blend in raisins. Stuff birds with this mix and truss. Dust with seasoned flour, top with bacon and roast at 325° for 1 hour, basting every 5 minutes for the last 20 minutes.
  SERVES 4.

GREEK BIRDS WITH ORANGES

2 partridges, split in half
½ cup olive oil
⅓ cup lemon juice
salt and pepper

½ tsp. minced fresh oregano
1 garlic clove, minced
honey
2 oranges, sliced with peel on

Wipe birds dry and put into large shallow dish. Mix oil, lemon juice, salt, pepper, oregano, and garlic, and pour over birds. Marinate at least 2 hours, turning occasionally. Broil or barbecue over hot coals, basting occasionally with marinade. For broiling, allow 15 minutes per side. Drizzle honey over orange slices and broil until just heated through; serve with birds. Pass additional oregano to be sprinkled on birds.
  SERVES 4.

TOLEDO PARTRIDGE CASSEROLE

4 birds
¼ cup olive oil
¼ cup cold water
2 carrots, chopped
1 leek, chopped
1 onion, chopped
1 bay leaf

1 sprig fresh thyme
3 whole cloves
salt and pepper
¼ cup minced tomato
1 tbsp. flour
wine vinegar

Pat birds dry and truss. Brown in hot oil in a Dutch oven. Add cold water all at once to stop cooking. Add carrots, leek, onion, bay leaf, thyme, cloves, and salt and pepper to taste. Cook, covered, for 30 to 40 minutes, or until tender. Transfer birds to a heated platter and keep warm. Strain sauce through a fine sieve and stir in tomato, flour, and a little vinegar to taste. Heat, stirring, until slightly thickened. Remove trussing cord from birds, split them, and spoon on sauce. Serve surrounded with steamed fresh vegetables.

SERVES 4.

POLISH PARTRIDGE

1 whole bird per person
salt pork or bacon
salt butter

sweet butter, seasoned with
lemon juice or anchovy

Lard birds well or wrap in salt pork or bacon, or baste with butter. Roast covered at 350° for 30 to 40 minutes. Slash breast before serving and fill with sweet butter spiced with lemon juice, or use anchovy butter.

BARBECUED PARTRIDGE

2 to 4 birds, cut into serving pieces
¼ cup flour
3 tbsps. sweet butter
1 medium-sized onion, sliced thin
2 tbsps. tarragon vinegar
3 tbsps. Worcestershire sauce

½ tsp. prepared mustard
1 cup water
½ cup chopped celery
½ tsp. salt
pinch of cayenne
1 cup catsup

Roll bird pieces in flour, and brown in butter. Remove birds, and drain off most of the fat. Brown onion in remaining fat. Add vinegar, Worcestershire, mustard, water, celery, salt, cayenne, and catsup, and simmer, covered, for 30 minutes. Add bird pieces and bake, uncovered, at 325° for 1 hour.

SERVES 2 to 4.

NEW ENGLAND PARTRIDGE FILETS

1 breast, boned and cut in half   4 slices bacon

Put a bacon slice under each breast half in a baking dish. Skewer a bacon slice on top of each. Bake at 400° for 10 minutes; remove top bacon slices and broil for 1 minute.

SERVES 1.

PARTRIDGE WITH ROYAL YORK SAUCE

1 plump bird, split and skinned
½ cup flour seasoned with ½ tsp.
  salt and ¼ tsp. white pepper
6 tbsps. sweet butter
1 tsp. chopped shallots
2 tbsps. dry white wine
½ cube of chicken extract

1 tbsp. hot water
salt and pepper
2 slices hot toast, buttered
2 tbsps. shredded almonds
2 tsps. chopped parsley
1 small garlic clove, minced

Roll bird pieces in seasoned flour; brown lightly in 4 tablespoons of the butter. Cover and cook slowly until done, about 45 minutes. Remove bird pieces and brown shallots in the same butter. Add wine and extract softened in hot water. Remove from the heat and blend in remaining butter; season to taste. Put bird on the buttered toast. Sprinkle with almonds, parsley, and garlic, and pour on the pan juices.

SERVES 1 or 2.

PARTRIDGE LEFTOVERS

JELLIED PARTRIDGE

1½ cups chopped cooked
  partridge
2 cups clear partridge or chicken
  broth, hot
1 tbsp. unflavored gelatin
¼ cup water

1 cup minced celery
2 tbsps. chopped pimiento
2 tbsps. chopped parsley
½ tsp. grated onion
dash of salt

Soften gelatin in water, then dissolve in hot broth. Cool. When aspic begins to set, fold in remaining ingredients. Pour into a 5-cup mold rinsed in cold water. Allow to set completely in the refrigerator.

SERVES 4.

PARTRIDGE PASTE

1 cold, roast partridge, boned and
  pounded to a paste

50 chestnuts, roasted and skinned
meat stock to cover nuts

Boil chestnuts in stock for about 2 hours or until softened. Add meat paste to nuts and liquid and work through sieve with wooden spoon. Bring to a boil again and serve with croutons.

SERVES 6.

BAKED LOAF

4 cups ground cooked partridge   1 small onion, minced
1 cup milk   2 eggs, beaten
1 cup bird or chicken stock   2 cups soft bread crumbs
1½ tsps. salt

Mix all ingredients and pour into a greased 8-cup loaf pan. Bake at 375° for 1 hour, or until firm and lightly browned. Unmold and serve hot with sliced tomatoes and parsley.

SERVES 6 to 8.

PIGEON

Along with turkey shoots, pigeon shoots were a favorite sport in most colonial villages. Partially as a result, the carrier pigeon was wiped out long ago.

Today pigeon shooting as a sport is limited to the western United States, where the band-tail pigeon is a well-known sporting bird. In the East pigeon shooting is apt to be limited to helping a farmer reduce the mess around his barn.

Not many easterners think of pigeon as food, yet they will pay a respectable price for squab under glass, and that's young pigeon, usually raised for the market. The trouble with pigeon is that when it gets beyond the squab stage—and a pigeon can live for a goodly number of years—it definitely is tough. The best solution for an old pigeon is a good strong marinade, such as The Red Marinade. Pigeons should marinate for a fair length of time; a young one for 12 to 24 hours, older birds for a couple of days. Pigeon meat is fine-grained and lean; it takes well to strong-flavored sauces.

Depending on appetites and the place in the meal, 1 or 2 squabs may serve 1 person. One older, larger, bird may be enough for 1 entrée. Pigeons weigh 7 to 10 ounces.

ENGLISH PIGEONS

1 pigeon per person, marinated   butter
   in The Red Marinade for an   lean bacon strips
   appropriate time   brown stock
onion, sliced   bouquet garni of herbs of your
carrot, sliced   choice
celery, chopped   salt and pepper

Mix equal amounts of sliced onion, sliced carrot, and chopped celery, enough to make a 1-inch layer in a casserole. Steam in butter until soft. Line the casserole with the leanest possible bacon, and spread steamed vegetables on top. Set birds on top, breast up, and pour on strained marinade, enough to come halfway up the birds. Barely cover birds with brown stock. Add a bouquet garni of fresh herbs of your choice, and season as desired. Simmer very slowly for about 1½ to 2 hours for young birds, longer for older birds, until tender.

NEW ORLEANS SQUAB

6 young squab   mixed, sliced vegetables (onions, celery, carrots)

Roast unmarinated squab on a bed of vegetables in a 325° oven for 30 minutes. Remove squab and put into a deep casserole. Pour 1 recipe of Sauce Paradis over. Cover and bake for an additional 15 minutes.

SERVES 3 to 6.

CALIFORNIA BAND-TAILS

4 to 6 birds	2 to 3 tbsps. seedless raisins
flour	2 whole cloves
4 tbsps. butter	rinsed, preserved grape leaves, or
¾ cup (approx.) beef broth	fresh leaves dipped into boiling
¼ cup port wine	water for 1 minute

Roll birds (tie if necessary) in flour; shake off excess. Brown on all sides in hot butter; do not burn butter. Add about half of the broth, all the wine, the raisins, and cloves. Cover and simmer for 30 minutes, adding more broth as needed. Arrange birds on grape leaves and spoon sauce over them to serve.

SERVES 4 to 6.

BRAISED PIGEONS

6 birds, giblets removed and reserved	Kitchen Bouquet
	parsley, chopped
2 oz. bacon or salt pork	3 tbsps. flour
3½ tbsps. butter	1 tbsp. red-currant jelly
salt	½ cup heavy cream
chicken broth	

Truss birds and wrap breasts with bacon or salt pork. Brown birds and giblets in butter. Add a dash of salt, enough chicken broth to cover bottom of skillet, and enough Kitchen Bouquet to color lightly. Cover and simmer gently for about 1 hour, or until tender, adding more broth if necessary to prevent drying. Remove birds and keep warm; sprinkle birds with parsley. Measure cooking liquid and add enough more broth to make 2 cups; bring to a boil. Mix flour with a small amount of water until smooth, then add to boiling liquid and cook, stirring, until thickened. Add jelly and melt over low heat. Strain juices, discarding giblets. Add cream, adjust seasoning, and reheat to serving temperature.

SERVES 6.

BREAD AND BUTTER BIRDS

6 birds, dressed (pigeon, dove, or quail)
6 tsps. minced fresh parsley
½ cup flour seasoned with
½ tsp. salt, ¼ tsp. pepper, and
1 tsp. ground ginger

3 tbsps. vegetable oil
½ lb. sweet butter
2 eggs, lightly beaten
½ cup fine bread crumbs

Fill cavity of each bird with 1 teaspoon parsley. Dredge birds with seasoned flour and brown quickly in hot oil. Remove birds, discard oil, and wipe skillet dry. Melt butter over medium heat. Dip birds into eggs, roll in crumbs; repeat with eggs and crumbs. Add to skillet and dust with remaining crumbs, sifted. Cook, uncovered, at 350°, basting with pan juices every 5 minutes, for 25 to 30 minutes.

SERVES 6.

NEW ENGLAND POTTED PIGEONS

6 birds, stuffed (perhaps Mushroom Stuffing)
3 slices bacon, cut into halves
4 cups boiling water

1 carrot, diced
1 onion, sliced
4 tbsps. butter
4 tbsps. flour

Put birds breast up on slices of bacon in a Dutch oven. Add water, carrot, and onion. Cover and simmer slowly for 3 hours, adding boiling water as needed. Make a sauce by blending butter and flour and adding to 2 cups of the cooking liquid; stir until thickened. Serve birds on toast.

SERVES 6.

ROAST STUFFED SQUABS

6 tender young pigeons
1 lemon, cut into quarters
2 cups freshly cooked rice
¼ cup melted butter
salt and pepper

¼ tsp. Italian seasoning mix
grated rind of ½ orange
2 tbsps. seedless raisins
3 tbsps. soft butter

Plump raisins by soaking in hot water 10 to 15 minutes; drain. Dry the birds with a paper towel and rub the insides first with salt, then the cut side of the lemon. Make a stuffing of the rice, butter, salt, pepper, Italian seasoning, orange rind, and raisins. Stuff the birds loosely. Skewer or tie closed and spread the soft butter on the breasts and legs. Put birds onto a rack in a roaster and roast at 300° for about 1 hour, basting frequently with 1 cup hot water in which 1 tablespoon of butter has been melted.

SERVES 6.

ALLEGHENY BROILED PIGEONS

4 pigeons split down the back and
    flattened into butterfly pieces
½ cup flour seasoned with ½ tsp.
    salt and ¼ tsp. pepper

1 or 2 egg yolks, beaten
½ cup fine bread crumbs
melted butter

Dust birds with seasoned flour, brush with beaten egg yolks, and cover with crumbs. Put birds skin down under a 550° broiler for 5 minutes. Reduce broiler heat to 400°, turn birds, and cook until done, basting with melted butter. Serve with Pepper Sauce or Poivrade Sauce.

SERVES 4.

QUAIL

Bobwhite is probably the best known of the quail family, but others such as Gambel's and the desert quail have their devotees across the country. These are small birds, 5 to 6 ounces, with tender, flavorful dark meat. Since they are similar to dove in having a short life span, you'll rarely come across a tough one. If the age is important to you, use the wing feather test as with grouse. Being small, quail are usually served 2 to each diner for a main course, or 1 apiece for an appetizer.

POLISH QUAIL

1 whole bird per person bacon
salt butter

Hang birds for several days, pluck and dress. Season with salt. Roast, wrapped and tied in bacon, on a spit or in hot oven. Baste with butter. When the birds begin to brown, discard the bacon. Do not roast for more than 30 minutes from the time they begin to brown.

QUAIL SMETANE

6 whole birds salt and pepper
½ cup dry bread crumbs ¼ lb. butter
½ cup ground Brazil nuts or 2 tbsps. Cognac, warmed
  hazelnuts ½ cup chicken or bird stock
grated rind of 1 lemon ½ cup dry white wine
¼ cup dry sherry 1 cup sour cream

Make a stuffing by mixing crumbs, nuts, and lemon rind. Add sherry and squeeze mixture dry. Stuff birds with equal amounts; truss. Dust with salt and pepper. Brown birds on all sides in hot butter. Pour on the Cognac, ignite it, and let flames die out. Transfer birds to a casserole. Add stock and wine to the browning pan and deglaze it; pour deglazing mixture over birds. Cover and simmer gently for about 30 minutes, or until tender. Remove birds and keep warm. Add sour cream to casserole, stir sauce smooth, and heat for 10 minutes without boiling. Serve with birds.
  SERVES 6.

NEW ENGLAND ROAST QUAIL

1 bird per person 1 slice toast per bird
butter water
salt and pepper juice of 1 lemon
1 bacon slice per bird

Butter quails inside and out, and sprinkle with salt and pepper inside and out. Top each with a bacon slice, and roast at 400° with 1 tablespoon butter in the roaster, basting 3 times in 20 minutes. Serve on toast with sauce of pan drippings mixed with 1 tablespoon more butter, 1 tablespoon water, and the juice of 1 lemon, cooked for 3 minutes.

QUAIL OREGANO

2 birds, split	¼ tsp. pepper
4 tbsps. sweet butter	1 tbsp. dried oregano
2 tbsps. minced parsley	½ cup brandy
½ tsp. seasoned salt	1 cup fine bread crumbs (optional)

Melt butter and sauté birds until brown. Add parsley, salt, pepper, oregano, and brandy, and shake pan to blend well. Cover and cook gently for 30 to 40 minutes. If the birds are young and tender, after browning well, they can be dipped into crumbs and broiled until golden, instead of being simmered.

SERVES 1 or 2.

NEW ENGLAND QUAIL AND RICE

2 quail, split	1¼ tsps. salt
¼ lb. sweet butter	¼ tsp. pepper
1 medium-sized onion, sliced	3 cups canned tomatoes, warmed
2 celery ribs, chopped	½ cup raw long-grain rice

Melt butter in a Dutch oven and lightly brown the quail, turning from time to time. Remove quail and soften onion and celery in remaining butter. Return birds and add salt, pepper, tomatoes, and rice. Cover and bake at 350° for 1 hour, stirring once after the first 15 to 20 minutes.

SERVES 1 or 2.

ROAST QUAIL WITH WHITE GRAPES

4 quail	2 to 3 tbsps. Cognac
6 tbsps. butter	¼ cup dry sherry, white wine, or
salt and pepper	vermouth
about 30 Thompson seedless (or	1 cup chicken stock
Belgian White Muscat or	1½ tsps. arrowroot
California Emperor) grapes,	1 tsp. grated lemon rind
peeled and halved, and seeded	1 to 2 tsps. lemon juice
if needed	

Rub birds generously with butter, salt, and pepper. Put a lump of butter, salt and pepper, and 3 or 4 grapes in each cavity. Sprinkle birds with Cognac and place in a roasting pan. Roast at 450° for 12 to 15 minutes, basting well 2 or 3 times. Heat remaining grapes in sherry and stock. Remove grapes with a slotted spoon and add stock to birds; roast for 5 minutes more. Remove birds and keep warm while making gravy. Mix arrowroot into sherry and stock and add to pan juices with lemon rind and juice. Stir well to deglaze pan, and simmer until slightly thickened. Correct seasoning as desired.

SERVES 2 to 4.

TARRAGON QUAIL WITH WINE

2 or 3 birds per person
flour
butter

⅓ cup plus ½ cup sauterne
¼ cup melted butter
1 tsp. minced fresh tarragon

Dredge birds with flour, and sauté lightly in butter, turning frequently, until golden brown. Transfer to a rack in a shallow baking dish and put a small piece of butter in each cavity. Deglaze skillet with ⅓ cup sauterne and pour deglazing mixture over birds. Bake at 400° for 35 to 40 minutes, basting every 10 minutes with a mixture of ½ cup sauterne, the melted butter and tarragon. If you like, deglaze roasting pan with remaining basting sauce, and pour over birds.

OYSTER-STUFFED QUAIL

1 or 2 birds per person
oysters
butter

salt and pepper
1 lemon slice per bird
1 thin slice of barding fat per bird

Stuff each bird loosely with freshly shucked oysters; 1 large one will usually do. Add a lump of butter, salt and pepper, and a thin slice of lemon to each cavity. Top bird with a sheet of barding fat. Put on a rack in a shallow roaster and roast at 450° for 20 minutes. Remove barding fat and baste birds well with pan juices. Season with salt and pepper, and roast for 5 minutes more, basting once again.

QUAIL WITH GRAPE LEAVES

6 quail
olive oil
6 thin slices barding pork

12 to 18 fresh or preserved grape
  leaves, rinsed
6 squares cooked cornmeal
  mush, fried

Rub birds with oil, wrap in barding pork, then in 2 or 3 grape leaves. Tie each bird firmly and wrap in lightly oiled cooking parchment or foil. Roast at 375° for 40 to 45 minutes. Unwrap and serve in the leaves on a fried square of cornmeal mush. May be served with Giblet Cream Sauce or Giblet Gravy.

SERVES 6.

DOVE

Upland bird shooters rate the dove high. It's a tricky flier which, even out in the open, seems to evade shotgun pellets most of the time. Shotgunners who know how the dove challenges their skills can't quite comprehend the mental attitude of nonhunters of the bird. In some states, such as New Jersey and New York, the mourning dove is protected as a "song bird," while Pennsylvania has what we call a half season. In addition to a daily bag limit, you can't shoot dove until the afternoon, meaning that you're out in the grain or stubble fields during the hottest part of the day. Early in the season it can be mighty uncomfortable!

Some people insist that doves are migratory birds. That is partially true; hundreds of thousands of whitewings stream across Texas and lower California heading for the Mexican wintering grounds. On the other hand, near my home in Pennsylvania there's a country road with gravel shoulder where every day as long as snow is absent, mourning doves can be seen graveling. True, most of the birds migrate, but some stay all year around.

The life span of doves, as with most small birds, is short. Rarely do they live more than a year. Since this is a fact of their existence, it's unlikely that you will come across a tough dove, especially if you remember not to dry out the small bird in cooking. A mature dove will seldom weigh more than 4 ounces, so it will not take long to cook. Needless to say, you should figure on several doves per serving, depending on size and appetites.

Doves are particularly easy and quick to clean, especially if you wish to use only the breasts. (The legs make nibbling, as does the back, but they're definitely finger food.) The breasts are meaty and make attractive, even servings. As an average figure 4 breasts to a person.

To clean dove for just the breast meat, hold the bird on its back in one hand. Grasp the outside wing with the other hand and give a good twist; the wing will snap off. Repeat with the other. Lay the bird again on its back in one hand and poke your free thumb into the body cavity just below and up under the breastbone. All in the same movement pry the bird apart by moving the two hands apart. A quick jerk will separate the breast from the rest of the bird. All that's left to do is to pluck the breast feathers or peel off the skin and wash.

DOVES AND MUSHROOMS

4 birds	¼ tsp. white pepper
2 cups fresh mushrooms	1 cup condensed cream of chicken
4 tbsps. butter, softened	soup
½ tsp. salt	1 cup heavy cream

Boil mushrooms in 4 cups boiling water for 3 minutes. Drain and transfer to ice water; let stand for 5 minutes. Drain and slice. Rub doves with soft butter and season with salt and pepper inside and out. Put into casserole and pour on undiluted soup. Cover and cook at 350° for 1 hour. Add cream and mushrooms, mixed. Bake until mushrooms are tender, only a few minutes more.
SERVES 2.

DOVE LOUISIANA

2 doves	2 tbsps. butter, softened and
½ to ¾ cup cooked rice	seasoned with ½ tsp. seasoned
4 tbsps. melted butter	salt and ¼ tsp. white pepper
¼ tsp. ground sage	2 tbsps. sweet butter
½ tsp. onion salt	1 cup white wine
pinch of cayenne	1½ tbsps. brandy
	½ tsp. cornstarch dissolved in
	¼ cup cold water

Mix rice with melted butter, sage, onion salt, and cayenne; use to stuff birds, after rubbing them inside and out with seasoned soft butter. Melt sweet butter in a casserole, and sauté the birds until brown. Add wine and brandy; cover and simmer slowly for 1 hour. Add dissolved cornstarch to thicken pan juices.
SERVES 1.

CARMEL SAUTÉED DOVE

6 birds	1 cup white wine
4 tbsps. butter	1 cup water
2 small onions, minced	2 cups heavy cream
2 garlic cloves, minced	½ tsp. salt
½ bay leaf	⅛ tsp. pepper
1 tsp. peppercorns	1 tsp. chopped chives
3 whole cloves	

Melt butter; add onions, garlic, bay leaf, peppercorns, and whole cloves, and cook for 5 minutes, stirring. Sauté the birds in the mixture until brown. Add wine and water, cover, and simmer for 30 minutes. Remove birds and strain sauce into a casserole. Add cream slowly and smoothly. Add salt, pepper, and chives; return birds, cover, and heat briefly without boiling.

SERVES 2 or 3.

TEXAS BAKED DOVE

4 to 6 doves or young pigeons
½ cup flour seasoned with
   ½ tsp. salt, ¼ tsp. pepper,
   ½ tsp. ground oregano, and
   1 tsp. Spanish paprika

4 tbsps. sweet butter
1 cup tomato juice, heated
½ cup chili sauce, heated

Dredge birds with seasoned flour. Brown in sweet butter, and place in a buttered casserole. Sift on remaining seasoned flour; add blended tomato juice and chili sauce. Bake at 350° for 30 minutes.

SERVES 2 or 3.

DUTCH-OVEN POLENTA DOVES

6 to 8 birds
¼ cup flour mixed with ½ cup
   polenta (cornmeal)
¼ cup rendered salt pork

¼ cup water
½ tsp. dried savory
½ tsp. ground ginger

Roll birds in flour-polenta mixture. Brown quickly in drippings in a Dutch oven. Add enough water to keep from sticking, about ¼ cup, and simmer, covered, for 30 minutes. Sprinkle on savory and ginger, and continue to cook, basting frequently, for another 30 minutes.

SERVES 3 or 4.

CANADIAN DOVE SAUTÉ BONNE FEMME

4 doves or young pigeons, whole
   or split down the back
½ cup flour seasoned with ½ tsp.
   salt and ¼ tsp. pepper
4 tbsps. butter

2 cups diced mushrooms
1 cup light cream, scalded
2 egg yolks, beaten
½ cup chopped ripe olives
¼ cup sherry

Roll birds in seasoned flour and brown in hot butter. Add mushrooms, cover, and bake at 375° for 35 to 40 minutes, or until birds

211

are tender. Remove birds and mushrooms and keep hot. Pour off all but ¼ cup of fat from the pan. Add cream, egg yolks, and olives slowly, and stir over low heat until thickened. Add sherry, correct seasonings, and pour sauce over birds.

SERVES 2.

OVEN-BARBECUED DOVE

2 doves per person	salt and pepper
bay leaf, crumbled	Bermuda onion, sliced
poultry seasoning	bacon strips
onion	barbecue sauce
butter	½ cup water per bird

Prepare doves for roasting. Prepare a double thickness of foil long enough to wrap doves. Put doves breast up on foil and sprinkle several pieces of crumbled bay leaf on each. Sauté onion in butter. Sprinkle doves with poultry seasoning, sautéed onion, salt, and pepper. Top with Bermuda onion slices. Lay strips of bacon on top, and drizzle with barbecue sauce. Seal top and one end of package with drugstore fold. Pour about ½ cup water into open end and seal that with drugstore fold. Bake at 350° for 2 hours. To crisp bacon, open top and put under broiler for a few minutes before serving. Prepare 1 foil package for each serving.

FRENCH PICNIC DOVE

2 doves per person	salt
1 potato, sliced	paprika
1 apple, unpeeled and sliced	seedless grapes

Stuff doves with slices of raw potato and unpeeled apple. Sprinkle heavily with salt and paprika and allow birds to sit until they reach room temperature. Put into a 400° oven for 20 minutes. Remove birds; remove stuffing immediately. Let birds cool for 20 minutes. Stuff cavities with seedless grapes at room temperature. Wrap with foil to carry to picnic.

MINTED DOVE

6 young birds, skinned	¾ tsp. grated nutmeg
fresh mint leaves	¾ tsp. ground allspice
3 cups sour cream	¾ tsp. white pepper
7 or 8 fresh mint leaves, minced	¾ tsp. salt
¾ tsp. ground cinnamon	

212

Rub birds well with fresh mint leaves. Combine sour cream and minced mint leaves, cinnamon, nutmeg, allspice, pepper, and salt. Cut foil into 6 very large heart shapes and spread sour-cream mixture evenly on both halves of each heart. Put a dove on half of each heart, fold over foil, and pinch foil edges together. Bake at 375° for 40 minutes.

SERVES 2 or 3.

WOODCOCK

This bird, just about the smallest upland game bird, has rich, dark meat with a distinct flavor. Along with quail, woodcock apparently has a scent that humans do not catch; many hunting dogs are perfectly willing to hunt them and point for the guns, but they simply refuse to pick them up or hold them if the birds are forced upon them. Whatever it is that turns off a dog, however, does not come through for humans. They are delicious morsels, particularly when served pink and moist. To a true fan, 3 or 4 woodcock would be considered only an appetizer.

PINK WOODCOCK

3 or 4 woodcock per person   sherry
bacon slices

Put cleaned birds in a heavy iron skillet and top each with a half slice of bacon. Put skillet in preheated 450° oven for 5 minutes, then turn to full broil and broil birds for 5 minutes. Remove from broiler and cover skillet tightly; return to 450° oven and cook birds for 15 minutes. Sprinkle birds with enough sherry to cover pan bottom; cover pan tightly and cook at 450° for 5 minutes longer. Serve with pan juices.

CANADIAN BAKED WOODCOCK

3 or 4 woodcock per person   butter
milk   sweet or sour cream
flour seasoned with salt and
   pepper

Split each bird, then dip into milk and dredge with seasoned flour. Brown in melted butter. Arrange in a shallow casserole and cover with sweet or sour cream. Bake at 350° for about 30 minutes, or until tender.

CANADIAN PIMIENTO WOODCOCK

6 birds, quartered
¼ cup flour seasoned with ½ tsp.
　salt and ¼ tsp. pepper
½ cup cooking oil
6 small onions, peeled but
　unsliced
2 garlic cloves, mashed

⅛ tsp. ground saffron
3 medium-sized green peppers,
　seeded and cut into strips
½ cup sherry
3 pimientos, minced
2 cups chicken stock

Dredge birds with seasoned flour. Heat oil, add onions, garlic, and birds, and cook, turning often, to brown evenly. Put in a deep casserole, and add saffron, green peppers, sherry, pimientos, and stock. Cover and bake at 450° for 15 minutes.
SERVES 2.

NEW ENGLAND BAKED WOODCOCK

6 birds, split
1 cup milk
½ cup flour
3 tbsps. sweet butter
1 cup fine dry bread crumbs

½ tsp. salt
⅛ tsp. white pepper
½ tsp. paprika
1 cup sour cream

Dip birds into milk, then roll in flour. Melt butter and brown birds in it. Remove birds, dip again into milk, then dredge with bread crumbs. Season with salt, pepper, and paprika, and place in a casserole. Add sour cream and cover dish. Bake at 350° for 45 minutes, or until tender.
SERVES 2.

ROAST WOODCOCK

4 birds
salt and pepper
4 tbsps. butter

4 generous pinches of dried
　marjoram or thyme
4 slices bacon

Sprinkle birds inside and out with salt and pepper. Put 1 tablespoon butter with 1 pinch of herb in each cavity. Wrap each breast with bacon and tie it on. Put on a rack in a roaster and roast at 400°, basting frequently with melted butter, until tender. If they are plump birds, it should take 20 to 25 minutes.
SERVES 1.

214

SNIPE

Snipe, another very small bird popular with many hunters, is generally found around water, but because of its size and diet it is similar to woodcock in taste. Hence it is included in this rather than the next category. Woodcock recipes can be used if desired.

Note that some people eat snipe bills like pretzels, when they are roasted crisp.

GEORGIA BRANDIED SNIPE

4 to 6 birds, whole but cleaned,
  livers reserved
1 tsp. paprika
¼ tsp. salt
¼ tsp. pepper

4 to 6 strips bacon
¼ lb. butter, melted
½ cup boiling water
½ tsp. minced parsley
½ cup brandy, heated

Dust birds with paprika, salt, and pepper; wrap with bacon. Put birds in a small roaster pan and roast at 350° for 20 minutes, until done, basting with some of the butter. Mash the livers and cook in melted butter in a saucepan. Mix roaster drippings with ½ cup boiling water and add to livers. Correct seasoning, add parsley, and serve sauce separately with birds. Slice off the breasts, put breasts on a hot platter, pour on heated brandy, and flame.

SERVES 2 or 3.

NEW ENGLAND ROAST SNIPE LYONNAISE

1 snipe, stuffed with a
  marble-sized piece of salt pork
  rolled in celery seeds
½ cup flour seasoned with ½ tsp.
  salt and ¼ tsp. pepper

3 tbsps. sweet butter
½ cup thin onion rings
1 tsp. paprika
½ tsp. seasoned salt
1 cup sour cream

Dredge bird with seasoned flour, and sauté in butter. Put in a casserole and cover with onion rings. Dust with paprika and seasoned salt; spoon on sour cream. Cover and roast at 325° for 1 hour. Sauce can be thickened if desired.

SERVES 1.

BAYOU BÉCASSINES

1 snipe, undrawn	1 clove, crushed
stock or consommé	4 peppercorns, bruised
beurre manié	1 garlic clove, mashed
3 oz. claret wine	1 tbsp. olive oil
2 shallots, minced	juice of ½ lemon
bouquet garni of 5 parsley sprigs tied with 1 bay leaf	salt

Roast snipe briefly, no more than 5 minutes; it should still be very underdone. Remove legs and wings carefully and reserve. Discard head, gall, and gizzard. Bone the bird. Pound the bird meat to a firm paste, adding enough stock or consommé to give the consistency of thick cream. Press through a fine sieve. Knead a walnut-sized piece of beurre manié and add to bird paste. Add wine, shallots, bouquet garni, clove, peppercorns, and garlic. Bring to a slow boil, reduce heat, and simmer for 2 minutes. Strain and add olive oil, lemon juice, and salt to taste. Put the 4 limbs of the snipe into the sauce and heat. Serve on squares of fried bread, with sauce.

SERVES 1 as an appetizer.

SEABOARD BROILED SNIPE

1 or 2 snipe per person	2 tsps. butter, softened, per bird
1 tbsp. cooked bacon, crumbled, per bird	½ tsp. seasoned salt per bird
	¼ tsp. pepper per bird
1 tsp. sweet pickle, minced, per bird	1 tsp. paprika per bird
	1 slice raw bacon per bird

Fill cavity with crumbled brown bacon and sweet pickle, mixed. Truss birds, cover with softened butter, and dust with seasoned salt, pepper, and paprika. Wrap in bacon slice. Brown in the broiler. When browned, reduce heat to medium or lower rack and broil for 13 to 16 minutes more, basting and turning frequently.

SERVES 1 as an appetizer.

MISSOURI SNIPE

8 snipe, cleaned	1 can (3 oz.) mushrooms, chopped, with liquid
8 square, crisp rolls	pinch of dried thyme
5 tbsps. butter	1 cup chablis or sauterne
¼ tsp. minced parsley	½ tsp. salt
1 tsp. chopped onion	½ tsp. pepper
1 tbsp. flour	

Cut tops off rolls and scoop out interior to make a pocket large enough to hold a snipe. Butter inside lightly and toast in the oven, split side up, until just lightly browned. Sauté parsley and onion in 1 tablespoon butter until browned. Add flour and brown. Add mushrooms and liquid, thyme, wine, salt, and pepper. Simmer for 15 minutes. Meanwhile, brown snipe on all sides in remaining butter; then add sauce. Turn snipe breast down in the sauce and simmer from 20 to 25 minutes. Put a snipe in each roll cavity and ladle on the sauce.

MAKES 8 stuffed rolls.

SMALL BIRD EXTRAS

The following recipes use any of the small edible birds, including some that are not thought of as game birds. While the "4 and 20 blackbirds" in a pie are familiar in the nursery, adults rarely think of blackbirds as food. Nor does one think of eating thrushes or larks, although they and many others are edible and are eaten abroad. Of course, few of these species are legal game here, but any small, legal birds may be used.

POLISH CHAUD-FROID OF SMALL BIRDS

12 small birds with hearts, livers, gizzards
salt
¼ lb. calf's liver
1 lb. veal or pork
¼ lb. salt pork (optional)
3 or 4 dried mushrooms
1 onion, sliced
1 bay leaf
10 whole peppercorns
10 juniper berries
¼ cup chicken bouillon
¼ cup Madeira
pinch of ground juniper berries
½ tsp. salt
⅛ tsp. pepper
diced bacon
carrots, celery, and onions, sliced
1 envelope unflavored gelatin
½ cup cold water
1 cup hot water
1 bouillon cube
1 tbsp. cornstarch

Skin birds; remove backbones. Sprinkle with salt inside and out. Return each heart and liver to cavity before stuffing. Braise calf's liver, veal or pork, salt pork, bird gizzards, and dried mushrooms in very little water (just enough to cover bottom of pot), topped with the sliced onion, bay leaf, peppercorns, and juniper, until liver is tender, about 10 minutes; then remove liver. Cook remainder for 10 minutes more. Discard bay leaf and peppercorns.

Remove mushrooms and grind remainder through the fine blade of a meat grinder. Dice mushrooms and add to ground mixture. Add 2 tablespoons of the bouillon, the wine, and a pinch of ground juniper berries. Season with salt and pepper to taste, and mix. Use to stuff birds, reserving part for topping. Skewer birds, roll in oiled paper, and arrange in a pan lined with diced bacon and sliced raw vegetables. Cover with oiled paper and sprinkle with remaining bouillon. Roast at 450° for 30 minutes.

Meanwhile, make aspic: soften gelatin in cold water, then dissolve in hot water with bouillon cube and cornstarch. Chill and let thicken until syrupy. Let birds cool, and remove oiled paper. As smoothly as possible, spread birds with remaining stuffing. Dip each one into syrupy aspic, chill, and let aspic gel. Dip several times to build up aspic layers, chilling each time. Serve on thin, dry toast with tartar sauce.

SERVES 4.

POLISH SNIPE

3 birds per person, with livers   butter
bacon or salt-pork slices   toast
salt

Clean birds, reserve livers, and return each liver to cavity. Truss. Wrap with bacon or a thin slice of salt pork and tie. Sprinkle with salt and roast in a shallow pan or on a spit at high heat (450° in oven) for 20 to 25 minutes, basting with melted butter. Serve on toast.

POLISH BIRDS IN WINE

6 to 8 birds   ½ cup dry white wine
bacon slices   6 juniper berries
½ cup strong bouillon

Prepare birds as in recipe for Polish Snipe. Arrange closely in a casserole and simmer, covered, until bacon begins to brown. Add bouillon, dry white wine, and juniper berries. Simmer until birds are tender, about 30 minutes more.

SERVE 1 or 2 birds per person.

NEW ENGLAND BROILED BIRDS

4 or more small quail, snipe, or
    woodcock, split along the
    backbone
½ lb. butter, softened
2 tbsps. flour seasoned with ½ tsp.
    salt and ¼ tsp. pepper

4 strips bacon
½ cup brown gravy
2 tbsps. rhubarb jam or currant
    jelly
1 tbsp. minced parsley
2 tbsps. brandy

Rub birds with half of the soft butter and dust with seasoned flour. Put birds on a broiler rack and top each with a bacon strip. Broil for 15 to 20 minutes, according to size, turning at 3- to 5-minute intervals. Remove birds and keep warm. Blend remainder of seasoned flour with gravy, jam, and remaining butter; add mixture to pan drippings and stir well. Add parsley, mix, and heat gently. Pour brandy, heated, over birds and ignite. Let flames die out; serve birds on toast with sauce on the side.

SERVES 4 as an appetizer.

NEW ENGLAND ROAST BIRDS

4 or more small birds, split along
    the backbone and trussed
2 tbsps. flour seasoned with ½ tsp.
    salt and ¼ tsp. pepper

½ lb. sweet butter, melted and hot
1 tbsp. minced chives
½ tsp. seasoned salt
½ tsp. white pepper

Dust birds with seasoned flour and put in a baking pan. Cover with a double thickness of cheesecloth wrung out in water. Pour on the hot melted butter, and bake at 325° for 20 to 30 minutes. Increase temperature to 425° and bake for an additional 7 minutes. Add chives, seasoned salt, and pepper to the sauce just before serving.

SERVES 4 as an appetizer.

CANADIAN UPLAND FRICASSEE

3½ to 4 lbs. plump young small
    birds, giblets reserved and
    chopped
6 slices bacon, diced

2 tbsps. flour
1 cup dry red wine
1 cup boiling water
½ to 1 tbsp. mild paprika

Cook bacon bits until crisp; remove from skillet. Dredge birds with flour and brown in bacon fat. Add wine, water, and paprika, cover, and simmer slowly for 1 to 1½ hours, or until very tender.

SERVES 4.

BAYOU BLACKBIRD JAMBALAYA

30 blackbirds	salt and pepper
1½ lbs. pork sausage	4 cups water
1 large onion, chopped	2 cups raw rice
1 large green pepper, chopped	1 tbsp. green onion tops
1 cup chopped celery	1 tbsp. minced parsley

Brown birds and sausage in a Dutch oven; cook until birds are tender. Add onion, green pepper, and celery, and cook until onion browns slightly. Add salt and pepper to taste, then the water. Bring to a boil and add rice; be sure there is sufficient liquid to cook rice. Cover tightly and cook for about 40 minutes. Just before serving stir in onion tops and parsley.

SERVES 6.

WATERFOWL

Geese and ducks are handled in the field exactly as are other game birds; clean and cool as quickly as possible. Wing feathers, particularly of geese, are tough to pull out. The easiest way is to use pliers.

Hand plucking goose or duck down can be done if you'd like to preserve the down. Down is a valuable by-product but it is difficult to handle. It floats and flies all over the place, getting into your nose and hair, not to mention cracks and crevices. If you pluck the down, do it into a deep enough braced bag so that the whole bird is inside the bag.

The paraffin method of removing down and pinfeathers must be done at home. To paraffin a duck, melt 3 cakes (4 ounces each) of paraffin in 6 quarts of 160° water. (A goose requires proportionally more paraffin and water.) Dip the rough-plucked duck into the liquid, pull it out and let it dry. When the coating has hardened it can be peeled off, taking with it the pinfeathers and down. Depending on how complete the rough plucking was, you may have to dip a bird several times to build up a heavy enough layer of paraffin. Because of the size of a goose, most people generally pour the hot liquid over the bird, rather than dipping the bird into it.

It is true that leaving the skin on any game bird makes it moister for eating, yet many members of the duck family *should* be skinned. These are the fish-eating ducks. The fish flavor gets into the skin and fat and makes it quite unsavory. To skin a duck, tie it at the neck and hang it from a handy point. Slit the breast skin and peel off the skin with the feathers.

Geese and ducks are traditionally deluxe eating, and the wild breeds are favored over the domestic by many discriminating diners. Whether it is the restrictive living that the domestic bird is subjected to or the generous feeding, it is a fact that domestic ducks and geese are not only considerably fatter than their wild counterparts but frequently unpleasantly so. To eliminate excessive body fat, particularly from domestic geese, put the bird, at room temperature, into a 400° oven for 20 minutes; this should be long enough to soften the body fat and it can be drained off and pulled out of the cavity. But it will be rare indeed for you to have to remove fat from a wild bird.

In addition to the breastbone test, there is another way to tell if you have a young goose or duck—at least some of the time. In the young of both species, before they have their full adult plumage, the outermost tips of their tail feathers end in a V-shaped notch. During their first fall, these feathers are moulted one by one, being replaced by feathers with neatly rounded or pointed tips. The hunter who takes Tail End Charlie from a flight (rather than the wise *old*—emphasis on old—leader) is much more likely to bag a young bird, even though all its feathers may have been moulted, particularly if taken late in the season.

The waterfowl family consists of five subfamilies, numbering about 200 species including the mergansers (the fish-eating ducks), river and pond ducks, sea and bay ducks, geese and swans.

The mergansers include the American or goosander, the red-breasted, and the hooded. The river and pond ducks are the mallard, black or dusty, gadwall or gray, baldpate or widgeon, green-winged and blue-winged teal, shoveler, pintail, and wood. The sea and bay ducks are the redhead, canvasback, greater scaup or broadbill, lesser scaup or creek broadbill, ring-necked, golden-eye or whistler, Barrow's goldeneye, bufflehead or butterball, old-squaw or southerly, harlequin, American eider, American scoter or black coot, white-winged coot, surf scoter, and ruddy.

The goose family includes (although not all of them are legal in all flyways) the white-fronted, snow, lesser snow, Canada or wild, brant, and black brant.

The rail and coot family, popular gunners' targets in marshy areas, are also included in this section. The crane family, too, is part of the overall marsh-area picture, but these are legal game in very few areas. Texas friends say that the sandhill is as delicious roasted as a turkey, although I have not had the chance to try it. I understand it must be cooked using a moist method.

There are two species of the order Limicolae, the snipe and the woodcock, which, according to some experts, are technically shore birds. While this may be true, many consider the woodcock an upland bird because that is where it is hunted. Recipes for snipe and woodcock are in the section on upland birds.

GEESE

Geese range in size from the Ross, which will weigh around 3 pounds, through the brant (to 5 pounds) to the choicest Canada goose, which will run around 9 pounds for an adult male. Ducks are not only smaller, but have a relatively wider range of sizes. The European teal will go about 10 ounces, the most popular mallard about 2½ pounds, and the largest, the Pacific eider, about 5½ pounds.

Whatever waterfowl your hunter comes home with, the meat is dark, rich, and flavorful. This is one meat that should be served just as rare as your family will allow, even bloody rare. Older birds benefit from marinating overnight or for 24 hours to tenderize. Use red wine or a marinade that will blend with the final dish. Old birds, even though marinated, should have moist cooking, but they still can be roasted. Put about 1 cup of water in the roaster to be sure there is steam to moisten the bird.

As a general rule, waterfowl should be at room temperature when put into the oven. If the oven is preheated to 500°, a 6-pound goose will take 1 hour and 10 minutes or less; a mallard cooks for

20 minutes for very rare, 30 for medium rare. (These times are for unstuffed birds.) Serve hot or cold, with Lemon Butter.

ROAST GOOSE

1 goose, 6 to 8 lbs., cleaned
lemon juice
salt and pepper

wild-rice or other stuffing
chicken stock

Sprinkle goose with lemon juice (omit lemon if goose has been marinated); dust with salt and pepper inside and out. Stuff with moist wild-rice stuffing, or any moist stuffing of your choice, and put on a rack into a 325° oven. Cook for approximately 25 minutes per pound, basting with seasoned chicken stock until done.
SERVES 8.

SOUR GOOSE

1 goose, 6 to 8 lbs., cleaned
salt and pepper
Apple-Raisin Stuffing, or chopped
    unpeeled apples and pitted
    prunes, plumped in hot water
    for 10 to 15 minutes
vinegar

Rub bird inside and out with salt and pepper. Stuff with Apple-Raisin Stuffing, or fill cavity with apples and prunes. Put on a rack and roast in a slow oven (325°) for about 25 minutes per pound. If the skin seems fatty, prick in several places with a fork to drain off skin fat and pour off fat as it accumulates in the pan. Toward the end of roasting time, baste with pan drippings with a dash of vinegar to brown.
SERVES 8.

BRAISED GOOSE

1 goose, 6 to 8 lbs., cleaned
salt
North Dakota Stuffing
2 bacon slices
1 onion, chopped

1 cup dry white wine
1 tbsp. butter
paprika
freshly ground pepper

Rub cavity with salt. Stuff with North Dakota Stuffing or one of your choice. Put bacon in the bottom of a heavy casserole large enough to hold goose. Add onion, white wine, and 1 tablespoon butter in small pieces. Put goose on top; sprinkle with salt, paprika, and a bit of freshly ground pepper. Cover, and put into 375° oven for 1¼ hours for 6-pound goose. Remove cover and turn up heat to 400°; cook until nicely browned, or until juices run clear from fork test, approximately 20 minutes more.

SERVES 8.

CANADIAN ROAST GOOSE

1 older goose, 6 to 8 lbs., prepared for roasting	1 tsp. garlic salt
	1 tsp. onion salt
1 cup chopped celery	½ tsp. ground cloves
1 cup chopped onion	¼ tsp. white pepper
1 small bay leaf	choice of stuffing
1 tsp. celery salt	

Bring the goose to a boil in water to cover with the celery, onion, and bay leaf, and simmer, covered for 1 hour. Discard bay leaf and again simmer, covered, for 1 hour. Drain bird well and cool enough to handle. Mix celery, garlic, and onion salts, ground cloves, and pepper. Rub well into bird inside and out. Loosely stuff with your choice of stuffing, and truss well. Roast at 350° for 2½ to 3½ hours, until goose tests done. Make Brown Gravy.

SERVES 8.

NEW ENGLAND HOLIDAY GOOSE

1 goose, 6 to 8 lbs., cleaned
Prune Stuffing
salt and pepper

Wash goose thoroughly and sprinkle inside well with salt and pepper. Stuff lightly and truss; prick skin well with a fork. Bake at 325°, uncovered, for 2¾ to 3 hours, or until tender.

SERVES 8.

BAYOU ROAST GOOSE

1 goose, 6 to 8 lbs., giblets reserved	1¼ tsps. salt
	1 onion, chopped
garlic salt	4 tbsps. flour
paprika	1 cup sour cream
1 carrot, chopped	4 oz. canned mushrooms
1½ celery ribs, chopped	

Wipe goose as dry as possible inside and out with paper towels. Season with garlic salt and paprika. Put on a rack in a shallow baking pan and roast, uncovered, at 325° for 1 hour, or until goose is browned and fat is rendered. Pour off liquid fat, reserving 3 tablespoons. Meanwhile, simmer goose giblets, neck, and wing tips in water to cover with carrot, celery, and 1 teaspoon salt. In reserved 3 tablespoons of goose fat cook the onion soft and yellow; stir in 2 tablespoons of the flour, then blend in liquid from the giblets. If necessary, add water to make 1 cup. Stir remaining 2 tablespoons flour into sour cream and then blend into gravy; season with remaining salt, or to taste. Put goose back into roaster and pour gravy and mushrooms over it. Cover roaster and roast for another 2 hours.

SERVES 6 to 8.

OREGON ROAST YOUNG GOOSE

1 young 4-lb. goose, cleaned	½ tsp. pepper
stuffing of your choice	2 tbsps. dried thyme
2 cups water	2 cubes vegetable extract
1 tsp. salt	

Stuff goose loosely and truss. Put trussed goose on a rack in a Dutch oven or self-basting roaster with remaining ingredients. Put into a preheated 275° oven for 30 minutes per pound of unstuffed weight. As soon as the bird tests done, raise temperature to 400°, and uncover bird to brown. Make a gravy of the giblets in pan juices while keeping bird warm.

SERVES 2 to 4.

NEW ENGLAND ROAST YOUNG GOOSE

Hang a young goose for 2 to 5 days; then clean. Loosely stuff with potato stuffing. Put bird on a rack in a roaster with small amount of water in the bottom. Cover and cook on top of the stove, water simmering, for 1 hour. Lay strips of bacon over the top of the bird. Roast, uncovered, at 475° until bird is browned and tender, basting every 15 minutes.

POLISH ROAST GOOSE OR DUCK

cleaned goose or ducks (allow
  1 lb. per person)
boiling marinade (perhaps Beer
  Bird Marinade)
salt
1 small onion per bird

½ apple per bird
1 tbsp. (or 1 tsp. per duck)
  marjoram, crushed
larding salt pork
3 tbsps. butter, melted and mixed
  with ½ cup cold water

Pour boiling marinade over the bird(s); when cool enough to handle wrap in cheesecloth soaked in marinade. Refrigerate for 2 days. Salt birds well 1 hour before cooking. Put 1 onion and ½ apple in each cavity (to be discarded before serving). Rub skin with marjoram and lay a strip of larding salt pork over the breast-bone. Roast at 300°, basting with butter-water mixture every 10 to 15 minutes. Roast at 18 to 20 minutes per pound for a large goose, 15 to 20 minutes per pound for ducks (approximately 2 hours for a goose, 30 minutes for a duck). Increase heat to 400° toward the end of cooking time to crisp.

POLISH GOOSE OR DUCK CASSEROLE

cleaned goose or ducks (allow
  1 lb. per person)
2 to 3 cups marinade (perhaps
  Cooked Marinade)
1 tbsp. crushed juniper berries
salt

3 tbsps. butter
1 cup bouillon
1 tbsp. drained capers
6 fresh mushrooms, sliced
1 cup sour cream
1 tsp. flour

Marinate the bird(s), refrigerated, for 2 days. Drain and reserve marinade. Wipe the bird(s) dry, and rub well with juniper and salt 1 hour before cooking. Brown quickly in butter in a heavy skillet. Cut bird(s) into serving pieces and arrange in a casserole. Pour on butter in which birds were browned. Mix bouillon, 1 cup of the marinade, the capers and mushrooms, and pour on. Simmer, covered, for 1 to 1½ hours, or until tender. Mix sour cream and flour smoothly, add to dish, and allow to bubble up briefly.

Variation

Proceed as above, but add a dash each of dried thyme and grated nutmeg and 1 small bay leaf to the cooking liquid. Instead of using sour cream, blend 1 tablespoon of melted butter, 2 teaspoons flour, and 3 ounces of Madeira or sherry. At the same time, add 12 to 16 pitted ripe olives, and heat just until the liquid bubbles.

WILD GOOSE CASSOULET

1 goose, 8 lbs., cut into 8 to 10
  pieces
4 cups dried white navy beans
¼ lb. Italian salami, cut into
  ¼-inch cubes
3 cups dry white wine
4 tomatoes, peeled, seeded, and
  chopped
4 large onions, chopped

4 peppercorns
2 tsps. chopped parsley
¼ tsp. dried rosemary
2 garlic cloves, minced
1 bay leaf
salt and pepper
½ cup olive oil
6 garlic sausages
1 cup bread crumbs

Soak beans in water to cover for at least 10 hours. Drain, discarding any beans that float on the surface. Put into a large, lidded, earthenware casserole. Add salami, 1 cup wine, the tomatoes, onions, peppercorns, parsley, rosemary, garlic, bay leaf, and enough water to cover. Cover the casserole tightly and bake at 200° to 225° for 6 hours, adding more water if needed.

Rub goose pieces with salt and pepper. Heat oil to sizzling, add the goose, and brown lightly on all sides. Reduce the heat, add 2 cups wine and simmer, covered, for 30 minutes. Stir goose and sauce carefully into bean casserole. In another skillet sauté garlic sausages until well browned; remove, reserving fat. Stir sausages into casserole carefully; cover and bake in 250° oven for 1½ hours. Sauté bread crumbs in sausage fat and sprinkle over top of casserole. Bake, uncovered, for 10 minutes to brown crumbs.

SERVES 14 to 16.

NEW ENGLAND GOOSE AND BEANS

1 old Canada goose, 6 to 8 lbs.
juice of 1 lemon

4 cups dried pea beans, soaked
  overnight
½ lb. salt pork, diced

Remove breast meat and cut into finger strips. Simmer strips in water to cover with lemon juice for 30 minutes; drain. Put strips in bean pot with drained pea beans and salt pork. Bake in slowest oven for 8 hours.

SERVES 8.

DUCKS

Mallards are the choice of most duck fans, and mallard (raised for market) is frequently the duck served in restaurants. Unless specified otherwise, assume mallard or a comparable duck in the following recipes. Puddler ducks—mallards, blacks, shovelers, woodies, and teals—are best for roasting. Diving ducks such as redheads, canvasbacks, and scaup are stronger flavored and are usually preferred in dishes calling for heavier seasoning.

SMALL DUCK TIMETABLE

Smaller ducks can be roasted with skin on and require a shorter cooking time. Rub with softened butter, and season. Put a cut-up apple in the cavity after salting and peppering if desired. Roast unskinned in a 400° oven.

Teal: 7½ minutes for rare, 10 for medium
Ruddy: 9 minutes for rare, 12 for medium
Butterball: 9 minutes for rare, 12 for medium

ROAST MALLARD

Stuff with Orangeman's Stuffing (or your choice of moist stuffing) and roast at 350° for 20 to 25 minutes per pound, basting with pan drippings.

BROILED MALLARD

Split young birds, butter well, and rub with salt, pepper, and a pinch of dried thyme. Broil, basting once or twice with butter, for 8 to 10 minutes per side; or marinate older birds in Oriental Marinade for 4 to 12 hours, turning often. Broil as above, basting occasionally with the marinade.

SOUTHERN MALLARD EN DAUBE

4 mallards
chicken stock or water
salt
2 parsley sprigs
12 peppercorns, crushed
1 celery rib, cut into 1-inch lengths
1 onion, quartered
2 slices lemon

1 carrot, quartered
1 navel orange, unpeeled and
   sliced thin
1 tsp. Worcestershire sauce
dash of Tabasco
lemon juice
2 envelopes unflavored gelatin
½ cup cold water

Simmer the birds until fork tender in chicken stock or water to cover with a dash of salt, parsley sprigs, peppercorns, celery, onion, lemon slices, and carrot. Simmer for 45 minutes to 1 hour. Remove ducks and cool; reserve stock. When cool enough to handle, skin and bone. Arrange meat in a shallow bowl and arrange around it paper-thin slices of navel orange. Strain stock and reserve 2 cups; skim off all fat and season with Worcestershire sauce, Tabasco, and a little lemon juice. Bring this to a boil while soaking gelatin in cold water, then dissolve gelatin over hot water. Stir dissolved gelatin into seasoned stock and pour over meat. Refrigerate until set. Slice to serve.

SERVES 4 to 6.

MALLARDS IN CREAM

2 or 3 birds, 2 lbs. each	light cream
salt	3 slices rye bread, cubed
flour	2 tbsps. peach preserves
½ cup butter	

Sprinkle birds inside and out with salt, and dust outside with flour. Brown on all sides in butter in a Dutch oven. Add enough boiling light cream to cover ducks and simmer, covered, for 45 minutes, or until almost tender. Uncover and simmer for 20 minutes more. Remove ducks and keep warm. Add cubed bread to pan juices and cook, stirring, until thickened. Add peach preserves and stir in well. Serve carved duck with some of the sauce; pass the rest separately.

SERVES 2 or 3.

CAJUN WILD DUCK

2 mallards prepared for stuffing	1 cup fresh bread crumbs
butter	1 tsp. pepper
1 onion, sliced thin	¾ tsp. salt
¾ cup minced celery	¼ cup Armagnac
¼ cup minced parsley	½ cup claret
18 to 20 pitted ripe olives	½ cup duck or chicken stock
2 garlic cloves, minced	

Melt 4 tablespoons butter and sauté onion, celery, parsley, olives, and garlic, until onion is soft. Stir in bread crumbs, pepper, salt, and Armagnac; use mixture to stuff birds. Rub birds well with butter and put on a rack in a roaster with claret and boiling stock. Roast at 400°, basting every few minutes, for 30 minutes. If you want them better done, cook for an additional 10 minutes, basting. Serve hot or cold: if cold, remove stuffing and serve it on the side.

SERVES 2.

MALLARDS ZINFANDEL

1 or 2 mallard breasts per person, or 2 or 3 teal-sized duck breasts each
butter

salt and pepper
1 red onion, sliced thin
Zinfandel wine
Canadian bacon slices

Put breasts skin side up in a shallow baking dish. Dot generously with butter, and sprinkle with salt and pepper. Put red onion rings on top. Add enough Zinfandel wine to come halfway up breasts. Bake at 400° for 10 to 15 minutes for mallards, less for smaller birds. Cover breasts completely with thin slices of Canadian bacon and return to the oven for 10 to 15 minutes more. This is for pink duck; cook longer for medium.

BIRD PÂTÉ

1 lb. boned duck, pheasant, or other game bird, with livers, cut into slices or cubed
2 truffles or mushrooms, coarsely chopped
¼ cup Cognac
salt and pepper
2 tbsps. butter
½ cup minced shallots or onions
¾ lb. lean veal, ground
¾ lb. lean pork, ground

½ lb. pork fatback, ground
½ cup pistachios or pine nuts
½ cup Madeira or Cognac
2 eggs
½ tsp. ground thyme
½ tsp. ground allspice
1 garlic clove, mashed
4 (approx.) thin slices of pork fatback or bacon
1 bay leaf

Combine game meat, truffles, and ¼ cup Cognac, dust with salt and pepper, and refrigerate for at least 1 hour. Melt butter and cook the shallots in it for about 5 minutes. In a bowl, combine shallots with ground meats, fatback, nuts, wine or more Cognac, eggs, thyme, allspice, and garlic. Drain liquid from game, and add it to meat mixture. Beat smooth with a wooden spoon. Simmer sliced pork fatback or bacon in water for 5 minutes and dry between paper towels; line bottom and sides of 2-quart mold with some of the blanched fatback; reserve some for the top. Divide ground meat mix into thirds. Put one-third in prepared mold, and cover with half of the marinated game. Top with more ground meat, then rest of game, then remainder of ground meat. Put the bay leaf on top and cover with rest of blanched fatback. Cover with foil. Set in a pan with boiling water that comes halfway up the sides. Bake at 325° for 1½ hours, or until pâté has shrunk slightly from sides. Remove from oven but keep in hot water pan. Weight top of the pâté and let it cool completely before removing from the baking dish.

SERVES about 15.

BAYOU DUCK AND OYSTER GUMBO

1 duck, cut into 6 to 8 pieces	salt and pepper
1 tbsp. butter	2 qts. (approx.) water
2 tbsps. flour	24 oysters
1 large onion, minced	

Make a roux of melted butter and flour and brown. Add onion and cook until tender. Season meat with salt and pepper and add to onion. Let meat fry in the roux until duck blood disappears. Add water and boil slowly until meat is very tender. Add oysters with their liquid and cook only long enough to curl the oyster edges. Adjust seasoning if needed.

SERVES 4 to 6.

DUCK BURGUNDY

2 ducks, 2 lbs. each	½ garlic clove, minced
2 oranges, peeled and sliced	salad or olive oil
2 apples, peeled, cored, and sliced	salt and pepper
2 onions, chopped	1 cup red Burgundy wine
3 celery ribs, chopped	

Combine orange and apple slices, onions, celery, and garlic for the stuffing. Rub duck breasts with oil; sprinkle with salt and pepper. Put birds in a roasting pan and cook at 450° for about 45 minutes, or until tender and brown, basting frequently with wine. Use pan juices for gravy.

SERVES 2 to 4.

FLORIDA DUCK

2 ducks, 2 to 2½ lbs. each	¾ tsp. dry mustard
6 bacon slices	½ tsp. ground ginger
6 oz. orange-juice concentrate, thawed and undiluted	½ tsp. salt
	1 tbsp. cornstarch
1 garlic clove, cut into halves	1 cup water

Put ducks, breast up, in a shallow roasting pan. Lay strips of bacon over breasts and roast at 450° for 20 to 25 minutes. Meanwhile, combine orange-juice concentrate, garlic, mustard, ginger, and salt, and heat to boiling. During last 10 minutes of roasting, remove bacon and brush sauce generously over birds. Mix cornstarch and a little of the water and stir into remaining sauce; add remaining water. Stir over low heat until thickened. Serve separately with the duck.

SERVES 2 to 4.

ALLEGHENY BREADED DUCKS

2 young ducks, cut into serving pieces
½ cup flour seasoned with ½ tsp. salt and ¼ tsp. pepper
1 egg, beaten with 1 tbsp. cold water
1 cup fine crumbs seasoned with ¼ tsp. ground sage
fat for browning

Roll bird pieces in seasoned flour, then dip into beaten egg, then dredge with crumbs. Brown completely in hot fat. Reduce heat and cook, uncovered, until done, turning carefully as needed.

SERVES 4 to 6.

HUNTER'S POINT BARBECUED DUCK

2 ducks, 3 lbs. each
4 tsps. lemon juice
1 tsp. Worcestershire sauce
2 tbsps. catsup
1 tbsp. melted butter
1 tsp. salt
1 tsp. paprika

Put birds on a rack in a roaster. Combine remaining ingredients and use as basting sauce. Roast birds at 375° for 1 to 1½ hours, basting every 15 minutes.

SERVES 4 to 6.

SUPREME ROAST DUCK

Brush each mallard-sized duck with mixture of ¼ cup sherry, 1 tablespoon Worcestershire sauce, and 1 teaspoon salt. Let stand at room temperature for 4 hours. Roast on a rack at 350° for 1 to 1½ hours, basting every 15 minutes with melted sweet butter.

NEW ORLEANS DUCK JAMBALAYA

2 young 2-lb. ducks, cut into
    serving pieces
1 tbsp. bacon drippings
½ cup flour seasoned with
    ½ tsp. salt, ¼ tsp. pepper, and
    1 tsp. ground ginger
1 tbsp. lard
3 tbsps. butter

1 medium-sized onion, sliced
1 lb. fresh mushrooms, sliced
1½ cups raw rice
1 cup diced cooked ham
⅛ tsp. crushed dried rosemary
⅛ tsp. dried savory
2 cups rosé wine

Grease birds with bacon drippings, and dust with seasoned flour. Melt lard and butter and brown ducks in this. Remove ducks and sauté onion and mushrooms in same skillet. Butter a casserole and put in the rice. Add pieces of duck, ham, drained mushrooms, and onion. Season with rosemary and savory; pour on the wine. (Add enough more to cover, if needed.) Cover dish tightly and bake at 350°, without removing lid, for 2¼ to 2½ hours.

SERVES 2 to 4.

ORIENTAL GINGERED DUCK

meat from 3 to 4 lbs. young duck,
    cut into 1½-inch cubes, skin
    left on
2 eggs, lightly beaten
¾ cup flour
2 tbsps. water
½ tsp. salt
fat for deep-frying

¾ cup water, boiling
½ cup cider vinegar
½ cup sugar
1 tbsp. cornstarch
1 tbsp. soy sauce
¼ cup cold water
½ cup pickled ginger root, sliced

Make a frying batter of eggs, flour, water, and salt. Stir until smooth. Dip duck cubes into batter and fry, a few at a time, in deep fat heated to 350° to 365°, until golden brown. Drain on paper towels; put into a warm dish. Make a hot sauce with boiling water, cider vinegar, and sugar, and stir until dissolved. Make a smooth mixture of the cornstarch and soy sauce with cold water, and stir into vinegar-sugar mixture. Cook, stirring, over low heat until thickened. Add the ginger root, stir well, heat, and pour over fried duck.

SERVES 6.

CANVASBACK ITALIENNE (good for any badly shot-up duck)

2 cups duck, skinned and cut into
    bite-sized pieces
flour
salt and pepper
butter

1 cup tomato sauce
½ cup beer
1 onion, diced
½ tsp. dried oregano

Sprinkle meat with flour, salt and pepper, and sauté lightly in butter. Put meat into a Dutch oven and add tomato sauce, beer, onion, and oregano. Cover and cook over low heat until tender, which will of course depend on age of bird—anywhere from 1 to 2 hours. Serve on buttered noodles with Parmesan cheese and parsley.

SERVES 2 to 3.

KEYS-STYLE DUCKS

2 black ducks, 2½ lbs. each
salt and pepper
6 medium-sized onions, chopped
3 tbsps. bacon fat

3 celery ribs, diced
2 apples, pared, cored, and cubed
3 or 4 slices bread, torn apart
8 crackers, crushed

Season birds generously with salt and pepper, and let stand while making stuffing. Simmer onions in bacon fat until soft. Add celery, apples, bread, and crackers with barely enough water to moisten and hold together. Stuff into birds loosely and truss. Put in a heavy Dutch oven with ¼ inch of water. Put uncovered into hottest oven for 15 minutes; reduce heat to 300°, cover, and cook for about 1 hour, until tender, basting every 15 minutes.

SERVES 2 to 4.

STEWED BUFFLEHEADS

2 buffleheads, split
¼ cup seasoned flour
¼ tsp. celery salt

¼ lb. sweet butter
1 cup (approx.) boiling water
1 tsp. dried oregano

Dust meat with seasoned flour, then with celery salt. Brown meat thoroughly in butter in a Dutch oven, about 5 minutes per side. Add water to come up ½ inch in the pot, add oregano, and cover. Simmer until well done, about 1½ hours, checking water level and adding more as needed. Add seasoned flour to thicken gravy as desired.

SERVES 4.

Some waterfowl should always be skinned. This includes old-squaw, mergansers, coot, and mud hens. These are fish eaters and it can easily be proven at the table if you don't skin them.

The following recipe, the result of a very mixed bag of sea ducks—mergansers, old-squaw, and others that some think not worth eating—shows that even the fishiest duck is tasty when properly handled. In eating, you can tell that one piece is not the same as another when you try two different kinds, but they are all good.

MIXED DUCK BAG

duck breasts, boned and skinned, from sea ducks
seasoned flour
butter
cooking oil
dry white wine
dry red wine

Roll breasts in seasoned flour and shake off excess. Cook quickly to brown in half butter and half oil. Reduce heat and sprinkle on equal generous amounts of white and red wine—enough to cover the bottom of the skillet. Cover skillet and simmer until done, about 15 minutes.

NEW ENGLAND ROAST COOT

1 coot
1 slice salt pork
¼ cup heavy cream
¼ cup dry red wine

Discard wings and skin bird. Put in a covered dish in refrigerator overnight. Skewer a thin slice of salt pork over the breast and roast at 400° for 16 minutes. Make a sauce of the drippings in refrigerating dish, the pan juices, the heavy cream, and red wine in the top part of a double boiler over simmering water. Heat, stirring often. Do not let the sauce boil.

SERVES 1 or 2.

ALLEGHENY BAKED COOT

2 older birds, skinned, with wings removed
¼ lb. sweet butter
1 cup hot water
1 cube vegetable extract
1 tsp. paprika
½ tsp. salt
¼ tsp. pepper
½ cup plum jelly, slightly beaten

Put birds on a rack in a Dutch oven. Top with butter. Add hot water with vegetable extract cube. Bake, covered, at 350° for 2 hours. Remove cover, dust birds with paprika, season with salt and pepper, and spread with jelly. Bake, uncovered, for 30 minutes more, basting at least 3 times.

SERVES 2 to 4.

NEW ENGLAND FRIED COOT

2 coots, cut into serving pieces, skinned
½ cup flour seasoned with ½ tsp. salt and 1 tsp. paprika
3 tbsps. salt-pork drippings
1 tbsp. chopped onion

water
½ cup milk
duck giblets simmered in ½ cup seasoned duck or chicken stock until done; drained
1½ tbsps. sour cream

Dredge bird pieces with seasoned flour and brown in salt-pork drippings in a Dutch oven. Brown onion in drippings and remove. Put rack into Dutch oven, add water only to top of the rack and cover. Bake at 350° until tender, young birds 35 to 40 minutes, older birds 1 to 1¼ hours. Turn once and add more water if needed. Remove birds and keep them warm. To the pan, add browned onion, 2 tablespoons seasoned flour, the giblet stock, strained and heated, and the milk; stir until thickened. Season to taste with salt and pepper. Mince the giblets, and add to sauce with sour cream. Heat without letting sauce boil after adding sour cream.

SERVES 2.

SOUTHERN COOT BAKED WITH RICE

1 coot, cut into serving pieces, skinned
4 tbsps. flour seasoned with ½ tsp. salt and ¼ tsp. pepper
5½ tbsps. sweet butter
1 medium-sized onion, minced
1 tbsp. minced green pepper

¾ cup raw rice
2½ cups tomato juice
2 tbsps. catsup
1 tsp. ground sage
dash of cayenne
½ tsp. ground bay leaf

Dredge bird with seasoned flour; brown in melted butter. Remove to a heated casserole. Fry onion, green pepper, and rice in remaining butter for about 15 minutes. Add tomato juice, catsup, sage, cayenne, and bay leaf; bring to a boil and simmer for 10 minutes.

Pour over bird. Cover casserole and bake at 350° for 1½ hours, stirring twice and adding more liquid if needed.

SERVES 1.

DUCK STOCK

carcass from 5-lb. duck(s), broken
  up
1 onion, in chunks
2 parsley sprigs

1 carrot, quartered
1 celery rib with leaves
dash of salt
12 peppercorns

Combine all in a large kettle and add water to cover. Bring to a boil and simmer, loosely covered, for 1 hour. Strain and reduce liquid by boiling to 2 cups.

MAKES 2 cups.

DUCK SOUP

2 or 3 duck carcasses, with some
  meat attached
1 cup chopped celery
1 onion, chopped
½ cup chopped parsley

6 cups water
¼ cup wild rice
½ tsp. sugar
salt and pepper

Combine all ingredients, bring to a boil, reduce heat, and simmer, covered, for 2 hours. Remove meat from bones and return meat scraps to soup. Reheat to serving temperature.

SERVES 6 to 8.

WATERFOWL LEFTOVERS

SALMI OF DUCK

1 cold roast mallard, boned and
  cut into bite-sized pieces
duck frame and trimmings
1 small onion
2 sprigs fresh thyme
1 bay leaf
½ tsp. salt

¼ tsp. pepper
flour
butter
6 oz. claret
1 tsp. orange juice
1 tsp. lemon juice

Make a duck stock with frame and trimmings, onion, thyme, bay leaf, salt, pepper, and enough water to cover. Simmer at least 1 hour. Strain stock and measure. For each cup of stock, blend 2 tablespoons flour with 2 tablespoons butter, and brown in a heavy pot. Add strained stock and cook, stirring, until thickened. Add duck meat, claret, orange juice, and lemon juice. Simmer for 15 minutes.

MAKES 3 to 4 cups.

CANADIAN DUCK WITH RED WINE

1 cold roast duck, cut into serving pieces
2 tbsps. butter
1 medium-sized onion, chopped
2 tbsps. flour
2 cups condensed chicken consommé
juice of 1 orange
grated rind of 1 orange
¼ cup dry red wine
salt and pepper

Melt butter and soften onion in it. Stir in the flour and brown it. Add consommé and simmer for 10 minutes. Add orange juice and grated rind, wine and duck pieces. Season to taste and simmer gently for 30 minutes.

SERVES 2.

CANADIAN DUCK À LA HABITANT

2 cups cubed roast duck
2 tbsps. butter
1 tbsp. flour
2 tbsps. minced ham
2 tbsps. minced onion
2 tbsps. minced celery
2 tbsps. minced green pepper
2 tbsps. minced parsley
½ tsp. salt
¼ tsp. pepper
½ tsp. paprika
1 cup consommé
½ tsp. ground allspice
pinch of grated mace

Melt butter; mix flour in smoothly. Add ham, onion, celery, green pepper, parsley, salt, pepper, and paprika. Cook, stirring, for 2 minutes. Add consommé, allspice, and mace, and simmer for 1 hour. Strain, return to pot, and add duck meat. Cook slowly only long enough to heat meat through.

SERVES 4.

SAVANNAH LEFTOVER DUCK

2 cups diced roast duck
2 tbsps. butter
1 tbsp. flour
1 cup hot duck stock
½ cup diced Swiss cheese
¼ cup minced Italian salami
2 tbsps. each of minced ham, onion, parsley, celery, and green pepper
½ tsp. minced garlic
⅛ tsp. white pepper

Heat duck in butter; remove meat and keep hot. Blend flour and stock into butter and heat, stirring, until thickened. Add all ingredients except duck, stir well, and cook slowly over very low heat for 30 minutes, stirring from time to time. Add duck and heat only long enough to heat through.

SERVES 4.

BIRD VARIETY MEATS

While eggs are not a variety meat, and certainly I am *not* recommending robbing nests for them, if you have a commercial source nearby, or a friendly neighbor who may raise any of the birds in the game category, do try the eggs. Each one differs somewhat from the others—some stronger, some milder—but all that I've tried have been excellent. Quail eggs, should you have a source of them, are very small and make most polite bite-sized appetizers when pickled. Pheasant eggs are undoubtedly the easiest to come by and are, to my taste anyway, superior to chicken eggs, although smaller.

As with big game, the variety meats include the liver and heart. All bird livers are very similar to chicken livers and can be used in all the same ways. The famous *pâté de foie gras* of France is made from goose livers, from birds that are specially force-fed to enlarge the liver, but almost any pâté can be made from wild birds.

Pâtés need not be expensive or difficult to make. Perhaps the most familiar is the ubiquitous *pâté maison*, made to one individual cook's taste; no two cooks make it exactly the same way. Not only can the pâtés be made in various ways, they can also be served in different ways. Originally a pâté was most often served *en croûte* (in a crust), while a pâté served in a special covered dish in which it was cooked was called a "terrine" from its container. Pâté can also be coated with aspic, or can be served just plain for spreading on crackers or bread at a party. The following are just a few of the ways in which a pâté can be made. Note that the Basic Farce can use game meat *or* livers.

MY PÂTÉ MAISON

¼ lb. game-bird livers	1 tsp. dry mustard
½ cup rendered chicken fat or soft butter	⅛ tsp. ground cloves
¼ tsp. grated nutmeg	2 tbsps. minced onion

Simmer livers in water barely to cover for 15 to 20 minutes. Drain and grind through finest blade of a grinder. Beat in remaining ingredients. Pack into containers (I use miniature bread tins), and cover. Refrigerate, or freeze for up to 3 months. Dip briefly into hot water to slip out of containers.

MAKES 1 cup.

MY ALTERNATE PÂTÉ

1 lb. game-bird livers	½ tsp. salt
6 oz. butter	¼ tsp. pepper
1 large onion, chopped	¼ tsp. grated nutmeg
¼ lb. sautéed fresh mushrooms, or canned mushrooms	

Sauté livers in the butter until no longer pink, 4 to 6 minutes. Put into blender with remaining ingredients, and blend smooth. Can be frozen.

MAKES 2½ cups.

Variation

Sauté 2 garlic cloves with the livers, and add ½ tablespoon Worcestershire sauce and ⅓ cup dry sherry. Blend all until smooth.

Variation

Stir in 1 hard-cooked egg, sieved. If you prepare this variation, do not freeze the pâté.

MY NEIGHBOR'S PÂTÉ MAISON

1 lb. game bird livers	1 egg, beaten
½ lb. loose pork sausage	pinch of grated mace
½ cup minced fresh parsley	salt and pepper
½ cup minced celery leaves	bacon strips
2 onions, minced	

Put livers through the finest grinder blade. Mix with sausage, parsley, celery leaves, onions, egg, mace, and salt and pepper to taste. Sauté 4 strips of bacon until crisp, drain, and crumble fine; add to liver mix with bacon drippings. Pack into a loaf pan and cover top with several more strips of bacon. Bake at 300° for 2 hours; cool on a rack, then chill. Discard bacon strips after unmolding.

MAKES 4 cups.

PÂTÉ EN GELÉE

½ lb. game-bird livers	1 envelope unflavored gelatin
3 tbsps. brandy	1½ tsps. Worcestershire sauce
1 can (3 or 4 oz.) chopped mushrooms, liquid reserved	½ cup pitted ripe olives
	¼ cup minced parsley
1 can (10¾ oz.) condensed beef or chicken bouillon	¼ tsp. grated nutmeg

Combine brandy and mushroom liquid and add livers. Bring to a boil and cook rapidly until livers are done and liquid has evaporated, about 5 minutes. Remove from heat. Put ¼ cup bouillon into blender; sprinkle on gelatin and allow to soften. Heat ½ cup bouillon to a boil and add to blender. Cover and blend at low speed for 10 seconds, then at high speed for 20 seconds. Add remaining bouillon, mushrooms, Worcestershire, olives, parsley, and nutmeg. Cover and blend at high speed for 15 seconds. Pour into a small mold and chill until firm, several hours or overnight.

MAKES 2½ cups.

BASIC FARCE

1 lb. game-bird livers or meat,
    ground
1 lb. fresh pork fat, ground
1 lb. lean pork or boar, ground
1 lb. veal or antelope, ground
1 cup minced onion
½ cup sherry, Madeira, or port,
    or ¼ cup Cognac

3 eggs
¼ tsp. ground ginger
¼ tsp. ground cloves
¼ tsp. grated nutmeg
1 tbsp. salt
½ tsp. (scant) white pepper
3 or more garlic cloves

Cook onion in sherry until onion is soft and liquid evaporated. Mix with ground meats and remaining ingredients. Mix well. Use the mixture for the following recipes.

MAKES about 6 cups.

PÂTÉ BAKED IN TERRINE

1 recipe Basic Farce
1½ lbs. game meat or livers
    (optional)
1 cup pistachios, blanched, or
    almonds, slivered (optional)
¼ cup Cognac or sherry
    (optional)
pinch of ground ginger

pinch of ground cloves
pinch of grated nutmeg
dash of white pepper
unsalted fatback, sliced thin
bay leaf
sprig of fresh thyme, or pinch of
    dried

The Basic Farce can be cooked alone or it can be embellished with up to 1½ pounds of strips or diced game meat or livers. For strips, cut the meat ¼ to ¾ inch wide and thick, in 2- to 4-inch strips; for dice, make the pieces ¼ to ½ inch in size. Up to 1 cup blanched pistachios or slivered almonds can be added. Marinate the meat pieces in Cognac or sherry with ground ginger, cloves, and grated nutmeg, and a dash of white pepper, for 30 minutes. Farce plus meat pieces will equal about 9 cups.

Line the cooking pan or pans with fatback. Cut fatback ¼ inch thick, then pound thinner between sheets of wax paper. If you have to use salt pork, slice it ⅛ inch thick and soak in cold water for several hours to freshen. Bacon can also be used; about 1 pound will be needed for 9 cups of mixture. Line the pan with fat, allowing slices to hang over the edges. Press about one-third of the farce into the bottom of the pan; top with an attractive layer of half of the meat and nuts, then top with another third of the farce;

add another layer of meat and nuts, and top with remaining farce. Press each layer as flat and smooth as possible. Fold the fat slices over the top, covering the filling completely. Top with bay leaf and thyme, and cover with a double layer of foil and the pan lid, if available. Set filled mold(s) into larger pan with boiling water to come halfway up the side of the mold. Bake at 375° for 1½ to 2 hours, or until the fat that rises to the top is perfectly clear. A 5-cup loaf tin will take about 1½ hours. Leave mold in water pan and remove lid, if used. Weight top evenly, to make for easy slicing and compact texture, and allow to cool thoroughly. Serve from mold or turn out and slice, fat and all.

MAKES about 9 cups.

PÂTÉ IN ASPIC

1 recipe Pâté Baked in Terrine
2 cans (10¾ oz. each) condensed beef or chicken bouillon

⅓ cup sherry or Madeira
2 envelopes unflavored gelatin, softened in ⅓ cup water

Cook like Pâté in Terrine, but don't fill the mold(s) all the way up before baking. When pâté is baked and cooled, remove it from the mold and scrape away all fat. Wash cooking mold, rinse in cold water, and wipe dry. Make an aspic with condensed beef or chicken bouillon, sherry or Madeira, and gelatin softened in water; heat until gelatin is dissolved and cool until aspic begins to set. Pour about ½ inch of this aspic into original cooking mold and allow to set. Carefully place chilled, baked pâté on top, centering it in the mold. Pour on remaining aspic until it fills the sides and tops the pâté, preferably ½ inch deep. Allow aspic to set before slicing pâté.

MAKES about 9 cups.

PÂTÉ EN CROÛTE

Pâté is made in the same way as for Pâté in Terrine, but it is baked in a crust in a metal mold rather than in an earthenware or other pottery container, and served turned out of the mold. Puff paste, regular piecrust, or pâte brisée can be used. The best (because of pâté fat) is made by blending, with hands or pastry blender, ¼ pound butter (or half butter and half shortening) into 4 cups flour and 1 teaspoon salt. Gradually add enough cold water, about

½ cup, until dough holds together. Form into a ball and wrap in wax paper. Store in refrigerator for 2 to 8 hours. Roll out ⅛ to ¼ inch thick, and line a mold or pans with a sheet of the dough, pressing firmly to sides first. Cut a piece of dough to fit the bottom and press in, being sure to cover the side-bottom joint with dough; make sure that there are no holes in pastry. If mold has no bottom, as with a flan ring or special mold for this, put the mold on a baking sheet. Allow ¼ inch of pastry to hang over rim. Fill with farce and add meat and nuts. Moisten hanging edge of pastry and pinch on a pastry top. Cut off excess from the top edge; roll a rolling pin over it. Excess pastry can be cut into fancy shapes and used to decorate the top if desired. Brush top with slightly beaten egg. Make a hole in the top and insert a small ovenproof funnel or tube of foil. Bake at 375° until the fat in the funnel runs clear— 1½ to 2 hours. Cool. When pâté is completely cooled, aspic can be poured into the hole to fill up spaces left when meat shrinks. Unmold to serve.

Pâtés and terrines keep well if refrigerated. Terrines will keep for at least 2 weeks if they are removed from the molds, wiped of any juices that have jelled in cooling, and are then wrapped in foil or returned to washed terrines; these will freeze, although freezing changes the texture somewhat. If aspic is used, wait no more than 2 days before serving. *Pâté en croûte* will keep for a week or so, and can also be frozen. If I intend to freeze it, I use a standard pie dough made with lard and brushed with 1 egg lightly beaten with 1 tablespoon water.

MUSHROOM AND LIVER PÂTÉ

½ lb. livers
¼ lb. fresh mushrooms, chopped
3 tbsps. butter

½ tsp. garlic salt
¼ tsp. crumbled dried tarragon
1 tbsp. brandy or sherry

Sauté livers and mushrooms in 1 tablespoon butter with garlic salt and tarragon over medium heat for 10 minutes. Add brandy and cook for 2 minutes more. Purée in blender, or in a mortar with a pestle, mixing in 2 tablespoons softened butter, until smooth.

MAKES 2 cups.

GIBLET SOUP

giblets from 3 grouse, 2 pheasants,
   2 ducks, or 1 Canada goose
3 cans (10½ oz. each) condensed
   beef bouillon
2 medium-sized onions, minced

½ cup chopped celery
1½ carrots, chopped
⅓ cup cooked rice
½ cup dry red wine

Cover giblets with cold salted water and boil until very tender, 45 minutes to 1 hour. Cool in the broth, then strain, reserving the broth, and chop giblets fine. Add to bouillon with onions, celery, carrots, rice, and giblet stock, and simmer until vegetables are tender, about 20 minutes. Correct seasonings, add giblets and wine, and reheat.

SERVES 6.

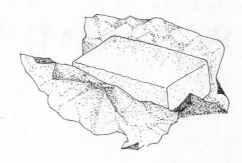

CHAPTER 5

MARINADES, SAUCES, STUFFINGS AND ACCOMPANIMENTS

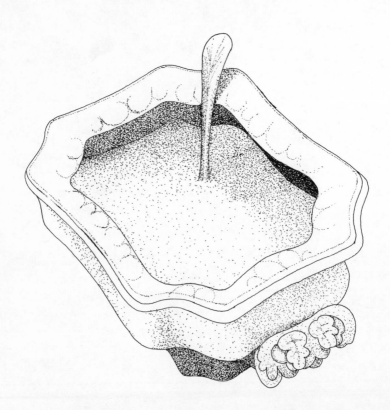

MARINADES

Some marinades are scattered throughout the previous chapters. Others, given below, are considered standard recipes and are widely adaptable. Some are simple and some take more time but freeze well.

Some cooks save the "ends" of wine used at the table (keeping reds in one bottle, whites in another) as a base for marinades. Of course this is thrifty, but keep in mind that the best results come from using the best ingredients available or the best you can afford.

Always marinate in glass or earthenware, or a stone crock or a container of unchipped enamelware.

BASIC RED-WINE MARINADE

⅘ qt. red wine (Burgundy or
  Bordeaux)
¾ cup red-wine vinegar
2 tbsps. olive oil
1 bay leaf

1 tsp. dried rosemary
1 tsp. dried marjoram
2 tsps. salt
½ tsp. whole black peppercorns
1 onion, sliced

Combine all ingredients.

VEGETABLE MARINADE

salt and pepper
4 onions, sliced
3 carrots, sliced
4 whole cloves
8 peppercorns, crushed
3 bay leaves

3 garlic cloves, mashed
6 parsley sprigs
4 juniper berries
6 cups red wine
2 cups olive oil
2 cups vinegar

Season meat with salt and pepper and cover with layers of onions, carrots, cloves, peppercorns, bay leaves, garlic, parsley, and juniper in a crock. Mix wine, oil, and vinegar and pour over all. Cover crock and set in very cool place for 5 days; if in the refrigerator, let it stand at room temperature for 2 hours each day. After 5 days remove meat and pat dry with cloth. Wrap meat for freezing, or refrigerate until ready to cook. Reserve strained marinade for cooking and sauces.

WINE-VINEGAR MARINADE

1½ cups red-wine vinegar
3 cups water
1 bay leaf
6 whole cloves
2 tsps. salt
¼ tsp. pepper

1 tsp. Italian seasoning, or a
   mixture of ¼ tsp. each of dried
   rosemary, marjoram, sweet
   basil, and oregano
1 carrot, diced
1 onion, sliced
1 celery rib, sliced
1 leek, sliced

Combine all ingredients.

SMALL GAME WHITE-WINE MARINADE
(very good for furred game)

1 carrot, sliced
1 onion, sliced
4 parsley sprigs
1 bay leaf
pinch of dried thyme

1 tsp. salt
8 peppercorns
1 tbsp. salad oil
¾ cup white wine

Combine all ingredients.

BIRD WHITE-WINE MARINADE (especially for pheasants)

⅘ qt. dry white wine
¾ cup white-wine vinegar
2 tsps. salt
1 tbsp. sugar
1 tsp. dried thyme

1 bay leaf
6 whole cloves
6 whole allspice berries
2 tbsps. olive oil
1 onion, sliced

Combine all ingredients.

BEER BIRD MARINADE (especially for pheasants)

¼ lb. butter
2 or 3 garlic cloves, minced
12 oz. beer

1 tbsp. salt
1 tbsp. pepper
1 tbsp. MSG

Melt butter; sauté garlic until translucent. Add beer slowly and mix in salt, pepper, and MSG. Pour hot marinade over bird and marinate at room temperature for at least 1 hour. Use to baste barbecuing bird as well.

THE RED MARINADE (excellent for pigeons)

⅘ qt. red wine
1 tbsp. olive oil
1 tsp. vinegar
1 tbsp. crushed pepper
6 whole cloves
1 garlic clove, crushed

4 whole bay leaves
pinch each of dried rosemary,
   tarragon, and dill
1 sugar cube, saturated with
   brandy

Combine all ingredients. Marinate young pigeons for 12 to 24 hours, older birds longer.

ORIENTAL MARINADE (excellent for ducks)

½ cup soy sauce
½ cup sherry or port
½ cup olive oil
1 onion, minced

1 tbsp. grated fresh ginger root
1 tbsp. grated tangerine or orange
   rind
dash of salt

Combine all ingredients. Marinate 2 ducks, cut into pieces, in mixture for 4 to 12 hours, as required.

COOKED MARINADE

4 cups water or part water and
   red wine
1½ cups vinegar
1 or 2 onions, chopped
1 carrot, sliced
1 garlic clove

1 tsp. dried thyme
2 bay leaves
4 parsley sprigs
12 to 15 peppercorns
1 tbsp. salt

Combine all ingredients in a saucepan and bring to a boil. Simmer for 1 hour. Cool before pouring over a venison saddle, or freeze in convenient amounts.

The following is really a beverage, popular in all Spanish-speaking countries, yet I have found that it makes an excellent marinade for steaks or chops; marinate them for 6 to 8 hours, or overnight. When strained, it makes an unusual sauce for broiled or grilled meats.

SANGRÍA (marinade or beverage)

⅘ qt. dry red wine
1½ oz. Cointreau
1½ oz. brandy

1 orange, sliced thin
1 lemon, sliced thin

Mix together red wine, Cointreau, and brandy. Add orange and lemon slices. Cover and chill for at least 24 hours. As a beverage, pour it over ice in a tall glass, leaving room to add 1 or 2 ounces of soda water. Stir.

SANGRÍA SAUCE

Make Sangría and chill 24 hours. Heat and simmer, uncovered, for 15 minutes. Strain out fruit. Can be thickened with cornstarch as desired.

BUTTERS

Butter is the most frequently used form of additional fat for game birds. While it is usually used plain, a flavored butter will add to the end results. Some follow the excellent practice of tucking a portion of butter, frequently herbed butter, under the skin of the breast of a bird. In this position it seeps all through the meatiest parts. Seasoned butters are also excellent on game steaks. Clarified butter is a very good cooking medium (it has a higher smoking or burning temperature than unclarified butter) and is excellent in sauces. This keeps well tightly covered in the refrigerator.

Beurre manié is easily and quickly made and keeps well under refrigeration. It is good to have on hand to thicken sauces and has the added advantage of doing it without "lumping" as the addition of plain flour will often do. To make *beurre manié*, work equal amounts of butter and flour well between your fingers. When it is smooth, store in a tightly covered container. Measure out as needed; about 2 tablespoons will moderately thicken 1 cup of thin liquid.

Margarine can be handled in both the same ways, although the flavor is not quite the same.

CLARIFIED BUTTER

Put sticks of butter on end into a heatproof glass cup so that they barely stick out at the top. Let them melt slowly without stirring. Pour off the clean, golden liquid into a jar with a tight top; it will keep for months, refrigerated. Discard the milky residue in the bottom of the cup.

Seasoned butters should be made ahead and allowed to absorb flavors before using. Each of these recipes makes slightly more than ½ cup. Always chill.

ANCHOVY BUTTER

Blend ¼ pound soft butter with 1 tablespoon anchovy paste and 1 tablespoon lemon juice.

CHIVE BUTTER

Blend ¼ pound soft butter, 2 tablespoons minced fresh parsley, 4 tablespoons minced fresh chives, and salt and white pepper to taste.

GARLIC BUTTER

Bring 3 garlic cloves to a boil in a small amount of water; drain and rinse under cold water. Put through press or mince. Mix with ¼ pound soft butter, 2 tablespoons minced fresh parsley, and salt and white pepper to taste.

SHALLOT BUTTER

Bring 3 tablespoons chopped shallots to a boil in a small amount of water, then drain and rinse under cold water. Mince and blend with ¼ pound soft butter; season to taste with salt and pepper.

DEVILED BUTTER

Cream 3 tablespoons of butter until light and lemon colored. Beat in 1 teaspoon dry mustard, 5 teaspoons Worcestershire sauce, 3 teaspoons Tabasco sauce, 1 teaspoon grated onion, and 1 teaspoon minced chives.

TOASTED ONION BUTTER

Combine 1 teaspoon toasted dried onion flakes and ¼ teaspoon each of salt and Worcestershire sauce with ¼ pound soft butter.

HERB BUTTER

Cream ¼ pound soft butter and beat in 1 tablespoon lemon juice, a bit at a time. Beat in 1½ teaspoons minced fresh parsley and ¾ teaspoon dried rosemary; season with salt and white pepper to taste.

LEMON BUTTER

Melt ½ pound butter and blend in the juice of 1½ lemons and ¼ teaspoon paprika.

MUSTARD BUTTER

Blend 4 tablespoons prepared mustard with ¼ pound soft butter.

MAÎTRE D'HÔTEL BUTTER

Combine ¼ pound soft butter, 1 tablespoon minced fresh parsley, 2 tablespoons lemon juice, ½ teaspoon Worcestershire sauce; season to taste with salt.

COLBERT BUTTER

Bring to a boil 3 or 4 tablespoons *Glace de Viande* diluted with 1 tablespoon water. Remove from heat and add ¼ pound soft butter. Season with salt, pepper, a pinch of cayenne, and a dash of grated nutmeg. Stir in the juice of ½ lemon, 1 tablespoon minced parsley, and 1 tablespoon Madeira wine.

BLEU CHEESE BUTTER

Blend ¼ pound bleu cheese with ¼ pound soft butter.

ROQUEFORT BUTTER

Cream together 5½ tablespoons each of soft butter and crumbled Roquefort cheese until smooth. Stir in juice of ½ lemon and 2 tablespoons minced fresh chives. Season to taste with salt and white pepper.

SAUCES

BROWN STOCK (for sauces and gravies)

2 lbs. or more of equal parts venison and veal bones with shreds of meat attached	3 qts. cold water
	1½ tsps. salt
	pinch of dried thyme
2 onions, sliced	bouquet garni (4 parsley sprigs,
1 carrot, sliced	2 celery ribs, 1 small bay leaf)

Spread out bones, onions, and carrot in a shallow pan. Brown bones well on all sides at 375°. Transfer all to a kettle and add water, salt, thyme, and bouquet garni. Bring slowly to a boil, skimming off fat as it rises. Cook slowly for at least 4 hours, or until reduced to 2 quarts. Strain through a fine sieve and store in refrigerator (or freezer) until needed. If refrigerated, keeps best if brought to a boil every 2 days.

MAKES 2 quarts.

GLACE DE VIANDE
(highly concentrated meat glaze or extract)

Meat glaze or extract made from domestic meats can be bought at fine food stores under a variety of labels. While it is time-consuming to make, the resulting concentrate made from game bones really is worth the effort. For a quick cup of broth, dissolve ½ to ¾ teaspoon extract in a cup of boiling water. To intensify flavors in other dishes, add up to 1 tablespoon extract per pound of boneless meat or to 4 cups liquid. When using it this way, it is best not to add salt to the dish until it is finished, then add as desired. Since it is so highly concentrated, additional salt may not be required.

Make a quantity of Brown Stock as above, using your choice of game bones (bird carcasses can be used) and an equal amount of veal bones. Strain through a muslin or flannel cloth wrung out in cold water. Chill and remove any remaining fat that may have risen to the top. Return the stock to a clean kettle. Cook very slowly over an asbestos mat over lowest possible heat, stirring frequently until it is reduced to one-quarter its volume and will mound in a spoon. It can be further concentrated to the point where it can be cut with a knife if desired. As the extract reduces, it must be watched more and more carefully and stirred constantly, as it burns very easily. Store in tightly sealed jars or freeze.

QUICK BROWN SAUCE

1½ tbsps. butter
1½ tbsps. flour

2 cups brown stock or consommé
salt and pepper

Melt butter; make a roux with the flour, stirring occasionally, until roux is the color of wrapping paper. Gradually stir in stock, bring to a boil, and cook for 5 minutes, stirring. Reduce heat and simmer gently for 30 minutes, stirring occasionally. Skim off fat; strain. Season with salt and pepper.

MAKES 2 cups.

CLASSIC BROWN SAUCE (sauce espagnole)

½ cup beef drippings
2 onions, chopped
1 small carrot, chopped
½ cup flour
8 cups brown venison stock, hot
3 parsley sprigs

1 celery rib
1 small bay leaf
1 garlic clove, mashed
pinch of dried thyme
¼ cup tomato sauce or purée
salt and pepper

253

Melt drippings; add onions and carrot, and cook, shaking to coat evenly, until they start to turn golden. Add flour and cook, stirring, until all is a rich brown. Add 3 cups stock, the parsley, celery, bay leaf, garlic, and thyme. Cook, stirring often, until sauce thickens. Add 3 cups more stock and simmer slowly, stirring occasionally, for 1 to 1½ hours, to reduce to about 3 cups. As sauce cooks, skim off fat that comes to surface. Add tomato sauce and cook for a few minutes longer. Strain through a fine sieve. Add 2 more cups stock and cook slowly for 1 hour, skimming from time to time, until reduced to about 4 cups. Season with salt and pepper to taste. Cool, stirring occasionally. Seal with a layer of melted fat on top and store, covered, in the refrigerator up to 1 week. If kept longer, remove fat, and bring sauce to a boil. Cool and reseal.

MAKES 4 cups.

SAUCE DIABLE (for broiled meat or birds)

Add 2 shallots, chopped, and 8 peppercorns, crushed, to ⅓ cup dry white wine, and cook until reduced to a thick paste. Add 1 cup Brown Sauce, 1 teaspoon Worcestershire sauce, and ½ teaspoon minced parsley.

MAKES 1 cup.

SAUCE PIQUANTE (for leftover meats)

Cook 3 tablespoons dry white wine, 1½ tablespoons vinegar, and 1½ teaspoons minced shallot over high heat until reduced to half. Stir in 1 cup Brown Sauce and boil up twice. Remove from heat and stir in 1½ tablespoons minced sour gherkins, 1 tablespoon minced chives, 1 tablespoon minced parsley, and a generous pinch of minced tarragon.

MAKES 1 cup.

BORDELAISE SAUCE

Cook 2 minced shallots in ½ cup red wine until wine is reduced by three-quarters. Add 1 cup Brown Sauce and simmer gently for 10 minutes. Just before serving add 2 tablespoons poached marrow and ¼ teaspoon minced fresh tarragon.

MAKES 1⅓ cups.

VENISON SAUCE

1 lb. mushrooms, sliced	1 cup Brown Sauce or bouillon
1/4 lb. butter	1 tbsp. tomato paste
2 shallots, chopped	1/2 tsp. minced parsley
1 cup dry red wine	1/2 tsp. minced fresh tarragon
salt and pepper	1/2 tsp. minced fresh thyme

Sauté mushrooms in foaming butter, turning with a wooden spoon. Add shallots and wine, and salt and pepper to taste; cook until reduced by half. Add brown sauce, tomato paste, and herbs.
Makes 3 cups.

MADEIRA SAUCE (for meat and birds)

Cook 2 cups Brown Sauce to reduce further to 1 cup. Add 1/3 cup Madeira, bring just to boiling point, and remove from heat.
Makes 1 1/3 cups.

SHERRY SAUCE (for 2 turkey breasts, hot or foil-warmed, or other bird meat, sliced thin)

1 cup turkey or chicken stock	4 egg yolks, lightly beaten
1 cup heavy cream	lemon juice
1/4 cup sherry	salt and white pepper

Combine stock, cream, and sherry in top part of a double boiler; heat until hot but not boiling. Pour hot liquid, slowly, over yolks, beating constantly. Return to top of double boiler over simmering water and cook, stirring often, until mixture coats a metal spoon. Remove from heat. Add lemon juice, salt, and pepper to taste (and more sherry, if desired). Strain sauce over sliced meat.
Makes 3 cups.

MUSHROOM STEAK SAUCE

3 tbsps. butter	1/2 cup water
1 green onion, minced	2 bay leaves
1 garlic clove, minced	2 tbsps. minced parsley
12 mushrooms, sliced or quartered	1 beef bouillon cube
1 1/2 tbsps. flour	salt and pepper
1/2 cup dry red wine	

Heat butter and sauté onion, garlic, and mushrooms until onion is tender and most of the liquid is evaporated. Blend in flour. Gradually stir in wine and water. Add bay leaf, parsley, and bouillon cube. Cook, stirring to dissolve bouillon cube, until mixture boils and thickens. Season to taste. Remove bay leaves before serving.

MAKES 2 cups.

Some sauces can be made using marinade as an ingredient, as in Roast Leg of Venison. Poivrade Sauce or Pepper Sauce can also be used with steaks and chops or even with small game or birds.

POIVRADE SAUCE

2 tbsps. butter or cooking oil
½ cup diced carrot
½ cup diced onion
¼ cup diced celery
½ cup diced game meat or bird trimmings
sprig of fresh thyme or pinch of dried
¼ bay leaf
3 tbsps. butter

4 tbsps. flour
1½ cups rich stock (brown for red meat, small game or bird stock for those meats)
dash salt and pepper
½ cup wine-based marinade, strained, or ¼ cup each wine vinegar and red or white wine
6 peppercorns, roughly crushed
1½ tbsps. sweet butter

Heat the butter or oil and add carrot, onion, celery, meat, thyme, and bay leaf. Cover and simmer very gently without browning until very tender. Meanwhile, in another pan, melt the 3 tablespoons butter and stir in the flour smoothly. If a dark sauce is desired, cook gently, stirring frequently, until well browned. Slowly stir in the stock and cook until thickened and season lightly with salt and pepper if needed.

When the vegetables are cooked, drain off the cooking fat and moisten them with the marinade. Cook over high heat to reduce to two-thirds of the original volume, stirring constantly. Stir in the thickened stock and simmer very gently for 30 minutes, stirring from time to time. Add the peppercorns and simmer gently 10 minutes longer. Strain through a fine sieve and return to heat to bring just to a boil. Swirl in sweet butter just before serving.

MAKES about 2 cups.

PEPPER SAUCE

a few venison or beef bones,
cracked small, or 1 lb. uncooked
small-game or bird bones
1 tbsp. crushed peppercorns
3 tbsps. minced shallots
½ bay leaf

½ tsp. dried thyme, or 3 sprigs
fresh thyme
1 cup dry red wine
1 cup heavy cream
salt and pepper
1 tbsp. butter

Bring peppercorns, shallots, bay leaf, thyme, wine, and bones to a boil in water to cover. Cover and simmer for 1 hour. Strain through a sieve, discarding bones but pressing rest through. Chill and freeze. Reheat if frozen and add cream and bring to a boil. Simmer for about 15 minutes. Add drippings from cooking skillet if being used and salt and pepper to taste. Swirl in the butter and serve.

MAKES 1½ cups.

CUMBERLAND SAUCE

4 shallots
12 oz. red-currant jelly
⅔ cup port wine
1 tbsp. wine vinegar
1 tsp. Dijon-style mustard

thinnest possible rind from
1 orange and 1 lemon, slivered
juice of ½ orange
juice of ½ lemon

Parboil shallots, drain and mince. Melt jelly with port in top part of a double boiler over boiling water. Add vinegar, mustard, shallots, and slivered rinds. Stir in orange and lemon juices. Cook over boiling water until rind is tender but not mushy, about 10 minutes. Chill.

MAKES about 2½ cups.

SCANDINAVIAN GAME SAUCE

3 tbsps. red-currant jelly
1½ tsps. grated lemon rind
1½ tsps. red-wine vinegar

½ tsp. dry mustard
3 tbsps. dry sherry
3 tbsps. dry red wine

Break up jelly with a fork and mix well with lemon rind, vinegar, and mustard in top part of a double boiler. Put over boiling water to melt thoroughly. Just before serving stir in the two wines. Great for goose or grouse.

MAKES ¾ cup.

QUICK GAME SAUCE

Blend equal amounts of red-currant jelly, commercial hot catsup, and red Burgundy or Bordeaux wine in top part of a double boiler. Heat and stir until smooth.

PLUM SAUCE (especially for roast goose)

1 cup port wine
1/3 cup goose drippings from roaster
1 can (14 oz.) purple plums, drained and pitted

1/8 tsp. ground cinnamon
dash of cayenne
1 tbsp. cornstarch, blended smooth with 2 tbsps. water

Simmer wine, uncovered, until reduced to about 1/2 cup. Add drippings and cook for 5 minutes. Crush plums lightly with a fork and add to port with cinnamon and cayenne. Simmer for 5 minutes. Add cornstarch-water mixture and bring to a boil, stirring. Simmer, stirring occasionally, until sauce is thickened and shiny, about 20 minutes.

MAKES 3 cups.

HORSERADISH SAUCE (for hot meats)

Combine 1 cup port wine, 1/2 teaspoon ground cinnamon, pinch of grated nutmeg, and salt and pepper to taste. Cook over low heat until reduced to 2/3 cup. Add 1 cup red-currant jelly, melted, and 1 cup (or to taste) freshly grated horseradish.

MAKES 2 2/3 cups.

SAUCE PARADIS (especially for pigeons, young and roasted)

4 tbsps. butter
4 tbsps. flour
2 cups double-strength pheasant stock (simmer 4 cups to reduce to half volume)

1/2 cup Madeira wine
2 tbsps. red-currant jelly
2 cups seedless white grapes
2 large truffles (or mushrooms), sliced

Melt butter, add flour, and stir until smooth. Add stock and cook, stirring, until slightly thickened. Add wine and jelly and stir until jelly is melted. Add grapes and truffles.

MAKES 4 cups.

ALASKAN BARBECUE SAUCE
(or relish for meat, basting for duck)

1 lb. canned jellied cranberry sauce	2 tbsps. cider vinegar
	2 tsps. Worcestershire sauce
¼ cup minced onion	1 tsp. barbecue spice

Melt cranberry sauce over low heat. Add all other ingredients, blend thoroughly, and cook together for 2 minutes.

MAKES 2½ cups.

SMALL-GAME BARBECUE SAUCE

1 can (16 oz.) tomato purée	4 strips bacon, diced
½ cup catsup	2 large onions, diced
2 cups water	1 tbsp. brown sugar
4 tbsps. vinegar	2 tbsps. prepared mustard
1 tsp. Worcestershire sauce	salt and pepper

Combine all ingredients and bring to a boil. Reduce heat and simmer until sauce thickens, stirring occasionally. This freezes well. Cook game about halfway (bake, broil, or roast); then add it to warmed sauce and simmer for about 1 hour.

Enough to dress 3 to 4 pounds meat, to serve 6 to 8.

BIG-GAME BASTING OR BARBECUE SAUCE

1 cup chopped onion	2 tsps. brown sugar
3 tbsps. butter	2 or 3 dashes of Tabasco
1½ cups canned tomatoes with liquid	½ tsp. dry mustard
	1½ cups venison stock
1 cup slivered celery	1 tsp. salt
1 cup chili sauce	⅛ tsp. pepper

Sauté onion in butter for 3 minutes. Add all other ingredients, cover, and bring to a boil. Reduce heat and simmer for 2 hours. Can be used as is for basting; or uncover and simmer for 30 minutes more until very thick, stirring often, for sauce. Freezes well at either point.

MAKES 5 cups.

DUCK BARBECUE SAUCE

Combine 2 sliced onions, 1 cup sherry, 2 sliced lemons, 2 tablespoons Worcestershire sauce, 1 garlic clove, 1 tablespoon prepared mustard, 1 tablespoon flour, 2¼ cups water, 2 teaspoons salt, and

1 teaspoon pepper. Spoon over 2 ducks (split or in parts), and roast, covered, at 350° for 2 hours.

MAKES 4 cups.

BASIC DEGLAZING SAUCE (for sautéed meats)

For each individual steak or chop to be cooked, use 1 tablespoon butter and ½ tablespoon olive oil, and sauté meat. Remove cooked meat and keep warm. Spoon off excess fat. Turn heat high and add ¼ cup of any of the following: red wine, dry vermouth, Cognac (this can be flamed), Bourbon, vinegar, Marsala, port, lemon juice, unthickened meat juice, cider, water, or coffee. Bring to a boil, scraping bottom and sides of pan with wooden spoon to clean off browned bits. Add 1 tablespoon butter, reduce heat and season to taste with salt and pepper. Simmer for a few minutes and pour over steaks.

PAN OR BROWN GRAVY (from roast)

Put a few slices of onion or carrot into a roasting pan with meat or bird. Roast meat in usual manner; transfer to a heated platter when done. Carefully spoon off fat from roaster and remove vegetables. To remaining juices add ½ to 1 cup water or stock just to cover the bottom of the pan. Cook over direct heat, stirring to deglaze, and let come to a boil. Reduce liquid until it has good color and flavor. Season with salt and pepper; swirl in 1 to 2 tablespoons butter just before serving. Add any juices from the roast that have bled out while waiting.

CREAM GRAVY (excellent with steaks and chops)

The simplest and quickest way is to deglaze the broiling pan with light or medium cream, stirring constantly and carefully to prevent curdling. Or, for roasted meats, pour off fat from the pan the meat was cooked in and stir in 2 teaspoons minced onion, 2 tablespoons butter, and 2 teaspoons flour; cook, stirring, for 2 minutes. Slowly stir in 1½ cups heavy cream and cook, stirring, until blended and thickened. Add 2 teaspoons lemon juice and 2 teaspoons red-currant jelly and cook, stirring, until melted. (Jelly can be omitted if desired.) Season to taste.

GIBLET GRAVY (for 3 small pheasants, or equivalent)

Simmer 4 cups water with wing tips, necks, and giblets from 2 or 3 pheasants; 1 carrot; 1 onion; salt to taste, and 2 juniper berries (for pheasant) for 1½ hours. Strain; reserve broth. Slice and reserve giblets. After roasting birds remove all but ¼ cup of roaster fat and add ¼ cup flour to the roaster, stirring all the while. (Flour can be browned for color if desired.) Mix in reserved giblet broth and sliced giblets, and stir to combine well and to deglaze the pan. Season to taste and cook, stirring, until smooth and thickened.

MAKES 2½ cups.

GIBLET CREAM SAUCE

Make this like Giblet Gravy, but add with the reserved giblet broth the juice of ½ lemon and Madeira wine to taste. Cook, stirring, until smooth and thickened. Stir in about ½ cup heavy cream and sliced giblets.

MAKES 3 cups.

STEAK SAUCE (for panfried steaks)

For each steak to be fried, use 1½ teaspoons butter. When steaks are done and removed, add another 1½ teaspoons butter for each steak; also add 1½ tablespoons chopped shallots and sauté until shallots are soft but not browned. Add 2 tablespoons dry red wine for each steak and reduce over high heat until most of the liquid is evaporated.

Steak Sauce Alternative (for broiled steaks)

2 tbsps. A.1. Steak Sauce   1 tbsp. minced fresh chives
4 tbsps. sweet butter, melted   ½ cup dry red wine
10 large fresh mushrooms, halved

Stir Steak Sauce into melted butter and sauté mushrooms in it until lightly browned. Stir in chives and wine; increase heat and boil until liquid is reduced by about half and thickened somewhat. Stir in pan juices and heat.

MAKES 1 cup.

Sauces for burgers, meat loaves, and meatballs are too often limited to the basic tomato. There are many other choices. Here are a few, which are also good with broiled or grilled meat.

BEARNAISE SAUCE

Clarify ½ pound butter. Mix 1 tablespoon minced onion, 2 tablespoons minced shallots, ½ teaspoon crushed peppercorns, 1 tablespoon minced fresh tarragon (or 1½ teaspoons dried), and 3 tablespoons tarragon vinegar in the top part of a double boiler. Cook over moderately high direct heat until liquid is almost completely reduced. Remove and let cool slightly. Beat 2 tablespoons water with 3 egg yolks and add to saucepan. Set pan over hot water, and cook, whisking rapidly. When the yolks start to thicken, remove from heat and gradually pour in the warmed, clarified butter, beating well with a whisk. Season to taste with salt and cayenne pepper. Do not cook again; it will curdle.

MAKES 2 cups.

SOUR-CREAM SAUCE

2 tbsps. butter
2 tbsps. flour
2 shallots, minced
¼ cup white wine
2 peppercorns, crushed

1 cup sour cream, at room
   temperature
salt and pepper
juice of ½ lemon

Melt butter (best done in drained pan in which marinated venison steaks were cooked) and stir in flour and shallots. Mix well, scraping browned bits from pan if previously used. Add wine and peppercorns slowly, mixing well. Add sour cream, and salt and pepper if desired. Cook, stirring, until thickened. Just before serving stir in lemon juice.

MAKES 1½ cups.

STROGANOFF SAUCE

4 tbsps. butter
1 small onion, minced
4 tbsps. flour
2¼ cups venison or beef broth

1 cup sour cream
½ tsp. dried dillweed
salt and pepper

Melt butter and sauté onion until limp. Stir in flour and cook, stirring, until blended and bubbling. Slowly add broth and cook, stirring, until thickened. Stir in sour cream; do not let sauce boil after adding sour cream. Add dillweed and salt and pepper to taste.

MAKES 3½ cups.

BLEU CHEESE SAUCE

4 tbsps. butter
4 tbsps. flour
1 garlic clove, mashed
½ cup milk

½ cup cream
1½ cups chicken broth
4 oz. bleu cheese, crumbled
salt

Melt butter. Blend flour and garlic into butter and cook until well mixed and bubbly. Gradually stir in milk, cream, and broth, and cook, stirring, until thickened. Add cheese and stir only until blended. Add salt to taste.

MAKES about 3 cups.

CURRY SAUCE

4 tbsps. butter
1 large onion, chopped
1 garlic clove, mashed
2 tbsps. curry powder
4 tbsps. flour
1 tbsp. cornstarch

2 tsps. sugar
½ tsp. salt
dash of cayenne
2 cups chicken broth
1 cup heavy cream

Melt butter and sauté onion until limp. Stir in garlic and curry powder and cook for 1 minute. Add flour, cornstarch, sugar, salt, and cayenne and cook, stirring, until blended and bubbling. Gradually stir in broth and cream and cook until thickened.

MAKES about 4 cups.

CAPER SAUCE

2 tbsps. butter
2 tbsps. flour
2 cups venison or beef stock
2 thin slices of lemon
⅓ tsp. dry mustard

2 tsps. wine vinegar
1½ tbsps. heavy cream, hot
2 tsps. butter
4 tbsps. capers, chopped

Melt butter, add flour, and cook roux, stirring, until roux is well blended and begins to brown. Gradually add stock and stir until thick and boiling. Add lemon, mustard, vinegar, and cream, and cook for 1 minute. Just before serving swirl in butter and capers.

MAKES about 3½ cups.

GARLIC SAUCE

Heat ½ cup olive oil and 3 tablespoons salad oil to blend, then cool. Add ¼ cup (about 2 heads) garlic, minced, and slowly simmer but do not brown. Mix together with ½ cup minced parsley, ¼ cup prepared mustard, ¼ cup Worcestershire sauce, 3 tablespoons soy sauce, 2 tablespoons pepper, and 1 teaspoon salt. Blend together and simmer for 20 minutes. Serve hot.

MAKES about 2 cups.

GREEN PEPPERCORN SAUCE
(for skillet-cooked steaks and chops)

¼ cup minced onion
⅓ cup brandy
1 tbsp. (approx.) green
    peppercorns, rinsed and
    drained

½ cup heavy cream
2 tsps. Dijon-style mustard
¼ tsp. minced fresh tarragon

In a skillet in which steaks have been cooked in half oil, half butter, cook onion in remaining butter-oil mixture until soft. Add brandy and stir to deglaze pan. Crush 2 teaspoons of the green peppercorns and stir in to pan with cream, mustard, and tarragon. Boil sauce, stirring, until thickened, about 3 minutes. Stir in remaining peppercorns and pour over steaks.

Enough for 1 to 1½ pounds 1-inch-thick steaks.

SWEET-SOUR SAUCE

Mix 1 tablespoon cornstarch with ¼ cup sugar and cook, stirring, in 1 cup water until thickened. Add 1 tablespoon prepared mustard, 1½ tablespoons beef drippings or butter, and ¼ cup vinegar. Heat until blended.

MAKES 1¼ cups.

CHUNKY SWEET AND SOUR SAUCE

2 cans (14 oz. each) chunk
    pineapple in syrup, drained,
    syrup reserved
1¼ cups venison or beef broth
¼ cup brown sugar
¾ cup vinegar

1 tbsp. soy sauce
1 tbsp. catsup
4 tbsps. cornstarch
1 cup thin-sliced green onions
3 green peppers, seeded and cut
    into 1-inch squares

Combine pineapple syrup, broth, sugar, vinegar, soy sauce, catsup, and cornstarch; cook, stirring, until thickened. Add onions and green peppers and cook for 1 minute. Remove from heat. Reheat if needed, and add pineapple chunks just before serving; do not reheat after adding chunks.

MAKES 6 cups.

TOMATO SAUCE

Heat 2 tablespoons olive oil and sauté 2 tablespoons minced onion, 1 minced garlic clove, and 2 tablespoons minced green pepper until tender. Add 1 large tomato, skinned and chopped, a dash of salt, and 4 to 6 drops of Tabasco; simmer for 10 minutes. Stir in 1 tablespoon chopped parsley.

MAKES 1¼ cups.

TOMATO SAUCE (puréed)

Melt 2 tablespoons butter. Add 3 tablespoons minced onion and simmer until wilted. Stir in ¼ cup flour and 1 tablespoon paprika. Stir in 3½ cups coarsely chopped tomatoes, and salt and pepper to taste. Simmer for 15 minutes, stirring often. Put through finest strainer possible, or use a food mill. Reheat, remove from heat, and stir in 2 tablespoons sour cream. Swirl in 1 tablespoon butter.

MAKES 3 cups.

BREAD SAUCE

Season 2 cups milk with a dash of salt and a dash of cayenne. Add 1 onion studded with 2 cloves. Bring milk and onion to a boil and cook for 5 minutes; strain. Add 1 cup fresh bread crumbs to milk or enough to thicken it, and correct seasoning. Butter or cream can be stirred in to make a richer sauce.

MAKES 2 cups.

COCKTAIL SAUCE

Mix ¾ cup catsup, 1 tablespoon (or more to taste) prepared horseradish, 1 tablespoon lemon juice, 1 teaspoon Worcestershire, dash of Tabasco, and salt and pepper to taste.

MAKES ¾ cup.

HORSERADISH SAUCE (for cold sliced meat)

1½ cups sour cream	2 to 3 tbsps. drained prepared
3 tbsps. snipped fresh chives	horseradish
¼ tsp. salt	½ tsp. seasoned salt
	1 tbsp. lemon juice

Combine all ingredients well and refrigerate for at least 2 hours.

MAKES 1¾ cups.

MUSTARD SAUCE

Mustard is a particularly popular flavor with meats. This sauce, which will keep for weeks in a tight jar in the refrigerator or frozen for months, was originally served with cold smoked tongue. It is equally good with corned, broiled, or roasted meat, hot or cold in sandwiches. I also use it as a binder-flavoring in ground leftovers for spreads.

Blend ½ cup dry mustard with ½ cup white vinegar, 1 teaspoon salt, and 3 tablespoons sugar to a smooth paste. Refrigerate overnight. Cook in the top part of a double boiler over hot, not boiling, water, stirring from time to time until very thick. Transfer to a jar with a tight lid, cool, cover, and refrigerate or freeze. To serve, blend smooth with an equal amount of mayonnaise.

MUSTARD SAUCE WITH GREEN PEPPERCORNS
(excellent for pheasant, turkey, or ham)

1 tbsp. sugar	1½ tbsps. green peppercorns,
3 tbsps. Dijon-style mustard	rinsed and drained
2 tbsps. white-wine vinegar	1 tbsp. butter
¾ tsp. salt	½ cup cream
2 egg yolks	

In top part of a double boiler mix sugar, mustard, vinegar, salt, egg yolks, and peppercorns, and cook, stirring, over hot (not boiling) water until thickened, about 5 minutes. Remove from heat and stir in the butter. Cool. Whip the cream stiff, then fold into mustard mixture smoothly. Cover and chill. Will keep for about 1 week refrigerated.

Makes 1½ cups.

RÉMOULADE SAUCE

Mix 2 cups mayonnaise, ½ cup minced sour pickle, 2 tablespoons minced capers, 3 minced hard-cooked eggs, 1 tablespoon prepared mustard, 1 tablespoon minced parsley, and minced tarragon and chervil to taste.

Makes 3 cups.

MULLED CIDER APPLESAUCE (excellent with wild pig)

1 cup water	1 pt. cider, heated but not boiled
⅛ tsp. nutmeg	20 to 24 tart, juicy apples
4 whole cloves, bruised	1 cup sugar
⅛ tsp. ground cinnamon	

Bring water to a boil, remove from heat and immediately add spices. Let stand 10 minutes; strain and add the heated cider. (This is mulled cider and, with sugar to taste, makes an excellent cold-weather drink.)

Wash apples and cut into eighths, put into kettle and add just enough mulled cider to steam and keep from burning. Bring slowly to a boil, cover and cook slowly for 20 to 30 minutes or until the apples are soft. Stir in the sugar and cook only long enough to dissolve it. Rub the fruit through a strainer to eliminate skin, core, and seeds.

MAKES about 6 cups.

Latins make a variety of sauces that are delicious with broiled and grilled meats, and they are generally unknown to most North Americans.

ARGENTINIAN GREEN CHIMICHURRI SAUCE

Mix equal amounts of minced fresh marjoram, parsley, and coriander (Chinese parsley) leaves, and lace well with minced garlic. Dress liberally with white vinegar and oil, and let stand covered, at room temperature, for 24 hours.

ARGENTINIAN RED CHIMICHURRI SAUCE

Wash well a good handful of fresh parsley leaves, and purée while still wet in a blender with 4 to 6 mashed garlic cloves and 2 tablespoons chicate (sweet, red ancho chile peppers, dried and ground) or sweet Hungarian paprika, ½ cup pineapple vinegar, and enough extra water to run the blender. Add 1 or 2 hot chile peppers (fresh or pickled and soaked in water for 30 minutes, then stemmed and seeded) if desired. Season to taste with salt. Can be stored and served in a shaker bottle.

COLOMBIAN AVOCADO SAUCE

Mash with a fork 1 large seeded, peeled avocado and 1 hard-cooked egg yolk. Stir in 1 tablespoon minced fresh coriander (Chinese parsley), 1 seeded and minced fresh hot green pepper, 1 minced scallion, 1 minced hard-cooked egg white, 1 tablespoon white-wine vinegar, and salt and pepper to taste.

COLOMBIAN CHILE SAUCE

Remove seeds, stems, and ribs from ½ pound fresh hot green peppers; chop coarsely. Work through a food chopper with 1 teaspoon salt. Add 1 minced onion and mix well.

ECUADORIAN HOT CHILE PEPPER SAUCE

Seed a fresh hot pepper and cut into small thin strips. Combine with an equal amount of minced red onion in a glass jar with a tight lid. Cover with lemon juice (which can be diluted to taste with hot water). Add salt to taste and let stand for at least 3 hours.

MEXICAN JALAPEÑO SAUCE

Mince 1 garlic clove and sauté with 2 tablespoons minced onion in 1 tablespoon olive oil for a few minutes. Add 3 cups peeled, seeded, and chopped tomatoes (about 4 or 5 large tomatoes), ½ teaspoon dried oregano, and ½ teaspoon salt. Cook all for 5 minutes. Stir in 1 tablespoon minced canned green jalapeño chiles. Remove from heat. Cool, cover, and chill.

MAKES 3 cups.

MEXICAN RED AND GREEN SAUCE

Peel and chop 6 medium-sized tomatoes and mix with ½ cup (or more to taste) diced, canned California long, mild green chiles (seeds and ribs removed); add ⅓ cup minced onion, 1 teaspoon salt, and fresh coriander (Chinese parsley) or parsley to taste. Add minced canned jalapeño peppers (the hot ones) to taste; about 3 should do it for spicy tastes.

MEXICAN PRUNE STUFFING SAUCE

Soak 1 cup pitted prunes in port wine to cover overnight. Drain prunes and reserve port; use prunes for stuffing birds (particularly good for pheasant; enough for a 4- or 5-pound bird). Roast bird as required. Scoop out prunes and reserve. Skim excess fat from roaster and stir in ½ cup of the reserved port. Simmer until reduced by one-third. Add reserved prunes and about ¼ cup heavy cream; reheat without boiling, and serve with the bird.

SPANISH SALSA VERDE

Purée 2 shallots or scallions in a blender with ½ teaspoon minced garlic, 4 drained anchovies, 2 tablespoons rinsed capers, and 3 tablespoons minced coriander (Chinese parsley) or parsley. Add 3 tablespoons strained lemon juice, 4 tablespoons olive oil, and salt and pepper to taste, to make a paste-sauce. Can be used as a sauce or dip.

MAKES ¾ cup.

SPANISH SAUCE

Boil 2 cups tomato sauce, 1 cup venison stock, 2 teaspoons chile powder, ¾ teaspoon ground cumin seed, and a pinch of cayenne, for 5 minutes. Add defrosted frozen meatballs or cold sliced meat and simmer, covered, for 30 minutes.

MAKES 3 cups.

TEXAS SALSA (while not Latin it's close to it—but not hot)

Heat 2 cups chopped onions, 1½ cups chopped green peppers, 1 teaspoon unroasted cumin seeds, 1 teaspoon crushed garlic, and 1 teaspoon crushed peppercorns in ⅓ cup vegetable shortening, stirring until onions are slightly wilted. Add 2 pounds canned, peeled plum tomatoes, and simmer for 5 minutes, mashing with a fork. Season to taste with salt and pepper. Serve hot or cold.

MAKES 6 cups.

STUFFINGS

Stuffings need not be cooked inside a whole bird; there is no reason why you shouldn't have stuffing with a bird that has been cut into parts. Simply put stuffing into a greased baking dish and cook it at 350° to 400° until cooked through and, if you wish, crisp and lightly browned on top. Needless to say, stuffing can also be molded under a bird breast or half a bird and the whole dish roasted together.

Red meats are not often stuffed, yet stuffed pork chops are familiar to many. Try the same method with double-thick game meat chops. Any of your favorite stuffings can be used for either game meat or birds, keeping in mind that geese and ducks seem to benefit most from somewhat sharp or fruity stuffings.

269

NORTH DAKOTA STUFFING (for 6-lb. goose)

1 lb. bulk pork sausage	1 celery rib, minced
1 cup cooked long-grain rice	1 garlic clove, minced
¼ cup fine bread crumbs	1 tsp. minced parsley
2 tbsps. butter	¾ tsp. dried thyme
2 eggs, beaten	¼ cup chopped pecans

Break up sausage and cook in a heavy skillet until it loses its pink color. Pour off all fat and stir in the rice, crumbs, butter, eggs, celery, garlic, parsley, and thyme. Add a few grinds of a pepper-mill and cook over medium heat for 30 minutes. Remove from heat and stir in nuts. Use to stuff goose or other birds.

ALSATIAN STUFFING (for 5- to 6-lb. goose)

¾ lb. bulk sausage	2 small white onions, chopped
¼ lb. ham, ground	½ cup minced celery
¼ lb. tongue, ground	¼ tsp. grated nutmeg
gizzard, heart, and liver from bird, ground	salt and freshly cracked pepper

Blend all together and season to taste.

FRENCH CHRISTMAS SHALLOT STUFFING
(for 5-lb. goose)

5 shallots, minced	½ tsp. freshly ground pepper
1½ garlic cloves, minced	½ tsp. dried thyme
3 tbsps. goose fat or butter	1 egg, lightly beaten
3 cups fresh bread crumbs	1 or 2 truffles, or bird livers
2 tbsps. minced parsley	(optional)
½ tbsp. salt	

Sauté shallots and garlic in fat until barely wilted; add crumbs, parsley, salt, pepper, thyme, and egg. Check for seasoning. Add 1 or 2 truffles, sliced or chopped; or goose livers cut into scallops; or lightly browned chicken or pheasant livers, if you like. Cool before using.

ORANGEMAN'S STUFFING (for 6-lb. goose)

⅓ cup butter or chicken fat	½ to ¾ tsp. salt
2 tbsps. chopped onion	1 cup orange slices
½ tsp. dried savory	pepper
1 qt. bread crumbs	

Melt fat and cook onion in it for a few minutes; soften, do not brown. Add savory, crumbs, salt, and orange, and mix well but lightly. Season with pepper to taste.

PRUNE STUFFING (for 6- to 8-lb. goose)

1½ cups dried prunes, or half prunes and half apricots
1½ cups water
5 cups seasoned dry bread crumbs
¾ cup melted butter
½ cup chopped green pepper or celery or mixture of the two

Bring dried fruit and water to a boil, then simmer for 5 minutes. Drain, reserving the liquid. Pit and cut fruit into ½-inch bits. Combine with crumbs, butter, green pepper, and celery, and moisten with just enough of the reserved liquid to hold together.

CASHEW STUFFING (for pheasant)

Simmer 1 cup coarsely chopped cashews in 1 cup pheasant or chicken stock until cashews are tender and liquid is absorbed. Mix in 4 slices of bacon, cooked and chopped, 2 tablespoons butter, ½ teaspoon salt, and a dash of pepper.

SHERRIED NUT STUFFING (for 2 pheasants)

2 cups plain toasted croutons
1 cup coarsely chopped celery
1 cup coarsely chopped tart apples
½ cup coarsely broken walnuts or pecans
1 onion, minced
½ tsp. dried thyme
½ tsp. dried marjoram
melted butter
sherry
salt and pepper

Toss croutons, celery, apples, nuts, onion, thyme, and marjoram lightly to blend, then add enough mixed half melted butter and half sherry to moisten. Season with salt and pepper. Use any leftover sherry-butter as basting liquid.

WILD-RICE STUFFING (for 4 pheasants, 2½ to 3 lbs. each)

1½ cups raw wild rice
5 tbsps. softened butter
½ cup minced onion
livers of 4 pheasants, chopped
½ lb. mushrooms, chopped
¼ cup chopped celery
½ cup coarsely chopped pecans
¼ cup chopped parsley
½ tsp. dried thyme
½ tsp. dried marjoram
salt and pepper

Rinse rice 3 or 4 times in cold water, then pour in a stream into large kettle of boiling salted water. Boil rice, uncovered, for 20 minutes, then drain in a sieve. Set sieve in a pan with about 1 inch of boiling water; cover sieve with a lid and steam rice for 20 to 25 minutes, or until it is dry. Transfer rice to a shallow dish, add 2 tablespoons of the softened butter, and fluff with a fork. Sauté onion and livers in 3 tablespoons butter over low heat for 2 minutes, then add mushrooms and celery and sauté over medium heat for 3 or 4 minutes, or until mushrooms are cooked. Combine with rice; add pecans, parsley, thyme, marjoram, and salt and pepper to taste. Allow to cool before using as stuffing.

APPLE-RAISIN STUFFING (for turkey or goose)

1 cup chopped onions, with their juice
3 cups peeled, cored, and diced apples
7 cups soft bread crumbs
¾ cup melted butter
1 cup seedless raisins, parboiled and drained

1½ tsps. salt
¼ tsp. pepper
½ cup minced parsley
1 garlic clove, minced
½ tsp. grated mace
½ tsp. grated nutmeg
½ tsp. ground sage
½ tsp. ground cloves

Mix all thoroughly.

HAM AND SMOKED-OYSTER STUFFING
(for 8- to 9-lb. turkey)

2 cups chopped onions
½ cup chopped celery
¼ lb. fresh mushrooms, sliced
¼ lb. butter
1 qt. crumbled dried bread (crusts removed from 3 loaves; let dry on trays overnight after pulling apart)

1 cup diced cooked or canned ham
½ cup (3¼-oz. can) smoked oysters
1 tbsp. minced parsley
½ tbsp. poultry herbs mix
1 tsp. salt
¼ tsp. pepper
¼ tsp. MSG

Sauté onions, celery, and mushrooms in butter; toss with crumbs. Add ham and oysters and toss again. Add parsley, poultry herbs, salt, pepper, and MSG, and toss until well blended. Can be frozen for later use.

GREEK PINE-NUT STUFFING (for turkey)

¼ lb. each of beef and veal, ground and mixed
¼ lb. chicken or pheasant livers, chopped
1 turkey liver, chopped
6 oz. butter
1½ cup croutons, crushed
½ can (11-oz. can) water-packed chestnuts, drained and chopped
⅓ cup pine nuts
2 celery ribs, minced
1 medium onion, chopped
2 tbsps. minced fresh parsley
½ cup tomato sauce
½ cup dry white wine
1½ tbsps. dried currants
½ tbsp. salt
½ tsp. poultry seasoning

Brown meats and livers in 1 tablespoon butter. Remove and reserve. Add 1 tablespoon butter to pan and sauté crouton crumbs lightly; add to meat. Add 1 more tablespoon butter, sauté chestnuts and pine nuts; add to meats. Add remaining butter to pan, and sauté celery, onion, and parsley just until limp. Add tomato sauce and wine, cover, and simmer for 20 minutes. Add currants, salt, and poultry seasoning, and blend into meat mixture.
MAKES 5 cups.

GERMAN APPLE-HERB STUFFING (for turkey)

¼ cup milk
¼ cup lukewarm water
15-oz. loaf of firm white bread, cubed
1 lb. beef chuck, ground and crumbled
turkey liver and heart, minced
2 tbsps. butter
2 cups minced celery
1 large onion, chopped
½ cup chopped parsley
1 large tart apple, peeled, cored, and shredded
2 eggs, slightly beaten
1 tsp. salt
1 tsp. poultry seasoning
⅛ tsp. pepper

Add milk and water to bread; set aside. Brown beef, liver, and heart in butter; stir in celery, onion, parsley, and apple, and cook over low heat, stirring often, until celery is soft. Cool slightly and mix lightly with softened bread, eggs, and seasonings.
MAKES 10 cups.

MUSHROOM STUFFING (for 6-lb. turkey)

5 bunches of green onions, sliced (about 3 cups)

½ lb. fresh mushrooms, washed, trimmed, and chopped (about 3 cups)

¼ lb. butter

6 cups coarse, soft white bread crumbs

½ tsp. salt

Sauté onions and mushrooms in butter for 10 minutes, or until just wilted. Pour over crumbs, season, and toss lightly. If baking separately, bake in a greased dish, covered, at 325°.

ACCOMPANIMENTS

Potatoes, baked, boiled, mashed, and fried, are a natural accompaniment to meat. There are other starches as well such as pasta and rice. Dumplings, which can be cooked with the meat if it is cooked in liquid such as a stew, or cooked separately, are a delicious change.

Dumplings don't have to be plain. Saffron powder can be added for color and flavor, dried herbs can be soaked in the milk before adding it, or fresh herbs can be minced and added to the batter.

NEW ENGLAND DUMPLINGS

1 cup flour

2 tsps. baking powder

½ tsp. sugar

½ tsp. salt

½ cup (approx.) milk

Sift dry ingredients together and slowly stir in the milk to make a batter thick enough to take up by rounded spoonfuls; use either a tablespoon measure or a soup spoon. Bring meat cooking liquid to a boil; the liquid should just barely cover the solid ingredients so that the dumplings sit on them. Drop in formed dumplings and cook uncovered for 10 minutes, then cover and cook for 10 minutes longer. Do not remove lid for last 10 minutes.

Serves 4 to 6.

STEAMED DUMPLINGS

Mix batter for New England Dumplings, but use only enough milk to make batter as stiff as that for baking-powder biscuits. Pat dough out ½ inch thick, and cut into rounds. Arrange rounds close together in buttered top of a small steamer. Cover and cook for 12 minutes.

NORWEGIAN DUMPLINGS

4 tbsps. butter
½ cup water
2 oz. flour
2 eggs, separated

salt
dash of ground cardamom
(optional)

Bring butter and water quickly to a boil and add flour. Stir over moderate heat until dough comes away from the sides of the pan. Remove from heat and let dough get cold. Beat in egg yolks, one at a time, with a dash of salt and a pinch of ground cardamom (optional). Beat egg whites stiff and frothy and fold in. Shape into marble-sized balls and place in boiling water to cover well. Cover pot and simmer gently for 10 minutes until dumplings rise.

SERVES 6 or 7.

GYPSY DUMPLINGS (excellent on rabbit stew)

1 cup flour
2 tsps. baking powder
salt

2 eggs, beaten light
milk

Sift flour with baking powder and a pinch of salt. Add alternately eggs and enough cold milk to make a stiff batter. Drop by small spoonfuls onto boiling rabbit stew; let rise, then cover and cook for 12 to 15 minutes.

SERVES 4 to 6.

SUET DUMPLINGS
(traditionally served with English salted meat)

1 cup flour
½ tsp. baking powder
½ tsp. salt

½ cup grated beef suet
cold water

Sift flour with baking powder and salt. Mix in thoroughly beef suet (traditionally done with the hands by rubbing, but a pastry blender can be used). Add enough cold water to make a stiffish dough that comes away from the sides of the bowl. Form into 12 balls. Drop onto boiling broth and cook, covered, for 10 minutes.

SERVES 6.

GERMAN SPAETZLE (excellent with any goulash)

3 cups flour	4 eggs
1 tsp. salt	¾ cup water
dash of grated nutmeg	butter
dash of paprika	

Combine flour with salt; add a dash each of grated nutmeg and paprika if you like. Add eggs and water, and mix well, beating with a spoon until batter is thick and smooth. Dampen a portable cutting board and spread on a generous spoonful of dough; spread very thin with a spatula dipped into water. Cut into small strips and push off the end of the board into a kettle of boiling salted water. (Dip spatula into boiling water as needed for cutting.) If dough is too thin to hold together, add a little more flour. Cook 2 cut spoonfuls at a time, boiling for 5 minutes or until tender. Lift out with a slotted spoon, put into dish, and pour on a bit of melted butter while continuing with remainder. Add fresh boiling water to the kettle as needed. Serve hot. Can also be made ahead of time and heated in a buttered skillet.

SERVES 6 to 8.

YORKSHIRE PUDDING

Yorkshire Pudding, an English favorite with a roast, is also excellent with game, but easier to bake if the oven is unoccupied; it's great with steaks.

1 cup sifted flour	1 cup milk
½ tsp. salt	3 to 4 tbsps. beef drippings
2 eggs	

Mix at least 1 hour before baking for a lighter pudding. Sift flour and salt and mix into a batter with unbeaten eggs and milk, beating smooth and creamy. Heat beef drippings in an 8-inch-square baking pan in the oven until sizzling hot. (Can also be baked in large muffin tins, if desired.) Pour in the batter and bake at 450° for 15 minutes, then at 375° for an additional 30 minutes. For a savory version, add a little grated onion and a sprinkle of ground sage to the batter; or plumped seedless raisins can be added just before baking.

SERVES 3 to 4.

Rice is an excellent game accompaniment, but there are many of us who find it difficult to prepare well. There are two methods that

276

I find most satisfactory, one the Spanish method and the other, steaming, which will keep rice hot and fluffy for up to 1 hour for delayed serving.

SPANISH-COOKED RICE

For 1 cup raw, long-grain rice, melt 1 tablespoon hydrogenated shortening in a heavy skillet. Add rice and cook, stirring, until rice is opaque but not browned. Pour on 2 cups boiling water or stock; top pan with double thickness of paper towel and a tight lid. Reduce heat to lowest possible and cook until rice is dry, about 20 minutes. Fluff with a fork. Re-cover with a new paper towel and lid and turn off heat. Will hold about 15 minutes.

MAKES 2 cups.

STEAMED RICE

For 1½ cups long-grain rice, bring 3 cups water with 1 tablespoon salt to a boil. Gradually add rice; do *not* let kettle stop boiling. Boil, uncovered, for 15 minutes, or until grains are just tender. Pour rice into a heatproof colander, at least 1½-quart size, and set over a pan with about 1 inch of gently simmering water. Cover top of colander with clean, damp cheesecloth to keep rice warm until ready to serve.

MAKES 3 cups.

Wild rice, not the same thing as white, requires a different technique. Again I have two favorite methods, one of which requires only a tea kettle for heating; the other needs a warm, not hot, oven.

OFF-THE-STOVE WILD RICE

Put measured amount of washed wild rice into a heavy pot; pour on boiling water so that it is 2 inches above rice. Cover pot and let stand until cooled. Drain and repeat. Approximately 30 minutes before serving, repeat again. This can be done, at least the first two "settings," earlier in the day. It's the last one that heats the rice for serving. Also, if your rice is a bit old, you can give it 4 settings; each one will show you fuller rice kernels.

STANDARD WILD RICE

Wash 1 cup wild rice well and put into a heavy pan with 4 cups water and 1 teaspoon salt. Cook very slowly, without stirring, until rice is tender and all the liquid has been absorbed, about 45 minutes. Drain in a heatproof colander and dry in warm, not hot, oven.

MAKES 4 servings.

WILD RICE WITH PINE NUTS

Prepare ¾ cup wild rice as directed on the package or either of the other ways, substituting pheasant or chicken broth for the water and salt called for. When the rice is cooked, lightly brown ¼ cup pine nuts in 1 tablespoon butter and stir into rice.

Obviously wine goes well with game meat and it makes an excellent jelly; follow the directions with packages or bottles of commercial jelling products. Or try one of these jellies.

PARSLEYED VERMOUTH JELLY

Combine in top part of a double boiler, over hot water, 2 cups dry vermouth with 3 cups sugar. Cook, stirring, until sugar is dissolved and syrup is very hot, about 15 minutes. Skim off foam. Remove from heat and stir in 6 ounces liquid fruit pectin and ½ cup minced fresh parsley. Mix well and let stand for 5 minutes. Pour into jars; seal with paraffin.

RED-PEPPER JELLY

Remove seeds and ribs from 12 sweet red peppers, put through a food chopper. Sprinkle with 1 tablespoon salt and let stand for 4 hours. Drain and rinse in a sieve under cold water. Combine peppers with 3 cups sugar and 1 cup of white-wine vinegar, and boil for about 30 minutes, or until jelly sheets from spoon and a candy thermometer reaches 220°. Pour into hot sterilized jars and seal with paraffin.

ROSÉ JELLY

In top part of a double boiler over boiling water, combine 2 cups rosé wine and 3 cups sugar. Cook, stirring, until sugar is dissolved. Stir in lemon juice to taste. Remove from heat and stir in ½ bottle (6-ounce size) liquid fruit pectin. Pour into sterilized jars and seal with paraffin.

HORSERADISH JELLY

Boil 2 cups sugar with 1 cup white vinegar for 3 minutes. Stir in 1 cup grated fresh horseradish and return to a boil. Add ½ bottle (6-ounce size) liquid fruit pectin and stir over high heat until mixture comes to a rolling boil. Remove from heat and let stand for a few minutes, skimming surface constantly. Pour into sterilized jars and seal with paraffin.

PARSLEY JELLY

2 cups firmly packed parsley with stems removed
2¼ cups cold water
2 tbsps. lemon juice

3 or 4 drops of green food coloring
2½ cups sugar
½ bottle (6-oz. size) fruit pectin

Crush parsley well in a pan with a potato masher. Add cold water and bring to a boil. Remove from heat, cover, and let stand for 15 minutes. Strain through cheesecloth and return 1½ cups liquid to the cleaned pan. Add lemon juice, food coloring, and sugar. Mix well. Make jelly, following pectin directions. Pour into sterilized jars and seal with paraffin.

APPLE-BRANDY JELLY

Soften 2 envelopes unflavored gelatin in ½ cup cold water. Add 3 cups boiling water and stir until gelatin is dissolved. Add ¾ cup sugar, 2 tablespoons lemon juice, and a dash of salt. When slightly cooled, add ⅓ cup apple brandy (Calvados, preferably), then tint a delicate shade with 2 or 3 drops of red food coloring. Note that other liqueurs can be used instead of apple brandy. Tint accordingly.

MAKES about 4½ cups.

WINE ASPIC
(for garnish, or coating; particularly good with pheasant)

pheasant carcass, from uncooked, boned bird
2 calf's feet, or 2 to 4 veal bones
1 beef bone
1 tbsp. salt
1 slice each of carrot and onion
1 bay leaf
1 or 2 leeks
1 celery rib

3 qts. water
2 egg whites, beaten stiff
½ lb. lean venison or beef, chopped
peppercorns
2 or 3 parsley sprigs
3 sprigs fresh chervil
3 sprigs fresh tarragon
2 tbsps. Madeira, sherry, or port

Bring carcass, calf's feet, and beef bones to a boil with salt, carrot, onion, bay leaf, leeks, celery, and water. Skim as needed, and simmer for several hours to make a strong broth. Strain, cool, and remove fat from surface. Clarify stock by adding egg whites. Add chopped venison or beef, a few peppercorns, parsley, chervil, and tarragon. Add more salt if needed. Bring slowly to a boil, stirring. As soon as the stock boils, reduce heat as low as possible and simmer for about 30 minutes. Strain through a fine cheesecloth or muslin, and stir in the wine. Pour into molds rinsed out in cold water and let become firm or use as a coating.

MAKES 6 cups.

INDEX